YANKEE WOMEN

YANKEE WOMEN

WOMEN

GENDER BATTLES
IN THE
CIVIL WAR

ELIZABETH D.
LEONARD

W. W. NORTON & COMPANY

NEW YORK   LONDON

The text of this book is composed in 11/13.5 Goudy Old Style,
with the display set in Goudy Old Style.
Composition by Crane Typesetting Service, Inc.
Manufacturing by the Courier Companies, Inc.
Book design and ornaments by Margaret M. Wagner.

Library of Congress Cataloging-in-Publication Data
Leonard, Elizabeth D.
Yankee women : gender battles in the Civil War /
Elizabeth D. Leonard.
p.   cm.
Includes bibliographical references and index.
1. United States—History—Civil War, 1861–1865—Participation,
Female.   2. United States—History—Civil War, 1861–1865—Women.
3. Women—United States—History—19th century.   4. United States—
History—Civil War, 1861–1865—Medical care.   5. United States—
History—Civil War, 1861–1865—War work.   6. Bucklin, Sophronia E.
7. Wittenmyer, Annie, 1827–1900.   8. Walker, Mary Edwards,
1832–1919.   I. Title.
E628.L46   1994
973.7′15042—dc20   93-48813

ISBN 0-393-31372-7

W. W. Norton & Company, Inc.,
500 Fifth Avenue, New York, N.Y. 10110
W. W. Norton & Company Ltd.
10 Coptic Street, London WC1A 1PU

1 2 3 4 5 6 7 8 9 0

To my family
and to Steve

CONTENTS

ACKNOWLEDGMENTS

ix

INTRODUCTION

xiii

CHAPTER ONE
"NO PLACE FOR WOMAN"?:
SOPHRONIA BUCKLIN AND CIVIL WAR NURSING

3

CHAPTER TWO
"MEN DID NOT TAKE TO THE
MUSKET MORE COMMONLY THAN
WOMEN TO THE NEEDLE":
ANNIE WITTENMYER AND SOLDIERS' AID

51

CONTENTS

CHAPTER THREE
"A THING *THAT NOTHING BUT THE DEPRAVED YANKEE NATION COULD PRODUCE"*: *MARY WALKER, M.D., AND THE LIMITS OF TOLERANCE*
105

CHAPTER FOUR
THE WOMEN AND THE STORYTELLERS AFTER THE WAR
159

CONCLUSION
195

NOTES
203

SELECT BIBLIOGRAPHY
285

INDEX
299

ACKNOWLEDGMENTS

It is with much gratitude that I acknowledge the many people who have given generously of their time and energy to help bring this project from conception to birth. I begin by expressing my sincere thanks to all the skilled archivists whose efforts on behalf of *Yankee Women* have been immeasurable in their value. I thank the staffs of the Iowa State Historical Library in Des Moines; the Department of Special Collections at the University of Iowa in Iowa City; the DeWitt Historical Library of Tompkins County in Ithaca, New York; the Syracuse University Library Special Collections Department; the Oswego County Historical Society; the Department of Special Collections, Penfield Library, State University of New York, at Oswego, New York; the Archives and Special Collections on Women in Medicine at the Medical College of Pennsylvania in Philadelphia; the Huntington Library in San Marino, California; the Bentley Historical Library at the University of Michigan, Ann Arbor; and the National Archives and the Manuscript Division of the Library of Congress in Washington, D.C. I deeply appreciate your patient assistance as I worked against time at each of your institutions to find all the documents I could ever hope to incorporate into this manuscript. I would also like to thank the talented and dedicated staff of the Interlibrary Loan Department at the University of California, Riverside—Janet Moores in particular—for their unswerving determination to find me even the most obscure of the many obscure books I regularly requested. Their success rate was remarkable!

There are a number of scholars whose varied contributions to *Yankee Women* during the period of its gestation deserve recognition. I would like to thank the three members of my dissertation committee from the University of California, Riverside—Professors Sarah Stage, Roger Ransom, and Sterling Stuckey—for their insights as well as their support and encouragement, particularly in the early and tenuous stages of this project. I would also like to thank Professor Charles Wetherell, also of the University of California, Riverside, who although not a member of my dissertation committee, nevertheless did multiple readings of the theoretical portions of the manuscript, and made relentless, if usually good natured, demands for greater clarity and precision.

Professor Jane E. Schultz of the Department of English at the Indiana University-Purdue University at Indianapolis, merits special mention for assistance far beyond the call of institutional duty. Unquestionably the reigning authority on Civil War nurses, Jane not only responded readily to my often vaguely thought-out questions in the initial stages of the project, but then stuck with me through the dissertation process as a painstakingly careful outside reader, to become one of my most highly valued professional colleagues.

Professor John A. Phillips of the University of California, Riverside, similarly has earned a special place here, for his unbounded willingness to struggle with me from start to finish, line by line, idea by idea, to produce this book. It should be noted that John deserves credit for the book's title, which is a vast improvement over any and all of the hopelessly cumbersome titles that I was able to come up with on my own. I repeat what I have said elsewhere, that John's apparently tireless assistance, his unfailingly sage advice, and his respect for me as a colleague as well as a student, have given me courage all along the way, and have made the whole journey a delight.

To my good colleagues in the Department of History at Colby College, I give thanks for the enthusiasm with which you have both welcomed me here and also cheered the progress of this manuscript since I arrived in 1992. Professor Robert Weisbrot especially gave me some shrewd advice early on about my approach to the topic which proved prescient in relation to the critiques I would later receive from my editor.

Which brings me to Amy Cherry, of W. W. Norton & Company, who has simply been a splendid editor from the first moment she took my manuscript in hand. Her great care in reading the manuscript and offering wise counsel over the course of many months of revision and re-revision is deeply appreciated, as is the collegial approach she has always taken in our discussions. I also would like to thank Steve Forman, the first editor at Norton to see *Yankee Women*, who saw enough merit in it to then pass it on to Amy; and Margaret Farley, who copyedited the manuscript swiftly, consistently, and with a very sharp eye!

Finally, I would like to thank my husband Steve Bellavia, for the many ways in which, along with our two cats, Sumi and Tako, you have conspired over the years to sustain my good spirits. Our small but growing family is the context that made this all possible. I love you.

INTRODUCTION

From February 1862 to June 1863, Mary Warden Bingham of Kensington, Michigan, kept a diary in which she recorded—in brief entries that revolved around her only son, James—her very personal experience of the Civil War. Many of Mary's entries noted the receipt of a letter from, or the dispatch of a letter to James, who had left home early in the war to serve with Company H of the First Michigan Infantry, United States Army. "Received a letter from James," Mary penned on March 13, 1862. "How dear these letters are . . . ." Similar entries followed over the next weeks and months: "I wrote to James today" (May 13, 1862); "Wrote to James" (May 21, 1862); "Received a letter from James" (May 23, 1862); "Wrote to James" (August 28, 1862); "Wrote to James to Louisville [Kentucky] and put some dried cherries in the letter" (October 10, 1862).[1] Clearly, at any one time the Civil War's direct impact on Mary Bingham's life could be correlated with the situation of her soldier son at the front. Having lost her husband, Kinsley, to illness in October 1861, Mary fretted constantly about James's safety. In a letter to James, dated May 5, 1862, Mary counseled:

> I would suggest in case you are in a battle to have something about

your person that would bind up a wound, and I think you might have a bite of something to eat in your pocket—how many have almost died of starvation before any thing could be brought up.[2]

Privately, she confided to her diary a few days later, "May God grant me strength to bear whatever is in store for me. Spare my boy if it be thy will O God."[3]

Less than a year after Mary began her wartime diary, James was dead from typhoid, contracted in camp at Bardtown, Kentucky. "I do hereby certify that Lieut James W Bingham died on the 9th Inst after a protracted illness . . . ," read the letter from Dr. James Muir. Mary's nightmare had come true and, abruptly, her own life seemed drained of color. "It seems to me I never did anything worth remembering . . . . [M]y life seems very monotonous, and I wonder sometimes why I am left when of so little use," she wrote to her sister Lucina in February 1863, some three months after James's death.[4] Mary's words echoed the sentiment of countless thousands of women across America for whom the war meant nothing less than the grievous loss of beloved husbands, fathers, brothers, and sons sent off with combined fear and pride, in response to calls such as that issued in April 1861 by the Governor of Wisconsin to his state's "Patriotic Women":

> It is your country and your government . . . that is now in danger, and you can give strength and courage and warm sympathies and cheering words to those who go to do battle for all that is dear to us here. Bitter as the parting may be to many, I am assured that you will bid them go bravely forward for God and Liberty, to "return with their shields or on them."[5]

As is well known, far too few women who responded to such calls during the war would enjoy the relief of their menfolk's safe return. And it is poor consolation that these multitudes of Mary Binghams were for a long time consolidated in the culture's historical memory into *the* dominant paradigm of the intersection between women and the Civil War: Civil War women as the weeping widows of the dead.[6] As much as the paradigm reflects a crucial aspect of women's experience of the Civil War, is it in fact the case that there have been and are no other connections to be made?

For a long time, scholars have considered the Civil War a watershed event in American history. James M. McPherson has convincingly argued that the Civil War represented a clear turning point in the history of the United States, marking the end not only of slavery but also of the "old federal republic in which the national government had rarely touched the average citizen except through the post-office." In its stead, the war integrated and centralized the disparate states and sections around a single dominant (if still occasionally contested) economic vision and purpose—northern led, government subsidized, industrial capitalism. In other words, out of the vestiges of the Jeffersonian agrarian republic of the early nineteenth century, the Civil War produced a politically and economically unified nation from which secession was no longer conceivable.[7]

McPherson's *Battle Cry of Freedom* (1988) affirmed the Civil War's supremacy among the transformative events of the nation's past, but it gave scant attention to the question of the war's specific impact on the history of American women, a subject admittedly beyond the scope of McPherson's purpose. Still, McPherson's vigorous reiteration of the Civil War's political and economic repercussions for the nation provokes questions about its implications for women. Did the war represent a "watershed event" in American women's history, as it did in the history of the nation as a whole?

To date, most discussions of women and war in the United States have centered on the two World Wars and, to a lesser extent, on the American Revolution. Scholars generally agree that these wars, along with such developments as the mid-nineteenth-century abolition and suffrage movements, and the emergence of large numbers of women's benevolent associations, such as the Woman's Christian Temperance Union and the Women's Trade Union League, represent milestones in the history of American women, which clearly mark their progress toward social, economic, and political equality with American men.[8] Women's active participation in World War I, argued Dorothy and Carl J. Schneider, "helped the already swelling suffrage movement to crest" in the form of the Nineteenth Amendment. William Chafe contended, in turn, that World War II expanded employment opportunities for middle-aged, middle-class women and thereby facilitated popular acceptance of a growing female labor force in the decades after the war. By "creating a basis in social reality for the idea that a woman's 'place' is not in the home," and by "creating an audience of women who knew firsthand how unequal their treatment in the work force was," World War II contributed to the development of the feminist movement in the 1960s and 1970s. As for the American Revolution, it set the stage for the emergence of an ideology of Republican Motherhood, in which women as mothers bore responsibility for the moral training of their sons for citizenship, making necessary the expansion of educational opportunities for girls and women in the early national period and the popular acceptance of females as educable creatures.[9] One wonders if the Civil War, too, constitutes a milestone in the history of American women and, if so, what sort of milestone?

Yankee Women, a study of northern, middle-class women in the Civil War, attempts to answer this question by recasting the role of the Civil War in United States and women's history, simultaneously bringing women to center stage in the war story and bringing the war to center stage in the history of American women.[10] For women supported the war in a rich variety of ways, not least of all with an enthusiastic spirit that occasionally surprised themselves. Even women whose immediate personal lives saw few visible alterations as a result of the outbreak of hostilities demonstrated noticeable changes in their self-understanding in relation to the world of war. There were many, for example, who, in the privacy of their own diaries, began to apply military imagery to their experience. Watching the troops gather in early April 1861 in preparation for departure to the front, Lucy Larcom of Massachusetts confided in her diary: "I have felt a soldier-spirit rising within me, when I saw the men of my native town armed and going to risk their lives for their country's sake."[11] Larcom unquestioningly embraced a military image for herself, writing that she would be a "soldier" in the Union cause though she might never step beyond her own front porch. Instead, she would contribute her "mite" in the currency of martial spirit.[12]

Women also sustained the efforts of the Union and the Confederacy in forms concrete and practical. Perhaps most fundamental was their response to the war's removal of large numbers of men to the battle front, which created serious gaps in the social and economic fabric at home that women leapt to fill. Women who remained on the home front confronted daunting and unfamiliar tasks, as men's departure for the war required them single-handedly to hold together households and family businesses. In many cases, women necessarily acquired and implemented new "public" skills to cope with the challenges presented by the enlistment of their male relatives and friends. "Dear Wife," wrote army surgeon R. Curtis Edgerton from the Missouri Headquarters of the 26th Illinois Regiment in October 1861,

> Tell John Wilber to get notes of all those that do not pay those bills promptly. And where he sees a man can pay and won[']t get his note first then sue. Have Wright get Charlie a pair of Boots as soon as you can spare the money. . . .[13]

Like Lydia Edgerton, many women found themselves suddenly responsible for business-related bookkeeping and management activities to which they did not bring much useful knowledge from the household. The rest of what had typically been considered men's work they had to learn in practice. In any case, women's assumption of new responsibilities on the home front required the mastery and application of skills and behaviors previously reserved for men, evoking the obvious possibility of conflict with those men who remained behind out of incapacity, principle, or need, or who returned from battle expecting to resume their prewar positions as patriarchs.

In addition, thousands of women responded to news of the first shots being fired at Fort Sumter in April 1861 by joining what quickly came to be known as the "bonnet brigades," transforming their everyday church groups, sewing circles, and benevolent societies into organizations designed to support the war effort in very material ways.[14] Even to women already well-versed in benevolent work, the war raised the level of demand for their services to new heights. Moreover, the war drove some leaders of regionally important societies to national prominence, among them Mary Ashton Rice Livermore of the Western Sanitary Commission, who later wrote,

> If men responded to the call of the country when it demanded soldiers by the hundred thousand, women planned money-making

enterprises, whose vastness of conception, and good business management, yielded millions of dollars to be expended in the interest of sick and wounded soldiers.[15]

Iowa's Annie Wittenmyer, too, built a regional reputation in soldier relief on the foundation of her skills in sanitary supply distribution among the Iowa troops up and down the Mississippi River in the early stages of the war.[16] The realities of sanitary supply collection and distribution pushed a number of women beyond the doors of their own homes, churches, and benevolent societies out into the field, threatening popular images of the middle-class woman as an "angel of the household."

The unanticipated carnage of the war presented its own challenge to midcentury notions of gender-appropriate behavior, leading great numbers of middle-class women to exercise their supposedly unique caretaking talents on a new scale and in the new, violent, and profoundly public contexts of the military hospital and the battlefield. Some twenty thousand women performed nursing and other medical support services for the Union alone during the four years of war, their actions eliciting gratitude but also hostility on the part of the men who believed the war front to be their own special domain, and who had themselves assumed responsibility for wartime caretaking.[17] Approximately thirty-two hundred women, Sophronia Bucklin among them,[18] served as regular employees of the Union Army under the authority of Superintendent of Women Nurses, Dorothea Dix. Other women gained nursing appointments through the various local, state, and national relief organizations,[19] or through male relatives, who were formally employed by the medical departments or as regimental surgeons. Still others enlisted independently as "laundresses" and "cooks" with their husbands' regiments, helping to care for the sick and wounded soldiers in the course of their daily activities. A few women, such as the Union's Mary Ann Ball ("Mother") Bickerdyke and Clara Barton, eschewed official appointments and "red tape" altogether and simply attached themselves *ad hoc* to the troops who needed them most at any given time.[20] All of these women deliberately left home to add their strength to the war effort, collectively shattering images of the battle front as man's special sphere, and establishing a virtually new field of labor for themselves and their daughters and granddaughters.[21] One woman, Mary Edwards Walker, struggled to combine her contribution to the Union's cause with a professional career as a physician.[22]

Yankee Women focuses on the stories of three northern, middle-class women—Sophronia Bucklin, Annie Wittenmyer, and Mary Edwards Walker—to provide answers to a multitude of questions about the intersection of American women's history and the history of the Civil War: Did the massive female presence in hospital and camp alter the course of the war? Did it affect popular perceptions of middle-class women's abilities? Did women's home front production of valuable commodities for the prosecution of the war significantly contribute to the health, welfare, and battle-readiness of the soldiers? Did such home front activities generate new respect for women's organizational talents or open up new professional opportunities? Did middle-class women's participation in the Civil War encourage self-reliance and self-esteem, and did it stimulate new ambitions for a life beyond the home?

Yankee Women responds to these questions, and also to recent debates in the history of gender concerning the processes that underlie the construction and reconstruction of cultural definitions of "maleness" and "femaleness,"[23] and the organization of these definitions into compelling gender systems[24]—ideological models for human behavior and interaction on the basis of sex—that have profound implications in any given time or place for men's and women's relative social power.[25] Somewhat paradoxically, historians of women and of gender who once shunned the study of wars as the heart and soul of "traditional history" have begun to include wars among the historical events receiving their greatest attention, because they represent the kind of social upheavals that highlight the arbitrary and changing nature of gender systems.[26] Wars produce abrupt, conscious, and concentrated adjustments in the behaviors considered appropriate for men and women and allow for some crossing of gender lines otherwise considered inviolable. Women, for example, may be required for the duration of a war to take jobs that are normally filled by men, increasing their access to (male) public-sphere rewards and enhancing their socioeconomic status; men on the battlefield may be permitted to display a degree of emotional tenderness for their fellows that in peacetime would be considered excessive, allowing them to enjoy uncommon freedom of expression in the private (female) realm of intimate social relations. Although any and all such changes take place with the general understanding that they represent "unnatural" and "abnormal" arrangements to be abandoned at the moment peace is restored, the likelihood is great that these "temporary" alterations in societal expectations with regard to men's and women's "natures," abilities, roles, and interaction will have certain long-term consequences for gender redefinition.[27] To study the Civil War—a war that erupted in the midst of an era in United States history perhaps unprecedented for the apparent rigidity of prevailing ideals of manhood and womanhood—from the perspective of gender issues, not surprisingly yields significant insights.

To be specific, antebellum Victorians typically characterized middle- and upper-class men as "strong," "passionate" (in the sense of being vibrant and sexual), and guided by their intellectual capacities, and thus assigned to them all ongoing responsibilities in the harsh, demanding "public" realm. To middle-

and upper-class women, characterized as "weak," "passionless," and overwhelmingly emotional, midcentury ideology assigned all responsibilities in the "private," safer realm of the home. The result of all this, of course, was to confirm antebellum middle- and upper-class men's access to public institutions and to the professions—higher education, medicine, law, the ministry—while simultaneously barring most women from these same opportunities on the basis of their theoretically crippling emotionality.[28] Stern notions of men's capacity (and women's incapacity) for worldly challenges, and the practical expression of these notions in terms of the conferral or withholding of social opportunities and status, undergirded a power relationship between antebellum Victorian men and women in which men maintained a strong element of dominance and control over "naturally" frail, dependent, and rightly subordinate women.[29]

But, in addition to the many consequences described at length by James McPherson and others, the April 1861 attack on Fort Sumter and the Civil War that followed it triggered a degree of social uproar that rapidly made untenable the strict adherence of northern, middle-class Americans, at least, to this very particular, and in many minds apparently fixed and perfectly harmonious web of ideals about the social roles and relative power of men and women and about their proper interaction. By drawing tens of thousands of middle-class women out of their familiar contexts of home and community into the alien and very public space of the battlefield, the war compelled adjustments by men whose desire to guard the physical territory of war yielded out of raw necessity. Prewar judgments about middle-class women's frailty and emotional instability, and about the impropriety of their dealing with blood, wounds, ailing bodies, and death outside of the family gave way to increasingly positive evaluations of women's various strengths, and of the potential benefits the sick and wounded might derive from exposure to women's "natural" caretaking talents. By requiring women who had previously devoted their managerial skills to the proper maintenance of bourgeois households or to the efficient accomplishment of local benevolent activities, to apply those skills in the administration of military hospitals and the gathering and distribution of sanitary supplies, the war also dictated men's adaptation to women's sharing of bureaucratic power. Moreover, the emergence of middle-class women from their more circumscribed prewar contexts, and the assumption by many of them of new and various civic responsibilities, generated (or at least intensified) their aspirations for concrete recognition in the form of professional status. Women who had formerly satisfied themselves with the accolades bestowed upon them as good, generous, and voluntary servants of Christ in their communities, and as faithful, devoted, and "true-to-woman's-nature" wives, sisters, and mothers at home, in their new wartime contexts sought, expected, and sometimes simply demanded the accoutrements of professionalization. This meant the granting of titles, training, and salaries. Perhaps most important, the professionalization of women as nurses, medical personnel, sanitary agents, and so forth, meant the sharing of a type of public stature and power previously reserved for men.

Pressure exerted at one point in a system demands some kind of response at another, and the intense wartime pressure applied to the antebellum system of middle-class gender expectations by northern women such as Bucklin, Wittenmyer, and Walker—respectively, a nurse, a leader in ladies' aid and soldier relief, and a physician—prompted much shifting and grinding among the various component parts. Like thousands of other northern, middle-class women, Bucklin, Wittenmyer, and Walker dedicated themselves to the Union war effort in ways they believed appropriate. In so doing, they each defied prevailing Victorian gender standards, with disparate results. Bucklin's and Wittenmyer's persistence, along with thousands of other women, in the fields of Civil War nursing and soldiers' aid, ultimately succeeded in shifting some of the boundaries of acceptable middle-class behavior between women and men, although the shifts were hard won and painful and provoked much resistance. In contrast, because Mary Walker's definition of appropriate female behavior strayed considerably farther from mid-nineteenth-century middle-class standards, her demands on the Victorian gender system challenged the very limits of its flexibility. Each of the three women took up a role in the war for which she considered women well suited, but what seemed reasonable to them did not, however, necessarily seem reasonable to others.

Their stories also reveal a great deal about the power wielded by the writers of the war histories to reconstruct and anchor prewar gender ideals once more in the effort to stabilize postwar society. Through its focus on Bucklin, Wittenmyer, and Walker, *Yankee Women* explores the ensuing anxiety among historians over the possible long-term consequences for middle-class culture of women's participation in the war effort. The book thus addresses further questions concerning the models and methods employed by interpreters of the past, and the goals that underlie their endeavors. Like their counterparts in the wake of other wars, post-Appomattox American historians confronted the problem of how to address the Civil War's effects on prewar gender roles and systems of gender interaction. Should they treat wartime changes in men's and women's roles and relations positively, throwing their weight behind permanent change in the middle-class gender system? Or should they encourage a quick and effective return to a prewar model? Historians who favored a return to antebellum gender roles and relations tailored their descriptions of women in the war—Bucklin, Wittenmyer, and Walker among them—in such a way as to

conform to prewar ideas of social order. The subsequent elevation of this particular war narrative to the first rank in the
popular postwar mind reflected the victory, albeit fleeting, of
those who sought to contain any possible cultural "damage"
from wartime violations of Victorian ideals of manhood and
womanhood. This narrative, which focused on middle-class
women's unrelenting selflessness and their harmonious cooperation with (and subordination to) men for the sake of the Union,
to a large extent, masked the realities of wartime gender interaction, flexibility, and conflict at the same time that it clearly
reflected a conscious prescription for postwar society's revitaliza-
tion of the prewar status quo. *Yankee Women* examines the
retelling of Civil War women's stories in order to expose the
hidden purposes of the storytellers in their function as "social
architects."

It is with the specific experiences of Civil War nurse
Sophronia Bucklin that *Yankee Women* begins. Her wartime
story, like the stories of Annie Wittenmyer and Mary Walker
that follow, quickly brings to light not only women's vital contributions to the Union effort, but also the gender battles that
resulted from women's necessary intrusion upon the presumedly
male sphere of war. After exploring these three stories, we
turn to the immediate postwar period and the valiant efforts of
historians and others to ban the conflictual aspects of women's
Civil War service from popular memory in order to foster a
return of middle-class gender arrangements to their status quo
antebellum. *Yankee Women*[30] closes with an extended evaluation of the postwar writers' success, and an interpretation of
the meaning of such efforts for the ongoing construction and
evolution of gender ideals in American culture.

YANKEE WOMEN

Photo reprinted from *In Hospital and Camp*.

CHAPTER ONE

"NO PLACE FOR WOMAN"?

SOPHRONIA BUCKLIN AND CIVIL WAR NURSING

The women who did hospital service . . . were an exceptional

class . . . representing no social grade, but coming from all—

belonging to no rank or age of life in particular . . . but in all

cases, women with a mighty love and earnestness in their

hearts—a love and pity, and an ability to show it forth and to

labor in behalf of it, equal to that which in other departments

of life, distinguishes poets, philosophers, sages and saints, from

ordinary or average men.

—HENRY BELLOWS, *WOMAN'S WORK IN THE CIVIL WAR*

Sophronia E. Bucklin of Auburn, New York, began her Civil War memoir, *In Hospital and Camp*, with a powerful statement of the emotions that inspired women such as herself to enlist as Army nurses.[1] Following the attack on Fort Sumter, she wrote, women experienced the "same patriotism" as the hundreds of thousands of men who leapt to respond when President Abraham Lincoln called for 75,000 militiamen to join forces in national military service to restore the Union.[2] It was this love of country that "lent also to our hearts its thrilling measure, and sent us out to do and dare for those whose strong arms were to retrieve the honor of our insulted flag."[3] Northern women, like northern men, had long anticipated the nation's collapse into war, and the exploding cannon at Fort Sumter only brought to the surface men's and women's passionate feelings of indignation and loyalty, the determination to punish the errant South.

The writings of nurses other than Bucklin reflected the same enthusiasm and eagerness she described, the same willingness to perform any kind of service for the Union cause for which they might be qualified. At the outbreak of hostilities, Mary Newcomb, who would soon become a nurse for the Eleventh Illinois Regiment, longed to be a mother providing soldier sons for the army. She wrote, "I was at the time [of the firing on Sumter] so full of patriotism that if I had had a dozen boys I have no doubt I should have said, 'Go! the country needs you.' "[4] Instead, she sent her husband, and then followed herself. Anna Holstein, who also later became an army nurse, threw her initial energies into the work of soldier relief. "As the soldiers went out from among us," she wrote,

> there came the yearning wish to lessen somewhat the hardships of their lonely camp life, especially when sick in hospital or wounded. . . . With all loyal women of the land, I worked zealously in their behalf; worked, because there was irresistible impulse *to do, to act.* Anything but idleness, when our armies were preparing for combat, and we knew not who should be the first to fall, who be called *widow*, or who *fatherless*.[5]

Sarah Palmer, who became the Ninth New York Regiment's hospital matron, described the anxieties that had plagued her journey to join the troops at the front, but then wrote of the return of "better feelings," those feelings that had prompted her to accompany the Ninth New York in the first place. "I knew," she wrote, "if they [the soldiers] could suffer so much, and *die* for their country, I could at least give some years of my poor life in the attempt to alleviate their sufferings."[6]

In Hospital and Camp reveals little of Sophronia Bucklin's private life before 1861, although it is clear that at the time of the war's outbreak she was probably in her late twenties or early thirties and was living in Auburn.[7] From other sources comes the information that she was unmarried at the time of her enlistment as a Union Army nurse, and remained so for the rest of her life.[8] Bucklin belonged neither to the elite nor to the working class. She was neither a highly esteemed woman of the upper crust, nor was she a hardy and heroic woman of the masses.[9] Rather, Bucklin entered the ranks of the military service from her position as a young, single, independent seamstress in a small town in central New York state, a position to which she would return in the postwar years.[10]

The opening words to her memoir demonstrate that Bucklin was driven by the same loyal devotion to the Union that motivated thousands of women to leave home and hearth to travel to the front. One wonders why, then, it was seventeen months—from April 1861 to September 1862—before Bucklin actually reported for her first nursing assignment. Although it is true that the physical consequences of the war became apparent only several months after Sumter—during the war's first real battle in July 1861 at Bull Run in Virginia, which resulted in 400 Confederate and 625 Union deaths, as well as a total of approximately 2,500 wounded[11]—still, Bucklin reported that her enthusiasm for war service had materialized immediately in the wake of the bloodless Confederate attack on the fort three months before. At that moment, when "it became necessary for armed men to assemble in multitudes, to become exposed to the hardships and privations of camps and the deadly peril of battle fields" she instantly became aware of the "necessity for woman to lend her helping hand to bind up the wounds of the shattered soldier, and smooth the hard pillow of the dying hero," and her heart warmed instantly to the call to duty. [12]

Why then was there more than a year's delay for Bucklin in reaching the battle front? For one thing, in contrast to what would become the dominant postwar image of northern men's and women's rapid, unhindered advance to fill their preordained places in the ranks of the Union's soldier and civilian armies, Bucklin and women like her experienced surprising difficulty simply finding out about nursing opportunities. According to Bucklin, neither personal inquiries nor close study of newspapers and journals provided the information she was seeking. [13] Mary Phinney von Olnhausen's memoir indicated that she, too, began seeking a nursing position immediately after the attack on Fort Sumter, but that an entire year passed during which her inquiries received no response whatsoever. [14] Elvira J. Powers noted the newspapers' frustrating focus, at least for the first year of the war, not on the opportunities available to women in nursing, but on "terrible stories" about women's "duties and trials" in military hospitals. [15] Apparently, the eagerness of many women to begin caring for the sick and wounded soldiers they knew the war would produce was not met with equal eagerness on the part of certain "authorities" to provide the necessary information to permit them to do so.

Ironically, the obstacles that blocked the way of Bucklin and others into Civil War nursing service, although they reflected strong popular resistance to the idea of such service, did not reflect any real paucity in the opportunities available. Opportunities for women to join the Union Army as nurses had technically existed virtually from the start of the war, in part thanks to one woman prominent, forceful, and timely enough to convince the War Department to recruit women early for military hospital duty. Four days after the attack on Fort Sumter, four members of the Sixth Massachusetts Volunteers were killed and several others wounded by Confederate sympathizers as they passed through Baltimore on their way to defend the Capital.[16] In response to news of the attack, reformer Dorothea Lynde Dix of Massachusetts, already famous for her vigorous work in the nation's insane asylums, boarded a train for Washington, to which the wounded had been removed.[17] Having apprised herself of the situation and having made adequate immediate provision for the wounded men, Dix went directly to the War Department to confer with officials there. Within six days, on April 23, 1861, Secretary of War Simon Cameron issued a formal document accepting Dix's offer of her free services in the organization of military hospitals for the care of sick and wounded soldiers, and in the supply of female nurses as well as the "substantial means for the comfort and relief of the suffering" from private as well as government stores. Two months later, on June 10, Cameron conferred upon Dix an official military commission, naming her the Union Army's first Superintendent of Women Nurses, and delegating to her the responsibility "to select and assign women nurses to general or permanent military hospitals, they not to be employed in such hospitals without her sanction and approval, except in cases of urgent need."[18]

Although Dix's commission seemed an early victory for women hoping to lend their caretaking skills to hospitalized Union soldiers, the stipulated conditions of that commission themselves were grounded in predominantly negative feelings about women at the front. For, according to her commission, Dix had jurisdiction only over those few general hospitals that had been established in and around the Capital to "care for cases with which the regimental facilities could not cope." These hospitals only were to be "the concern of Miss Dix and her staff of volunteer nurses, and their organization was to be largely her responsibility."[19] As the theater of war expanded and the numbers of sick and wounded increased, various emergencies soon pushed the women nurses out into field hospitals across the war front as well,[20] and these developments extended the geographical range of Dix's influence, such that she soon found it necessary to appoint James E. Yeatman in St. Louis and Mary A. Livermore in Chicago to assist her.[21] But, initially, the War Department's intentions appear to have been to keep Dix and her nurses under close scrutiny and, probably, close supervision.

Moreover, in the first weeks after Sumter, both the government and the general public anticipated a short war. It was only the July battle at Bull Run that alerted the Union—whose troops were deeply discouraged by their own humiliating and disorderly retreat—that the Confederacy did not mean to surrender as easily as early predictions had suggested they would and that the war would likely be long and brutal.[22] But Dix's commissioning preceded this crucial battle and may, in fact, have been above all a diplomatic move to appease her elevated sense of duty, rather than an acknowledgment of her assertion that the army's medical department would soon need women's services. Still, Dix's appointment meant that, in theory at least, the opportunity for women to join the Union as nurses in the general hospitals in and around Washington had been created.

A second possible avenue for women's entry into Union Army nursing lay in the regiments themselves, as they quickly formed across the north in response to Lincoln's April call to arms. In the early weeks of the war, the government expected each regiment to provide its own medical equipment and staff to serve its soldiers in the field.[23] Throughout the war many women found their way into Civil War nursing by enlisting with their soldier-husbands, either as nurses or as laundresses or cooks. Catherine Oliphant, for example, mustered in with her husband to the Third Maryland Cavalry. A letter of tribute dated long after the war and written by a lieutenant noted that,

> *while she was enrolled* as a *laundress*, she *served, in fact, as an army nurse*, and her constant and faithful ministrations in such capacity endeared her to the hearts of every member (officers and men) of the Third Maryland Volunteer Cavalry. . . .[24]

As Oliphant's case suggests, women might follow their husbands and other male relatives into the military in a variety of capacities. Once in the field, however, they typically functioned as nurses, either intentionally or by default. Similarly, Mary Newcomb wrote that after her husband had departed with the Eleventh Illinois Infantry, she became lonesome and set off to visit him in camp. While there, black measles broke out among the regiment, and she unhesitatingly took up the work of nursing "the boys." Like Oliphant, Newcomb never sought or received a commission from Dix, but she remained with the regiment, despite the February 1862 death of her husband, until the end of the war.[25] On the other hand, unmarried Julia S. Wheelock of Ionia, Michigan, wrote, "My object in going South [initially to Alexandria, Virginia] was to help care for a wounded brother." When she arrived in the fall of 1862, Wheelock discovered that her brother had already died from his wounds. Nevertheless, she wrote, "I resolved to remain and endeavor, God being my helper, to do for others as I fain would have done for my dear brother." She continued in the service until July 1865 as an agent of the Michigan Relief Association, a nurse and a hospital visitor, identifying Michigan soldiers in the hospitals in and around Washington, determining their needs, and supplying them with goods forwarded by the Association.[26]

In the early months of the war, the Woman's Central Relief Association (WCRA) in New York City afforded yet a third avenue for women into the military's nursing service, besides those provided by Dix and by the regiments themselves. Established as a civilian operation on April 26, 1861, three days after Secretary of War Cameron formally accepted Dix's offer of help, the WCRA included among its stated goals the initiation of "relations with the Medical Staff of the army" and the organization of a "bureau for the examination and registration of [female] nursing candidates."[27] From mid-April until mid-June, the WCRA project was spearheaded by the well-known Dr. Elizabeth Blackwell, a licensed physician since her graduation in 1849 from the Geneva Medical College in Geneva, New York, as the nation's first degreed woman doctor. Blackwell hoped, by virtue of her professional status, to influence the Union Army to allow women chosen by the WCRA to serve as military nurses, and she even offered to design and implement nurse-training programs for those women selected. At this point in the nation's history, no formal medical training existed for female nurses, and women who felt a call to serve the soldiers typically perceived nursing less as a profession requiring special education than as an extension of their domestic responsibilities.[28] Blackwell herself had a somewhat different vision, which augmented the common conception of women's "natural" ability to nurse with the notion of modern nursing as a "health science," as articulated by Florence Nightingale in the aftermath of the Crimean War of the 1850s.[29] Conceivably, Blackwell considered formally trained female nurses not just more useful to the troops, but also more likely than the untrained wives and sisters of Union soldiers to receive acceptance from the public and from a military medical community still demonstrably resistant to the idea of women at the front.[30]

Ironically, the War Department's formal appointment of

Dorothea Dix to the position of Superintendent of Women Nurses by mid-June seems to have undermined the efforts of Blackwell and the WCRA to recruit, train, and deploy trained women nurses to military hospitals, which raises further suspicions about the real reasons behind Dix's commission.[31] By appointing a laywoman to head the female nursing service, was not the military intentionally undercutting any possible advance in authority of the woman physician who had sought to deliver nurses with her own imprint to the Medical Department? In mid-June, President Abraham Lincoln also formally established the United States Sanitary Commission (USSC), which, under the firm hand of a clergyman, the Reverend Henry Bellows, rather than a doctor, quickly embraced and then absorbed the WCRA, leaving behind little trace of Blackwell's influence and extending the government's hand into all sanitary affairs, including nurse recruitment. In any case, in the spring of 1861, and regardless of the ambiguous purpose of the War Department's conferral of authority upon her, Dix considered herself to be the provider of the most "proper" route for northern women's entry into Civil War nursing.

From the beginning of the war, then, various opportunities existed for women such as Bucklin to obtain nursing positions within the Union Army, either through the offices of Dorothea Dix or through the USSC (and later the other Commissions as well) and the regiments themselves.[32] It was the newspapers' reticence on the topic of women army nurses, at least in the first year of the war, that effectively slowed the progress of prospective nurses to the front. "I was led by Providence into the right channel," wrote Bucklin later of her discovery that Dix held the key to her appointment as a Union Army nurse.[33] In the silence that met their inquiries about military nursing, Bucklin and others confronted a major barrier to their firsthand participation in the care and healing of the sick and wounded soldiers, and a clear sign of popular and official resistance to the possibility of women overstepping antebellum gender boundaries.

The lack of widespread public information about the opportunities for women in military nursing was indeed a consequence and a symbol of common attitudes about women in the military service. The newspapers' restraint reflected dominant northern, middle-class public opinion that decent women, especially "ladies," did not belong in the military in any capacity. According to the popular argument, such women had no place being anywhere near the fighting because, being naturally delicate, they could not possibly cope with the harsh conditions of the battle front, nor with the ugly consequences of combat. Bucklin herself addressed the difficulty she experienced adjusting to the proximity of war and its carnage, when she wrote of her arrival in the fall of 1862 at the Capital. Describing first her bedazzlement with the grandeur of colorfully uniformed officers and the impressive, massive mobilization of national resources, Bucklin turned to her initial response to the sight of wounded men, "lying on blood-stained stretchers, under fly tents, being borne in at every hand where a sheltering roof made it possible to establish a hospital. . . ." Seeing her countrymen thus, she confessed, quickly

> recalled to my mind the errand on which I had come, made all the courage in my soul recoil at one dread bound. A strange sense of suffocation oppressed me, as if the air by which I was surrounded was filled with poisonous vapors, and for a few minutes I doubted my own strength.[34]

Bucklin's acknowledged sensation of "suffocation" at the sight of the bloodied soldiers mirrored common Victorian ideas about women's frailty, and would have lent itself well to the argument that the presence of feeble women at the war front constituted nothing other than a serious hindrance to those "properly" engaged in medical activities for the sake of the sick and wounded. That women nurses might steel themselves to the task at hand—Bucklin later noted that she herself hardly imagined that the feeling of incapacity "would wear off so soon"[35]— was not perceived to be a possibility. Nor was it conceivable that Victorian women could learn to live, even thrive, in the often harsh physical circumstances for which military hospitals were famous. Bucklin described winter at the Hammond General Hospital at Point Lookout, Maryland, where she was stationed from November 1862 to March 1863:

> [T]hrough the cold dreary weeks . . . we endured the cold without sufficient bedding for our hard beds, and with no provision made for fires. On bitter mornings we rose shivering, broke the ice in our pails, and washed our numb hands and faces, then went out into the raw air, up to our mess room, also without fire, thence to the wards. . . .[36]

Prevailing ideals of Victorian womanhood defied the prospect that Bucklin and others might accustom themselves to such conditions.

Indeed, in the mid-nineteenth-century, middle-class mind, the exigencies of military life contrasted sharply with notions of female gentility. Middle-class women who travelled to the war front theoretically traded the security and the responsibilities of the household for a violent and bloody world considered by many to be completely inappropriate, and destructive, to their tender natures. Sarah Palmer testified graphically to the opposition women nurses faced. "Standing firm against the tide of popular opinion," she wrote,

> hearing myself pronounced demented—bereft of usual common sense; doomed to the horrors of an untended death-bed—suffering,

torture, hunger, and all the untold miseries of a soldier's fate; above all the loud echoed cry, "It is no place for woman," I think it was well that no one held a bond over me strong enough to restrain me from performing my plain duty. . . .[37]

Women who sought nursing positions with the army confronted impassioned popular condemnation.

Single women such as Bucklin also faced popular suspicions about the propriety of young, unmarried women placing themselves in the midst of large groups of men for whom the isolation of the war from the influences of home automatically implied a collapse into moral depravity and sexual license.[38] Objectors found it easier to assume the sustained virtue of older widows or "spinsters" such as Dix herself, or married women who followed their enlisted husbands into the service and who received the permission of regimental officers to join a company in the official or quasi-official capacity of company nurse. Advanced age, or even better, the proximity of her husband, protected and even guaranteed a woman's integrity and her reputation against accusations.

Unmarried women such as Bucklin, however, contended with the specter of immorality. Would they be able to resist the advances of lonely men far from home? To many observers, wartime nursing constituted a greater threat to the presumed innocence of single women than it did to the integrity of the family, so that a woman who left her child at home with relatives in order to follow her husband's regiment typically evoked less criticism than a woman who had no such commitments.[39] It would, after all, be the single woman's fault if she gave in to male sexual pressure. And, as Bucklin's memoir indicated, the military hospital afforded the women little physical privacy—or safety—sometimes providing "only the length of an unpainted board for the partition walls between wards, halls, nurses' quarters, and all other officers."[40] Cornelia Hancock of Pennsylvania, young and single, wrote home to her mother and her concerned community in 1864 to reassure them that her "virtue" was safe. "No soldier," she wrote, "would be allowed to come into my house without knocking even in the daytime, and at night they could not get in without sawing out the logs. There is no danger from anything in the army. . . ."[41] Some years after the war, Julia Wheelock noted, "I know it was thought and even said by some, that a lady could not be associated with the army without losing her standard of moral excellence. I pity those who have such a low estimate of the moral worth and true nobility of the soldier."[42] Such reassurances betrayed the anxieties of families and friends back home about women in general, and single women in particular, at the war front, surrounded by men who, at least when healthy, had been gathered together in camps where cards, liquor, and license abounded. Popular resistance to women's presence on or near the battlefield was so strong in the early months of the war that "Providence," as Bucklin had described it, rather than human hands, seemed the only guide for those women who sought a way to serve the Union in a nursing capacity.

Even the War Department's appointment of the highly respected, austere, middle-aged, and morally correct Dorothea Dix failed to dispel popular concern about the propriety of women at the front, nor did it evoke hearty send-offs by her appointees' anxious relatives and friends or resounding welcomes from the surgeons and staff of the hospitals to which she assigned them. Dix's insistence on rigid moral standards among her recruits, to which she lent the credibility of her own widely recognized integrity, eased but did not entirely clear their path.

Indeed, in some ways the high and uncompromising moral standards by which Dix measured the worth of her recruits, and which reflected her concerns about public opinion, themselves paradoxically presented another potential obstacle to aspiring army nurses like Bucklin. Once women knew of Dix's appointment, they began to flood her with letters of application. But Dix had very clear ideas about the sort of women she could appropriately place in military hospital service. She stated these ideas for the first time in an April 1861 letter, written less than a week after her initial agreement with Secretary Cameron, to Louisa Lee Schuyler of the WCRA. "No young ladies should be sent at all," she wrote,

> but some who can give their services and time and meet part of their expense or the whole, who will associate themselves by two to be ready for duty at any hour of day or night—those who are sober, earnest, self-sacrificing, and self-sustained; who can bear the presence of suffering and exercise entire self control, of speech and manner; who can be calm, gentle, quiet, active, and steadfast in duty, also who are willing to take and execute the directions of the surgeons of the divisions in which they are stationed.[43]

In a July 1862 circular issued by the Surgeon General's office, Dix reiterated her requirements. A female nurse, according to Dix, must be between the ages of thirty-five and fifty and of strong health and "matronly" appearance, and must display "good conduct, or superior education and serious disposition," maintain "habits of neatness, order, sobriety and industry," and present "certificates of qualification and good character" from two individuals.[44] Notably, neither in the letter to Schuyler nor in the circular did Dix require anything in the way of medical or nursing experience—let alone training—from her female applicants. She, too, participated in the notion that a woman's "nature" prepared her for this work. Dix's demands instead revolved around a woman's age, physical constitution and appearance, her moral character, and her ability and willingness to follow orders. Dix perceived herself and her nurses as components in the military structure, subject at all times to military discipline. She also sought to assuage in advance critics who charged her or her nurses with impropriety or insubordination. Her goal was to provide the military medical establishment with an abundant supply of the able helping hands she believed that proper middle-class women could offer.[45]

Some women took Dix's stern requirements in stride. In 1863, Alice Ropes rushed to the Union Hotel Hospital in Washington, D.C., to tend her dying mother, a nurse under Dix's supervision who had succumbed to typhoid fever less than six months after her installment as matron. With more than a hint of humor, the young and probably modest Alice wrote home to her brother Ned: "Miss Dix does not allow young people in the hospital unless very ugly; but she lets me stay during the daytime, which is not very complimentary to my good looks. . . ."[46] But for many women, the requirements further threatened the possibility of their successfully fulfilling their patriotic objectives. Bucklin, who was too young by Dix's standards but who otherwise generally met the Superintendent's requirements—having a plain appearance and a serious attitude toward her work—seems to have taken advantage of her local screening board's failure to ask her age. They did not ask, and she did not volunteer an answer, having "resolved not to be kept from the great work because no wrinkles seamed my face, and no vestige of gray hair nestled among my locks." When Bucklin finally met Dix some time after she had taken her first nursing position, the Superintendent declared her "altogether too young" for military service but did not dismiss her, perhaps because Bucklin had already demonstrated her integrity, skills, and commitment.[47]

In Cornelia Hancock's case, however, Dix found it impossible to compromise as she had with Bucklin. Hancock encountered the Superintendent in Baltimore, where at first glance Dix insisted that Hancock return home. As Hancock wrote later,

> She immediately objected to my going farther on the score of my youth and rosy cheeks. I was then just twenty three years of age. In those days it was considered indecorous for angels of mercy to appear otherwise than gray-haired and spectacled. Such a thing as a hospital corps of comely young maiden nurses, possessing grace and good looks, was then unknown.[48]

Undaunted, Hancock, like numerous other women that Dix rejected, simply found an independent avenue to the front, in her case, through association with the Second Pennsylvania Regiment for which her brother-in-law served as a doctor.[49]

If Dix's requirements, which derived from prewar notions of middle-class womanhood and of appropriate gender interaction, themselves posed an obstacle to middle-class women's access to nursing positions, women's determination and ability to circumvent the requirements suggests the ultimate tenuousness of Dix's control over the whole nursing operation, and also highlights wartime stresses on the antebellum gender system. Instead of yielding to the limitations inherent in conventional notions of Victorian womanhood (as reflected in Dix's specifications, and in popular resistance to their presence at the front), women found avenues to Civil War nursing on their own, or they found ways to convince Dix to appoint them despite their "shortcomings." In so doing, they exerted pressure on the prewar gender system, pressure that gradually compelled it to adjust to the reality of wartime necessity.

Despite popular and official resistance, and beginning especially in 1862, women of all ages and appearances, and of all family and class backgrounds, found their way into nursing service in the Union's field and general hospitals, where they were able over time to demonstrate conclusively their competence. In many cases they found, as they had expected, that their work resembled the maternal chores for which they had been trained since birth. Bucklin wrote of her first appointment to the Judiciary Square Hospital in Washington:

> Our duties here were to distribute food to the patients, when brought up from the kitchen; wash the faces and hands and comb the heads of the wounded; see that their bedding and clothing was kept clean and whole, bring pocket handkerchiefs, prepare and give various drinks and stimulants at such times as they were ordered by the surgeon.[50]

Months later, at the Hammond General Hospital in Maryland, Bucklin's duties were similar. Assigned to care for ninety-six men, "mostly wounded," she was expected to feed and groom her charges, to ensure that their clothes and bedding were clean, and to "prepare what delicacies I could procure for their comfort."[51] At Hammond General, because the head surgeon permitted her to do so, Bucklin had the additional responsibility for dressing wounds,[52] a task that often amounted to a grisly test of her endurance. Describing the arrival of eleven hundred new wounded at the hospital, Bucklin revealed a conscious ranking of the many awful jobs to be done:

> Beds were to be made, hands and faces stripped of the hideous mask of blood and grime, matted hair to be combed out over the bronzed brows, and gaping wounds to be sponged with soft water, till cleansed of the gore and filth preparatory to the dressing. I busied myself with everything save touching the dreadful wounds till I could evade it no longer. Then with all my resolution I nerved myself to the task and bound up the aching limbs.[53]

As fearsome as hospital work seemed, women nurses quickly displayed their aptitude for it. And, as the war progressed, their contributions became increasingly apparent to the otherwise overwhelmingly male hospital personnel, usually consisting of a surgeon-in-charge, a series of assistant surgeons assigned to oversee hospital records, clerks and orderlies, ward physicians for every 75 to 100 patients, medical students, stewards who cared for general hospital conditions and who also dispensed medical and other supplies, ward masters, male nurses, and cooks.[54] As the women displayed their skills, a good deal of the early resistance to their presence at the front faded.

In fact, more than merely accepting the presence of women nurses in their hospitals, by the middle of the war, some military surgeons welcomed them to the point of lobbying the Surgeon General for the right to select their own as they saw fit. Late in 1863, Surgeon General William Hammond's office issued an order carefully worded to present the illusion of supporting Dix, but in fact diverting much of her power of appointment and dismissal to his own office, and to individual medical officials. In a letter to her sister, Cornelia Hancock discussed her interpretation of the order. "The Surgeon-General," she wrote,

> told me of that order before it was published . . .—said that he both could and would appoint ladies at the request of a surgeon *irrespective* of *age, size,* or *looks,* merely at the *request* of a Surgeon-in-Charge. He said that was particularly inserted to allow surgeons to choose their *own* nurses, as many objected to Miss Dix's.[55]

Of course, a surgeon-in-charge could potentially use such a regulation to avoid having to accept female nurses into his hospital at all. But Hancock's letter, and the action taken by the Surgeon General to limit Dix's power without in fact limiting women's access to nursing positions, suggests something else.

While on the one hand, female nurses in general had, by 1863, managed to make a place for themselves with the army at the front, on the other hand, something about Dix's nurses in particular continued to provoke strong negative feelings among medical officials. If Hancock was right, these negative feelings revolved in large part around the issues of "age, size and looks," and, by implication, the surgeons who objected to Dix's mature, "matronly" nurses did so merely because they sought to staff their hospitals with women who were young and attractive. Other matters, however, lay hidden beneath the surface of such demands for youth and beauty.

These issues can be summed up under the heading of the ongoing opposition among male physicians and others to the possibility of the women nurses' professionalization. The rigid standards that Dix applied to the women she approved for appointment demonstrated that although she asked for no financial compensation herself, she nevertheless took herself and her assignment very seriously. As the Superintendent of Women Nurses, Dix aimed to provide the Union Army with a steady supply of dedicated, efficient, and morally impeccable (and, by popular definition, necessarily middle-class) women who would perform their hospital duties with consistency and care. Her goal was not to decorate the military hospitals with attractive young women simply to bring "sunshine" into the lives of the sick and wounded. Dix's nurses, as part of the military service, had a specific, solemn job to do in assisting the medical staff to tend most effectively to the welfare of the soldiers under their care. The Surgeon General's action in 1863, and the resentment of the surgeons to which Hancock alluded in her letter, suggest that some of the women appointed by Dix were doing their job all too well.

From this point of view, the official limitations placed on Dix's authority from 1863 on, and the sentiment of the surgeons who favored younger, prettier, and theoretically less experienced and less self-confident women, both testify to the endurance of a broadly held vision of gender that isolated middle-class women from the medical profession. Even as the northern, middle-class public and the Union's military medical hierarchy, in response to the urgent practical need, were adjusting Victorian ideals of womanhood to permit women nurses at the front, the limitations of that adjustment were already tangible. Medical officials in particular, even as they came to welcome the women's help with gratitude and praise, provided strong indications of the extent of their support. For most, the acceptance of women as hospital nurses during the war did not imply open endorsement of nursing as a women's profession.

In other words, if, in the medical emergency that the Civil War represented, certain boundaries between men and women in the Victorian gender system could shift, this did not mean the shift should be permanent and that women's temporary foothold in this quarter of the public sphere should be sanctioned. Many of the same people who learned to praise the nurses for their undeniable contributions simultaneously manifested abiding resistance to long-term changes in the structure of the medical profession—to include women—or the antebellum Victorian gender order—which recognized no place for the ideal woman among the ranks of waged, professional workers. The development under Dix of a virtual "army nurse corps" of mature, serious women to whom military nursing had the air of a potential career, posed a significant threat to the monopoly held by men at midcentury on medical practice, which Civil War surgeons and others were unwilling to tolerate.

Within the war context, surgeons' objections to Dix's power reflected their basic desire to retain the authority of their positions in the military medical establishment. For Dix alone to have the official power to appoint and discharge, especially as the war continued and broadened, undoubtedly struck many as too strong a power to be in the hands of a woman. After all, did not the very nature of Dix's appointment suggest that the government itself recognized a temporary place for certain women in the military's medical system, but gave little credibility to trained nursing as a profession for women? Dix's personal qualifications for the position of Superintendent of Women Nurses constituted nothing more than her "twenty years' experience in public life, and a passion for efficiency and humanity."[56] Moreover, she provided her services *free*. One could argue that the conditions of Dix's own appointment and the growing desire among army medical men in particular for nurses who seemed more like the "girls next door" than matronly professionals—many surgeons, wrote former nurse Amanda Shelton Stewart after the war, longed for nurses who were not "elderly" and "homely" like Dix's recruits, but who were young, pretty, and dressed "like home folks"[57]—indicate the limits of gender system change that Civil War nurses would make possible. By placing emphasis on the importance of the women nurses' youth and beauty, male medical personnel focused attention not on the grueling work that middle-class women as a group continued to prove themselves capable of performing, but rather on individual women's transitory physical attributes, and thus implied the impermanence of individual women's usefulness as medical assistants and helped to undermine the credibility of nursing as a postwar profession for women.

The issue of professionalization was a complex one, involving not only status but also the problem of payment for services rendered. A sign of Dix's own early inability to think of her nurses as paid professionals had materialized in her April 1861 letter to Louisa Lee Schuyler, regarding the need for nurses to be prepared to finance themselves. In contrast, the July 1862 circular from the Surgeon General's Office, in which Dix had stated her requirements, included the stipulation that nurses would receive wages for their service, amounting to "forty cents a day and subsistence" plus "transportation . . . to and from the place of service."[58] Clearly, by the middle of 1862 Dix supported the idea of at least minimal remuneration for her nurses—what Bucklin later termed a "poor pittance"—if not for herself.[59] In fact, the shift in Dix's philosophy came far sooner than July 1862, as evidenced by the passage in August 1861 of a Congressional Act, entitled "For the Better Organization of the Military Establishment," which guaranteed the payment of wages to government nurses.[60]

It would, of course, be a mistake to interpret the act's passage as unqualified testimony to broad congressional support for the idea that women *should* be paid for their services to the army's medical establishment or that the women who served the Union Army as nurses constituted the core of a new women's nursing profession. In the case of Civil War nurses, as elsewhere, the issue of pay for labor cut two ways. By default, pay tangibly legitimizes and professionalizes labor. However, the issue of pay also reflects the grave problem of recruiting labor, especially in times of labor shortage, without the promise of remuneration. The Congressional Act of August 1861 indicated little more than Congress's realization that the availability of funds for service would have a significant influence on the average woman patriot's ability to commit herself to the task. Bucklin, an unmarried, independent seamstress from central New York state, for example, longed to serve her country in an active capacity. She could not, however, depend on a husband or her family's wealth to support her in that effort. Indeed, few women could have given their time and energy to the military without any concern for compensation. The great majority, including Bucklin, required some support.

It is not suprising, then, that Bucklin's letters contain repeated references to the subject of wages. In February 1863, Bucklin's sister, Almira, wrote, "let me know some items of what you are appointed to do and tell me how much wages you get a month."[61] In September 1864, she wrote again, "I want you to write soon and tell me all about the Hospital how you like it and how much you get a month. . . ."[62] Perhaps Almira herself was obsessed with money. But a November 1861 letter to Bucklin from Lewis Hawkins, a friend from Ithaca then at the front, strongly suggests that the question of wages factored into Bucklin's own thinking almost a year before she received her commission from Dix. Hawkins wrote,

> . . . you wanted to know if they wanted any more nurses in the hospital I have just seen too [sic] of our company that has been here most of the summer and they say they are fixing up the Mansion house with six hundred beds and they say the[re] will be a good chance for nurses I don't know how much wages they get but I have been told they get one dollar a month more than we do or one dollar less they dont know which and they say the work is very easy I wish you would come and try it. . . .[63]

From a practical standpoint, Bucklin had to confront the issue of money. One need not doubt Bucklin's patriotic fervor to acknowledge her financial concerns.[64]

Considerable tension persisted around the issue of the female nurses' wages, even among the nurses themselves. In her memoir, Mary Newcomb claimed that throughout the course of her service as a military nurse she was "not after money," but only desired to "be where the men were, and where I could do the most good."[65] Moreover, Newcomb numbered herself among those who could not justify women's receipt of wages for such service. She laid out her views in a discussion of a confrontation with Dorothea Dix in Helena, Arkansas, to which town she and a Miss Mertz had travelled with the Eleventh Illinois Regiment. Newcomb wrote,

> One day there walked in on us an elderly lady with quite an orderly appearance. She said: "Are you appointed to this work?" Miss Mertz said: "I am not." She then looked at me and asked the same question. I said: "No, I volunteer my services. I did not come for pay, and I will accept no commission from any one." She then said: "I am Miss Dix." "Oh!" said I: ". . . When the doctors don't want me they will say so, and I will go, but you can't give me a commission."[66]

Apparently, Newcomb believed it improper for decent women to take money for work that was rightfully and morally theirs to perform, and indeed she never directly drew wages herself. However, it is worth noting that in her later life even Newcomb gladly accepted a government pension on the basis of having been a Civil War nurse. Moreover, her pension file indicates that after the early-1862 death of her husband, Hiram A. W. Newcomb, a sergeant with the Eleventh Illinois, she began to draw *his* $8.00 per month pension, which certainly helped to subsidize her "voluntary" services.[67]

The author of the introduction to Bucklin's memoir vigorously addressed the clearly controversial topic of women nurses receiving pay and rations in return for their labor. "*Pay and rations!*" wrote the otherwise unidentified "S. L. C."[68] Soldiers also received pay and rations, and "Who says, because they were *paid*, the sacrifice which they laid on their country's smoking altar was not a voluntary blood-offering?"[69] For Bucklin's literary defender, the receipt of wages in no way diminished the degree of her devotion to the Union cause. The introduction went on to address with passion the tendency among some people to compare, unfavorably, women in the government's

employ during the war with the women of the various commissions (such as the USSC) who in theory worked voluntarily:

> Many women, possessed of independent means, were enabled,
> under the patronage of the Commissions, and under the pretence
> of aiding the work in the hospitals, to behold the grandeur of the
> Capitol, and gratify a taste for romantic adventure. But how many
> of these slept for nights under the white cover of a tent. . . . ?[70]

This line of argument intended to exonerate from the charge
of unsuitable behavior women such as Bucklin, who gratefully
and without any apparent reservations accepted the wages that
the government offered. It was wrong, the writer argued, to
belittle the accomplishments and sacrifices of women simply
because they accepted payment for their difficult work. To hold
Bucklin and others like her in contempt on the basis of standards
of personal philanthropy, possible only for the very rich, betrayed such women's loyalty to the Union. Pointing to the
common soldier for comparison, the writer boldly challenged
critics of paid women's army service.

The fervor of S. L. C.'s challenge testified to the presence
of strong popular sentiment against middle-class women as wage
earners. After all, Victorian America attributed caretaking
skills to women on the basis of their sex, and considered self-
sacrifice a female virtue.[71] Many, therefore, expected women
nurses to donate their labor to the Army. Especially among
people who remained uncertain about the propriety of women
working in military hospitals, a substantial proportion believed,
impractically, that only patriotic motives devoid of financial
undertones could serve as justification for such work. To writers
who later described the Civil War nurses simply as women "with
a mighty love and earnestness in their hearts—a love and pity,
and an ability to show it forth and to labor in behalf of it,"

the Civil War represented a context in which pure (meaning financially unrewarded) patriotism and love of country constituted the only acceptable incentives for women in the nursing service.[72] Restrictions such as these did not apply to the soldiers, but in the case of women, a current ran through the Victorian mind, which held that only those women who *donated* their energy to the war effort merited recognition and praise.

As the Union's casualties increased, however, the middle-class, northern public, like the Medical Department, knew that the war could not be won without women becoming more intimately involved with day-to-day operations closer to the front. If the military did not allow women to take nursing positions, those positions would have to be filled, as they previously had been, by men, typically convalescent soldiers.[73] How much better for the Union Army if those men could be taken off nursing duty, be allowed to heal properly, and be returned to the front lines. In 1867, Anna Holstein wrote that it was the mid-September 1862 battle of Antietam in Maryland that shocked the northern public, and the government, into a true understanding of the war's ongoing physical consequences. A "dreadful slaughter" in which over 60,000 Union soldiers struggled against less than half that number of Confederates to "expunge the dishonor of previous defeats," and in which some 23,000 men ultimately fell dead or wounded,[74] Antietam, wrote Holstein, "brought before us the horrors and sufferings of war as we had never previously felt it."[75]

Of course, not all the dead and wounded at Antietam were Union soldiers. But the enormity of the sacrifice on both sides only enhanced the Union's comprehension of the need to bolster the Army's medical services with all available hands, male and female. If Antietam offered any indication, the months and perhaps years that lay ahead would demand the utmost of the army's medical service personnel, including women nurses. Although they might not necessarily have to lay down their lives, nurses would be required to sacrifice even the most common comforts of life—regular food, shelter, clothing, rest—to the urgent tasks at hand. Logically, only the relatively wealthy, such as Dix herself, could make these sacrifices without pay. But elite women did not enter the nursing ranks in large numbers. Instead, thousands of average middle-class women like Sophronia Bucklin enlisted as the female "foot soldiers" of the Union Army's medical corps, expecting little more than wages of forty cents a day and rations in return for their patriotic contributions. As Sarah Palmer wrote,

> I learned to appreciate the noble-heartedness of the untiring nurse, whose duties were for humanity's sake, not surely for the 12 dollars a month, and soldier's rations.
>
> That was but a sorry recompense, so far as a return for the days of toil, and the haunted nights, and the scanty fare. Still there was no murmur of discontent—men needed a woman's hand to minister unto them, and in their sore need she withheld not her own, so strong with a brave woman's honest purpose. [76]

Palmer silently shared in the praise she meted out, for she herself served as a Dix appointee. Her words rang with the frustration experienced by Bucklin and every other female nurse whose dedication to the soldiers' welfare came under suspicion each time she collected her wages.

Unlike the writers of the postwar commemorative works, who did not address the issue of women nurses earning wages for their labor, the author of the introduction to Sophronia Bucklin's memoir brought the issue of wages to the forefront. The fact that Bucklin herself barely touched on the subject in the body of the memoir probably reflected her awareness of its controversial nature, as well, perhaps, as her own lingering discomfort with it. But if Bucklin hesitated to address to any great extent the issue of money and wages, she demonstrated considerably less restraint when it came to the sharp conflicts and tensions she experienced in the course of her work as an army nurse. Many women during and after the war chose, in their writings, to emphasize the positive aspects of their interactions with the male medical staff of the hospitals and to balance their criticisms with words of praise. Hannah Ropes wrote home to her daughter from the Union Hotel Hospital late in 1862, "We upon the whole have had goodish men to rule over us." But, she added, "between the surgeons, stewards, [male] nurses and waiters, the poor men in all the hospitals barely escape with life or clothes or money."[77] Amanda Stearns wrote to her sisters about the reception she received upon her arrival at the Armory Square Hospital in Washington. Apparently, the ward master, a man named "Jobes," did everything in his power to counteract the unpleasantness of the surgeon-in-charge. When the surgeon failed to acknowledge Stearn's presence, she wrote, Jobes "took the first opportunity to say, 'This is the lady who is to have charge of the ward.'" The surgeon, "evidently not approving of a lady's presence in a hospital," responded with a "little nod" and a "Humph!" and moved on. Throughout her stay, Jobes supported and encouraged her, but Stearns was the first to admit that "[i]t is not every nurse here that has a Jobes, who when Father Wilson at the cookhouse protests that 'there are too many special diets on Ward E's lists, and he will have to report the nurse there,' tells him 'to go to the d——l'. . . ."[78]

Some women stressed points of cooperation and mutual respect among the men and the women and glossed over points of conflict. As Elvira Powers confided to her diary in June 1865, "notwithstanding that there is much feeling upon the subject of her real or imagined interference with professional duties, yet there are many wise and noble surgeons in the service who rightly appreciate woman's influence in a hospital and have assisted her in every noble word and work." A woman could consider herself "amply repaid," she continued, if at the end a physician voiced his appreciation of her work, saying in effect,

> You have been a blessing to the patients and a help to me—have attended to your own duties as nurse without interfering with those of mine as physician. And there are those whose lives are due to your care. Some were very low with nervous prostration and nostalgia—another name for home-sickness—and your conversation and attention has aroused, cheered, strengthened and saved them.[79]

In conveying her vision of the harmonious cooperation among male doctors and women nurses in the military hospitals, Powers inadvertently exposed the rigidity of the unwritten rules that were meant to govern interactions among the various parties. Similarly, when Bucklin recalled that "No man of generous heart wished women shut out from the doors of either field or city hospitals. . . . It was only the ruffians . . . who wished to exclude [the female nurses] from performing the labors, which kept our feet on the round from early morn to the setting of the sun,"[80] she recognized that there were male hospital personnel who supported the women's work, but also made it clear that there were "ruffians" who most certainly did not. Surgeons-in-charge, in particular, who generally were (or at least tended to be) "a law unto themselves,"[81] commonly expected the nurses to confine themselves to specific assigned tasks and to refrain from meddling in other affairs. So long as the women understood and followed these rules, the system ran smoothly.

Certainly, there were hospitals where strong bonds of mutual appreciation between the nurses and their male colleagues developed. Emily Elizabeth Parsons wrote home from Benton Barracks Hospital in April 1863, "the Doctors find the wards where there are lady nurses get along so nicely that they are all anxious to have them. They keep asking me when they too shall have ladies in their wards."[82] Female nurses' pension files in the National Archives contain many letters from surgeons in support of the women's pension applications, praising them for work well done. In 1894, for example, former surgeon T. B. Hood wrote in support of nurse Harriet Sharpless's pension request that the "service rendered by Miss Sharpless was faithful & capable and efficient in the highest degree—if devotion to the sick and wounded during the late war could entitle any one to consideration, Miss Sharpless is entitled."[83] Men with lingering hostility toward women nurses would not have written such letters, designed as they were to help the former nurses gain benefits from the federal government, which explicitly acknowledged their military service.

However, as Elvira Powers's words suggest, and Bucklin's memoir clearly indicates, women nurses frequently failed or refused to understand and follow the rules laid down by surgeons-in-charge and others, contributing substantially to strained relations among male and female hospital personnel. Indeed, antagonism and conflict between the nurses and the male staff were regular features of at least some Civil War hospitals. At the Wolf-street Hospital in Alexandria, Virginia, Bucklin's appointment in the spring of 1863, even staff eating arrangements provided a source of friction, and a symbol of contested hierarchy. Nurses and surgeons used the same "mess," but at different times, an arrangement that meant the nurses' food "had to be prepared first, to allow them [the surgeons] ample time to grow hungry. . . ." Because male cooks cared more about pleasing the surgeons than the nurses, they frequently served the women scanty, undercooked meals in order to guarantee sufficient quantity and the proper degree of cooking for the surgeons who would follow them. Thus, Bucklin wrote, at noon,

> One thin slice of bread was laid by our plates—we could get no more until another meal. A nice roast would be served for dinner, and, when twelve o'clock arrived, the beef would be cooked only sufficiently for the blood to ooze out under the knife. From this raw material, thin slices were shaved, which were placed upon our plates, together with potatoes cooked in the patients' soup, another round of bread, and a draught of the filthy Potomac water. The roast went back into the oven, and, of course, was "delicious," when the surgeons' mess hour arrived.[84]

At Wolf-street, the miserable meal situation was only one element in a generally hostile environment that left Bucklin convinced of the surgeons' determination, in this hospital at least, "by a systematic course of ill-treatment toward women nurses, to drive them from the service." In consequence, Wolf-street saw a high turnover of female nurses—more than ten in one year, "many of them recognized and efficient helpers of the Government. . . ."[85]

Bucklin related such vivid tales of the struggles between women nurses and the male medical establishment, not just at Wolf-street but at all the hospitals where she was stationed, that her memoir—along with its expression of her obvious joy in caring for the soldiers—leaves the impression not of the overwhelming harmony among men and women in wartime hospital service that others would later emphasize, but rather of cacophony. *In Hospital and Camp* sharply depicts doctors' and nurses' opposing views and goals, not simply in regard to the best care for the sick and wounded soldiers, but also in terms of their own places in the military medical system. Although many women later wrote only of their experiences of men's favorable adjustment to women's presence, and kept relatively silent on the subject of conflicts encountered on the job, Sophronia Bucklin chose to reveal both the positive and the negative aspects of a female nurse's hospital life during the war. As the memoir's introduction noted, Bucklin had generally borne her frustrations with the "insolence" and the "tyranny" of numerous "shoulder-strapped officials" in silence in order to avoid risking dismissal. ("*We* were not cowered from any fear of corporeal punishment being inflicted," she wrote later, ". . . but rather [from the] thought of usefulness cut off, of the disgrace of dismissal, of being shut out where our hands could not minister unto the brave wounded."[86]) Once the war was over, however, she felt morally bound to speak as openly of the conflicts and injustices she had witnessed, as she did of the real pleasures of wartime service. Ostensibly a simple remembrance of her years as a Union Army nurse, Bucklin's memoir also unwittingly became her testimony to a gender system under stress.[87]

Among other things, Bucklin wrote about the arbitrariness of the orders given by surgeons with respect to where the nurses could go within a hospital. At her first assignment at the Judiciary Square Hospital in Washington, for example, she found that women nurses were forbidden to enter the kitchen, which deprived them of the possibility of selecting food items they deemed necessary for their patients. Because the idea that a woman might be prevented from entering the kitchen in a typical mid-nineteenth-century middle-class home was so utterly absurd (was not the kitchen the center of woman's domain?), nurses like Bucklin neither understood such a regulation nor did they feel compelled to obey it. "We devised many ways to relieve their [the soldiers'] wants," she wrote vaguely. Elsewhere, she seemed to allow the possibility that nurses occasionally even pilfered from hospital stores.[88]

Bucklin also wrote of the frustration the women nurses often experienced in their attempts to accomplish the work they had come to do—tending the sick and wounded—as male officials frequently assigned them to duties that had little to do with the soldiers' medical care or that seemed designed to erode the women's resolve. On one occasion, Bucklin and her female co-workers found themselves charged with "washing the dishes for the whole ward . . . [so that] we wielded the dish cloth for days, soiling our clothing, and [were] often busily employed when we knew we needed the hours for rest." At the Wolf-street Hospital, the surgeon-in-charge determined to deny Bucklin and another woman nurse of the possibility of doing any real labor at all. "On inquiring what work was to be given to my hands to do," wrote Bucklin,

> the surgeon in charge remarked, that there was very little to do; if I found little to do, do that—if I found less, to do that. Then we wandered aimlessly about, forbidden to enter the wards; the only employment presenting itself being the care of the linen with the ironing and mending—long and irksome tasks, which we felt were not the ones we had come out to perform.[89]

Later, this same surgeon dismissed her. As female nurses frequently explained, a hospital's surgeon-in-charge determined not only the duties of the nurses but the conditions and comfort of each nurse's situation. "It was in his power to make our paths smooth, or to throw disagreeable things in the way which would make our positions extremely unpleasant, and subject us to no ordinary annoyance," wrote Bucklin. The surgeon-in-charge also freely set the terms of a nurse's attachment and discharge, at least until the Surgeon General's Office declared in October 1863 that the "*reasons* for the discharge of any woman nurse would be endorsed upon the certificate of her removal," eliminating some of the potential for the individual surgeon's capriciousness. Until then, wrote Bucklin, "Miss Dix was subject to much annoyance by the frequent appearance of her competent nurses, who had been ordered to report to her by some domineering surgeon, whose love of power had been thwarted in some manner."[90]

And it was not just surgeons who tried to exert this sort of control over the nurses. Earlier, at Hammond General Hospital in Maryland, Bucklin's wardmaster and the hospital steward tried to engineer her removal—on charges that she unlawfully held a key to the cupboard containing the hospital's stimulants. Apparently, they failed in their efforts, but the struggle left Bucklin painfully aware of the fundamental tenuousness of her position.[91]

Not even the bloodiest battle or the severest hospital conditions seem to have been able to ease completely the tensions between the men and women who worked to save the war's fallen soldiers. For Bucklin, the summer of 1863 began with several weeks of frustrated idleness following her involuntary departure from the Wolf-street Hospital, during which time she raged over the thought "of the treatment to which loyal women had been subjected, when patriotic zeal had nerved them to leave home and its comforts to endure privation, sickness, hunger, and fatigue—and, after all, they were held from the good which they were eager to do."[92] Soon, however, the ghastly July battle at Gettysburg, Pennsylvania, in whose wake over 50,000 Union and Confederate soldiers lay wounded or dead,[93] cleared the way for her reassignment, this time to a field hospital close to the site of the massacre that had sealed the doom of the Confederacy. Bucklin described the scene that greeted her arrival at the battle site: "Everywhere," she wrote, "the grass had been moistened with blood," and everywhere,

were evidences of mortal combat, everywhere wounded men were lying in the streets on heaps of blood-stained straw, everywhere there was hurry and confusion, while soldiers were groaning and suffering. . . . It seemed impossible to tread the streets without walking over maimed men, who had fallen in the shock of that July's fire. . . . They lay like trees uprooted by a tornado, . . . they lay on the bloody ground, sick with the pains of wounds, grim with the dust of long marches and the smoke and powder of battle, looking up with wild haggard faces imploringly for succor.[94]

As one of the first women nurses to reach Gettysburg, Bucklin quickly set about "raising the wounded": grooming, bandaging, and feeding the hundreds that lay before her. "I washed agonized faces," she wrote, "and combed out matted hair, bandaged slight wounds, and administered drinks of raspberry vinegar and lemon syrup."[95] In the first few days after the guns fell silent, in the scramble to cope with the consequences of a three-day slaughter, male and female workers rushing to serve at the field hospital—little more than five hundred tents set in rows across a wide field[96]—can have had little time to revive dormant tensions that plagued them in other places. As emergency triage gave way in subsequent days to the establishment of routines and duty rosters, however, Bucklin and some forty other women nurses, who rapidly appeared at the hospital, found themselves on an increasingly structured schedule—"[b]eef tea was passed three times a day, stimulants three times, and extra diet three times—making nine visits which each woman nurse made a day to each of the two hundred men under her charge."[97] The very regularization of hospital life, as summer faded into fall, meant that each worker was expected to learn and uncomplainingly fill his or her place in an emerging system.

As time went by at Gettysburg, and the field hospital's internal workings came to resemble those of hospitals across the theater of war, Bucklin acknowledged that "[t]here was no conflicting of duty" among the various caretakers. But the lack of overt friction belied the antagonism kept hidden beneath the surface of hospital personnel relations. Indeed, Bucklin noted the same tensions at Gettysburg as had been present elsewhere, but here, at least, perhaps because of the inescapably awesome nature of the soldiers' sacrifice, all felt "constrained to keep in utter silence the many thoughts, which [might otherwise] have been given forth without restraint."[98] Even so, Bucklin later reported that some unnamed "foolishness" at one point prompted the surgeon-in-charge to consider releasing her from duty, and it was only with a vigorous apology on her part for whatever she was believed to have done (but denied doing) that she managed to convince him to keep her on. "I smothered my pride of spirit," she wrote with obvious distaste, "believing it would hurt me less to make the humiliating statement than it would to go, and thereby leave the boys to other hands."[99] Bucklin's words displayed her resolve to continue with the army, as well as her firm belief that the "boys" belonged in her own and the other women nurses' hands. In contrast to those who claimed that women's caretaking abilities should be confined to the members of their households, Bucklin argued for women's rightful presence wherever human suffering demanded it.

Surgeons and other men in positions of greater or lesser authority in the medical establishment frequently felt threatened by the women nurses' presence, not least of all because of the women's often calculated rereading of prewar cultural assumptions about the inherent right of women to care for the sick. If the men did not fear actual replacement by the women, they nonetheless felt their authority coming under question as the women nurses competed for a measure of control over the soldiers' care. Bucklin described a number of situations in which she attacked a surgeon's abuse of his diagnostic and prescriptive powers in relation to the patients. Although the bulk of the medically untrained female nurses did not regularly involve themselves in a critique of medical techniques, Bucklin figured among those who challenged the surgeons' overzealous use of amputation. She sadly remembered a soldier who had died as a consequence not of his wound, but of the surgery performed to remove his arm. "I shall never out live the feeling," she wrote,

> that his was an unnecessary amputation, although I do not mean to censure or arraign the judgment of any one; but his wound was only that of a bullet through the fleshy part of the arm, and it seemed to be doing as well as could be expected. After the amputation, which did not discharge properly, his symptoms grew fatal. . . .[100]

Bucklin's self-effacing tone did not hide the boldness that underlay her questioning of the surgeon's judgment.

The issue of unwarranted amputations provoked other female nurses as well. Mary Newcomb not only wrote about it in her memoir, but also confronted it head on during her nursing service. At Mound City Hospital, she wrote, she asserted herself against a group of doctors intending to amputate a boy's arm. Shocked by her intervention, one angry older doctor reminded her of her place. "We are sent here to take care of these fellows," he told her, "and we don't propose to have anyone interfere." To this Newcomb brazenly responded,

> I am well aware of that fact . . . but I persist that that boy's arm shall not come off. I don't care who sent you nor what authority you work under. . . . I wear no shoulder-straps, but that boy's arm shall not come off while I am here.

In Newcomb's account, the old doctor then reexamined the boy's arm, declared it worth saving, at least for the time being, and moved on.[101] Newcomb, it should be recalled, was not an external appointee of Dix or any of the commissions, but was nurse to her husband's regiment. Her willingness to confront the old doctor may well have reflected the relative security of her position.

In any case, by taking independent action on behalf of the soldiers' welfare, women nurses sought simultaneously to "make the front truly a home-front" and to make a place for themselves in a world otherwise dominated by men, a world in which they believed they had a proper place.[102] Women did not want to take over men's jobs, but wanted to be recognized for the special skills they brought to their own. Where recognition was denied, women nurses increased the friction by finding numerous, often evasive ways to do what they considered right.[103] In contrast, doctors sought to protect their authority over the untrained, to maintain their prominence in the medical hierarchy not just for the duration of the war, but with an eye toward the profession as it would develop in the future.[104] These men railed against women's interference, women's incompetence, and women's unsuitability for hospital work in order to drive the women away. Those women who did not buckle under the hostility of the male officials with whom they had to work, in turn asserted their usefulness, their skills, and their natural fitness for the tasks at hand. Sarah Palmer inadvertently summed up this response: "I found it *was* a place for woman," she wrote.

All of man's boasted ingenuity had been expended to devise terrible engines with which to kill and maim God's own image and if war was right, it was right for women to go with brothers, and husbands, and sons, that in the time of peril the heart might not faint with the thought of an untended death-bed in the crowded hospitals, where no hand but the rough soldiers' should close the dead staring eyes. . . . Had there been more women to help us, many a brave man, whose bones moulder beneath the green turf of the South, would have returned to bless the loved ones left in the dear old home behind him.[105]

Men had made this war, she seemed to say, and the proper place for women, with their tender hands and their depth of caring, was precisely at the point where they could best cope with and counteract the effects of men's awful creation.

Bucklin did not hesitate to record in her memoir the many conflicts she and other female nurses experienced with their male co-workers and superiors, and she dealt with similar candor with the struggles among women in the hospital hierarchy. Bucklin wrote, for example, of the arrival at Hammond General Hospital of a Mrs. Gibbons, who had previously served as the hospital's matron, and who boldly indicated her intention to reestablish herself in that position and proceeded, apparently unchallenged, to do so. In the weeks that followed, Mrs. Gibbons systematically replaced Dix's nurses with nurses of her own choosing, and before too long Bucklin found herself jobless. Given her keen awareness of the gender conflict that surrounded her, it comes as no surprise that Bucklin characterized Mrs. Gibbons in male terms, recalling her "masculine contempt for all women not endowed with her energetic, unyielding will," and admitting that it was "impossible for me to attempt to see anything lovely or feminine in the character of the new matron."[106] Bucklin also wrote of the hostility between herself and another woman nurse at City Point Hospital in Washington, aroused, according to Bucklin, by the other nurse's resentment of Bucklin's generosity towards her patients. Irked that Bucklin's soldiers seemed content and her own merely complained that they wished she would treat them as well, the unnamed nurse complained daily to the surgeon-in-charge, and generally "manifested a very unkind feeling . . . [although] I could conscientiously disavow having anything but the best good of those suffering men in view."[107]

Discord in Civil War hospitals clearly extended beyond the issue of gender boundaries. Other memoirs, too, record conflicts between women in the hospitals, not least of all between the regular nurses like Bucklin and those women who approached military hospitals with a desire not to take up nursing, but simply, and briefly, to extend their benevolent influence among the soldiers. Interestingly, such women met little criticism from male medical personnel. The same Victorian ideals that characterized women as morally superior doers of good but restricted the context of women's benevolent activity to the home or the local community, freely allowed that such women might legitimately visit a military hospital on occasion, especially if they brought with them items reminiscent of peacetime and home, such as once familiar foods that the war had turned into luxuries, to comfort the hospital-bound. As one nurse wrote, doctors often welcomed women who "came in bands, bringing and distributing through the wards their gifts of delicacies to tempt the appetite, reading matter, paper and envelopes, always with such words of cheer, comfort, praise, and gratitude, that fainting hearts were reassured. . . ."[108] Doctors reserved a different attitude for women who chose to spend days, weeks, months, even years in a bloody, foul-smelling, pest-ridden military hospital filled to capacity with men in the most physically degraded condition, performing for these soldiers duties considered far too intimate or too hard or too grimy for a woman's hands. Nurses, in turn, resented female outsiders who were obviously unwilling to make the harsh and long-term commitment to soldier care.

In their reports of encounters with female United States Sanitary Commission agents and other visiting, nonmedical elite women, middle-class nurses displayed an attitude of cold disdain. In June 1864, Amanda Stearns, serving at the Armory Square Hospital in Washington, D.C., wrote with irritation in her journal about a visit from "a troop of ladies." They "came with strawberries," she wrote, "to treat the hospital," and as a result, the nurses were, "as usual . . . obliged to submit to their fashionable airs and want of sense."[109] A similar tone of contempt crept into a letter Katharine Wormeley wrote in June 1862: "to-day, at the close of such a week, comes an 'excursion party' from Washington,—Congressmen and ladies in silks and perfumes and lilac kid gloves! 'Sabbath-breaking picknickers on a battle-field!' as Georgy [Georgeanna Woolsey] called them in a rage."[110] And a May 1863 letter by Mary von Olnhausen read,

> A lot of women came in to-day just as I was dressing "Blue Beard's" wound. One of them, as she saw it, just gave a stagger and fell up against the wall. She was pale as could be, and I thought would faint. All the women crowded around, and one young one said, "Oh, I always thought I should so like to be a nurse." She looked about as much account as a yellow cat.[111]

At different times, different "ladies" were the recipients of the army nurses' scorn, but at all times the scorn itself shone through, directed at women who presented themselves as "superior" in some way, indeed, who clung to precisely those traditional notions of woman's proper sphere that the nurses, by definition, defied. Nurses felt only contempt for those women who, from their perspective, pursued ways of contributing to the war effort that would leave their hands clean, be it of blood, dirt, or perhaps the exchange of money for labor that repulsed them. Sarah Palmer wrote with disgust of a visit to her field hospital of some "ladies," after which she "turned to my tent, sick of folly—sick of fashion—sick of that species of my sex which trailed costly silks and laces in the dry dust, when the help for which many died even, could not be given from their hands."[112]

Less obviously, perhaps, but no less certainly, tensions among women constituted further symptoms of a gender system crisis provoked by the war's unsettling influence on the prewar definition of middle-class womanhood. In essence, the army nurses rejected a model of womanhood that they had come to experience as confining, a model epitomized by Palmer's useless "ladies" in their "costly silks and laces." Simultaneously, Bucklin and others rejected the uneven system of power relations between men and women for which such a model provided a fundamental component. Instead, they pressed, with varying degrees of strength, for an altered system in which their demonstrated abilities and contributions could be acknowledged and rewarded with gratitude, with pay, with respect, and perhaps even with a share of undisguised power. Sophronia Bucklin's uniqueness lay in her keen awareness and her bold confrontation of these issues, not only in her memoir, but also on the job.

It must be noted, however, that although Bucklin and other female nurses frequently found their routes into army service obstructed, and their work in military hospitals frustrating and rife with conflict, they took great pride and derived great pleasure from the nursing experience. Bucklin regularly reminded her readers that she loved her work and wished to do no other. Of her sentiments at the end of the war and the termination of her nurse's commission, Bucklin wrote,

> Among the sad memories of these years in hospital and camp, of some fast friendships formed when the dead lay around us, with the suffering and groaning on every hand, there remain some pleasant ones,—the cherished of my life. In the silent watches of the night and the peaceful hours of the day they come to me as ministering angels to soothe my soul, when troubled with life's many little perplexities, and awaken in me a charitable view of earthly affairs.[113]

Clearly, Bucklin's labor in the Union cause gave her great satisfaction, above and beyond any conflicts she experienced and any wages she earned.

For most middle-class women, service in the Army medical corps was distinctly different from any work they had done before, and it required countless physical and emotional adjustments. "It was no small matter for me to apply the wet towel to the faces," wrote Bucklin of her first days at the Judiciary Square Hospital in Washington. "I had been nurtured in quietude. . . . I did not fancy it would wear off soon."[114]

Nevertheless, these women perserved against the mental and emotional obstacles that they discovered within themselves, as well as against all obstacles posed by others from without. Not surprisingly, the soldiers who experienced the benefits of the women's presence and care accepted them with appreciation. Bucklin wrote, "Woman's help had not been counted upon . . . [a]nd when her hand with its softer touch pressed on the aching forehead . . . words failed in the attempt to express the gratitude of a full heart."[115] A journal entry by Emily Elizabeth Parsons, a Hospital Transport Service nurse and later matron of the Jefferson Barracks Hospital in St. Louis, confirmed the truth of Bucklin's words. Parsons wrote of the arrival of herself and several other female nurses on board a ship sent to the battlefield to convey soldiers to safer ground:

> The poor men on the boat . . . were so glad to see women round them. They had not seen a woman for weeks and weeks. One of the ladies heard one of the men say to another, as she went by, "Tom, is it not good to see the women round?"

And she added, "If those who object to women in hospitals could only hear the speeches that are made to us, I think their objections would be answered."[116] In an 1864 report to the Western Sanitary Commission, Eliza Chappell Porter wrote of the arrival at a battle site of a group of women nurses like herself: "Never was the presence of women more joyfully welcomed. It was touching to see those precious boys, looking up into our faces with such hope and gladness."[117] Certainly, the gratitude of the soldiers constituted a key element in the women's satisfaction. "It was wonderful to see the universal childishness with which each threw himself upon our sympathies," Bucklin wrote.[118] Julia S. Wheelock concurred. "It was pleasant," she wrote, "to know that your efforts, however humble, were gratefully appreciated—yea, an hundredfold. And there was a melancholy pleasure even in administering to dying wants. . . ."[119]

But perhaps even more satisfying than the appreciation of the soldiers was a woman's sense of being a soldier herself, the awareness that she had sacrificed the comforts of home to contribute powerfully to the Union cause. Daydreams of peacetime and home, wrote Bucklin, frequently dissipated when the groans of the sick and wounded pierced her thoughts and caused her mind to turn to the work at hand. "My heart held my country and its heroes dearest, and I turned . . . to bend over the beds of some who had been very nigh to death, and give a little ray of comfort to others, who were fast drifting into the cold current."[120] Emily Parsons wrote home in an uncompromising tone to those who questioned her service: "I am in the army just as Chauncy [her brother] is, and I must be held to work just as he is; you would never think of requesting he might not be sent on picket duty because it was hard work."[121] Explaining herself to her sisters in a letter home, Amanda Stearns wrote simply, "I could not remain at home inactive when there was so much need of service."[122] Likewise, Hannah Ropes wrote home to her daughter Alice, "I miss you and mother very much, but I can't go back unless you need me more than the soldiers do."[123] With the end of the war in sight, Cornelia Hancock wrote a letter to her sister, which captured the intentions of many women like her. She wrote, "I shall come home when the 12th N. Jersey is mustered out of service. . . ."[124]

Women who wrote about their experiences in Civil War nursing expressed great satisfaction in the work, in their realization that they were contributing directly to the war effort, and in the soldiers' profound gratitude for their care. The tone of many verged on absolute delight, reflecting the joy of adventure and the exhilaration of activity. "To have a ward full of sick men under my care is all I ask," wrote Emily Parsons in a letter of January 1863. "I should like to live so all the rest of my life."[125] Cornelia Hancock wrote her mother from Gettysburg, "I like to be here very much, am perfectly suited to the suffering and the work just suits me."[126] Amanda Stearns wrote to her sister, "This life is one of constant interest and excitemer̃t, like a journey through foreign lands."[127] *"This is life,"* wrote Katharine Wormeley to a friend. And a few days later she continued,

> As for the ladies among whom my luck has thrown me, they are just what they should be,—efficient, wise, active as cats, merry, light-hearted, thoroughbred, and without the fearful tone of self-devotion which sad experience makes one expect from benevolent women. We all know in our hearts that it is thorough enjoyment to be here,—*it is life*, in short; and we would n't be anywhere else for anything in the world.[128]

After the war, the Reverend Henry Bellows, President of the USSC, wrote of the army nurses,

> . . . the rewards of these women were equal to their sacrifices. They drew their pay from a richer treasury than that of the United States Government. I never knew one of them who had had a long service, whose memory of the grateful looks of the dying, of the few awkward words that fell from the lips of thankful convalescents, or the speechless eye-following of the dependent soldier, or the

pressure of a rough hand, softened to womanly gentleness by long illness,—was not the sweetest treasure of all their lives.[129]

Bellows was right to point out that Civil War nurses such as Bucklin relished their work in ways they themselves could not have foreseen. He was wrong, however, to suggest that there was a simple equation between what the women gave to the Union cause and what they took away with them, and that women who had sacrificed freely when the war emergency had presented itself to them, having received ample spiritual payment for their sacrifices, would now joyfully return to the home front satisfied with their consciousness of the good they had done. "[T]he rewards of these women," wrote Bellows, "were equal to their sacrifices."[130] Such a statement smoothed over the complexities of the women nurses' experiences, and implied that they had already received in full measure the compensation they deserved and could now return quietly to their homes.

Bellows's statement contained elements of truth, but it excluded many of the aspects of women nurses' wartime experiences that Sophronia Bucklin's story reveals: issues such as the northern, middle-class public's initial (and in many cases persistent) objection to women in military hospital service; the need for the great bulk of the women nurses to receive real wages for their service, in addition to the more "spiritual" pay that the soldiers' thankfulness could provide; and the nurses' early and repeated conflicts with surgeons and other officials and staff regarding their presence and relative status in the hospitals, the tasks they could be assigned, their assumptions of moral superiority, their roles in patient diagnosis and care, and the possibility that their wartime service might generate a new women's profession.[131] Bellows glossed over these points, the points at which the prewar gender system, with its guidelines for proper behavior and for gender interaction, suffered great pressure.

By glossing over such issues, Bellows contributed to an early postwar image that cleansed the topic of women in Civil War nursing of its unpleasant and threatening aspects and simultaneously dismissed the notion that middle-class women might or could derive some sort of permanent benefit from their participation as nurses in the war effort. What if women like Bucklin struggled after the war to continue in paid hospital service, putting another wedge in men's domination over professional health care? What if they sought to extend past Appomattox their wartime license to function in new ways in the public sphere? Postwar historians such as Bellows attempted quickly to seal off the doors to change that Bucklin and the military nurses had opened.

Photo courtesy of the State Historical Society of Iowa,
Des Moines.

CHAPTER TWO

"Men Did Not Take to the Musket More Commonly than Women to the Needle"

Annie Wittenmyer and Soldiers' Aid

Iowa had two armies serving the nation—the great column, 78,000 strong, of boys in blue at the front, and that other army of men and women who furnished the muscles of war here at home. . . . Nations are not saved by muskets alone, but by the great, strong hearts that beat in one impulse, and whose sacrifices are not in the smoke of battle, but in the loyal duty that lies nearest, and without visible reward.

—S. H. M. Byers, *Iowa in War Times*

Bits and pieces of information about Annie Wittenmyer's life prior to the outbreak of the Civil War in 1861 combine to present the impression of an energetic, well-to-do merchant's widow in the town of Keokuk, Iowa, long dedicated to local benevolent activities. Nearly a decade before the war, Wittenmyer spearheaded the establishment of a free school for the underprivileged children in Keokuk, first in her home and later in a warehouse. Ultimately, she enrolled some two hundred children.[1] Although most midcentury schools charged tuition, automatically precluding attendance by the less fortunate, Wittenmyer aimed to redress this wrong in her town, in part, perhaps, because she herself had received a more advanced training than was usual for young women at that time, having attended a girls' seminary as a child in Ohio.[2]

Wittenmyer felt a strong commitment to education. She derived additional motivation for founding the school from her belief in Christian responsibility. More than one biographer later described Annie Wittenmyer as a prominent, zealous churchwoman.[3] Wittenmyer and others who helped to organize the free school no doubt saw the school as a vivid expression of Christian duty. "Many of the young scholars," wrote one historian, "were ragged, dirty and neglected waifs from off the streets. The good women of Keokuk cooperated with Annie and helped wash and clothe them."[4] For women like Wittenmyer, education of the poor went hand in hand with Protestant Christian benevolence, and thus it comes as no surprise that, within the free school, Wittenmyer also developed a Sunday school class, which in 1857 formed the nucleus of Keokuk's new Chatham Square Methodist Episcopal Church.[5] The free school was continued in one form or another until Keokuk established its own public school system some years later.[6]

Perhaps it is to be expected, then, that thirty years after the war ended, in her preface to *Under the Guns: A Woman's Reminiscences of the Civil War*, Wittenmyer addressed the commencement of her wartime activities in soldier relief in a rather mundane tone, as if to suggest that the war itself brought to this longtime philanthropist not so much a break with her normal life as a shift into a new field of labor. "Camps and hospitals," she wrote,

> were established near my home in Keokuk, Iowa, early in April, 1861. I began at once my ministrations to the sick in these newly established hospitals, and, during my daily visits, closed the eyes of the first Iowa soldier who died in the war. From that time on till the close of the war I was actively engaged all along the lines.[7]

Unlike Sophronia Bucklin, Wittenmyer recalled no sudden surge of emotion, no rush of patriotic fervor. For Wittenmyer, service to Iowa's soldiers constituted nothing more than an extension of the benevolent work in which she been engaged for years. Such was a woman's Christian duty, to care for those in need. In the war, for Wittenmyer as for countless other middle-class women whose patriotic roots ran deep, responsibility to country merged with responsibility to God. And so, with women across the Union, she moved quickly into action after the firing on Fort Sumter.[8]

In comparison with other women who sought to commit themselves in various ways to the Union's cause, Wittenmyer had distinct advantages. For one thing, her late husband, William Wittenmyer, had left her wealthy enough to pursue her work voluntarily, as she did for many months. In addition, the presence in her two-story brick home of her parents and her married sister (whose husband had enlisted) made it possible for her to leave her son behind with a clear conscience.[9] Moreover, Wittenmyer's widowhood itself limited the challenges she might anticipate as she moved into an ever wider scope of activity. No one accused her of licentious behavior or of abandoning her proper role in her family. The combined influence of these advantages by no means guaranteed Wittenmyer absolute freedom of movement, nor did it dictate her future prominence, for certainly many women relief workers of similar background and condition remained in the shadows. Her personal and financial independence, however, minimized for Wittenmyer specific obstacles to wartime service that others, such as Sophronia Bucklin, encountered full force.

On the 31st of May, 1861, the following news item appeared in Keokuk's daily newspaper, *The Gate City*:

> *Volunteer Aid Society*: The Ladies of the city are requested to meet on Saturday afternoon at 3 o'clock in the Medical College Hall, for the purpose of forming a Volunteer Aid Society.[10]

This formal summons masked the range of relief activities in which many of the town's women had already been engaged for troops passing through and stationed in Keokuk, strategically located at the southeastern corner of the state on the Mississippi River. Indeed, as soon as Iowa's soldiers had begun to gather in Keokuk, in response to President Lincoln's call to arms, townswomen had dedicated themselves to their support, supplying beds, bedding, clothing, food, and other essential items, regularly visiting soldiers' encampments and hospital bedsides, and gathering materiel of all sorts, including "200 needle-books, filled with the necessary appliances for repairing the wardrobe," to forward to regiments in the field.[11] But, in the six weeks between the attack on Fort Sumter and the end of May, it became clear that a systematization of women's individual and frequently disparate efforts could only serve the troops better. The result was the establishment of the Keokuk Ladies' Soldiers' Aid Society. The Society immediately named Wittenmyer its "Corresponding Secretary," assigning her responsibility for establishing and maintaining contact with sister societies throughout the state of Iowa.

Once organized, the Keokuk Society began in earnest to live

up to its initial proposal "to furnish . . . the Hospital stores needed for the comfort and recovery of our sick and wounded soldiers from Iowa," as a supplement to the inadequate supplies being furnished by a Federal Government unprepared for the massive mobilization a Union victory would require.[12] From the start, the Society's members did not stint on the attention they gave to the local military hospital. As a published report later explained, women of the Keokuk Society considered the support of the hospital and its patients—already numerous, due to outbreaks of camp illness, even before any real fighting began—their unique responsibility, and they took to the task with vigor, detailing individuals to visit the wards and determine what needs existed, in order to supply them as quickly and efficiently as possible. On one occasion, when sick soldiers far exceeded the number of beds available at the hospital, on the request of the surgeon in attendance, Society members produced overnight twenty-five "ticks"—straw-filled mattresses common wherever soldiers were quartered. Moreover, relief workers connected with the hospital regularly found themselves involved in matters beyond those of strict material demand and supply, as they

> stood over the beds of those very low, administering cordials and stimulants; . . . bathed fevered brows; and when all nursing was in vain . . . procured, made up, and sent in the burial shroud for many, that the friends of the deceased might feel that all respect has been paid to the honored dead. . . .[13]

For most of the Society's women, Keokuk's military hospital was as close as they would get to the battle front, although attendance at the death of soldiers from around their state undoubtedly seemed to bring the front very close indeed.

The horizon of the Society's activity, however, lay far beyond this one local military hospital. Although the Society's explicit purpose—to supply the needs of Iowa's regiments—seems to reflect a relatively narrow orientation toward the state rather than the nation, from a different perspective the Keokuk Society's goals appear quite broad. For Wittenmyer and her colleagues aimed at coordinating not only one town's relief activities, but the relief activities of women across Iowa. In fact, with Keokuk as the hub of Iowa's military activity—the point from which the state's regiments not only embarked for the war, but also the point to which they returned for medical care[14]— it was logical that the townswomen envisioned their Society as the state's central organization for soldier relief. It made sense in their minds to encourage Iowa's women to organize their efforts and funnel their supplies through Keokuk.

And so, in September, the state's newspapers widely circulated the following notice "To the Ladies of Iowa":

> We address you in behalf of the "Soldiers' Aid Society" of this city, and invite you to organize in your respective districts and cooperate with us in providing the Iowa volunteers, and especially in furnishing their hospitals with such comforts and conveniences as the Government does not provide.
>
> As our society will be in direct communication with the troops, they will, through their Secretary [Wittenmyer], transmit to you from time to time such items of intelligence as will advance the interests of your associations. . . .
>
> All packages sent to the "Soldiers' Aid Society," Keokuk, express pre-paid, will be forwarded to their destination free of charge.[15]

Even before the September notice, women's societies had been springing up around the state of Iowa, and many had already begun to channel their supplies through Keokuk as a result of Wittenmyer's effective fulfillment of her job as corresponding secretary, and of Iowa women's recognition of Keokuk's geographic centrality.[16] Immediately, the Society began keeping track of its dispersals of goods, at one early date some $35 worth to the Second, $8.20 to the Fifth, and $22.40 to the Seventh Iowa Regiments.[17] More than a desperate cry into a vacuum of inactivity, the September notice constituted an affirmation of the Keokuk Society's willingness to control a system of statewide soldier relief efforts that was rapidly falling in place.

The Society's September notice had another meaning, however, in light of the establishment of the United States Sanitary Commission (USSC) in New York City three months earlier, in mid-June 1861. The USSC—formed as a national umbrella organization for the coordination of soldier relief—attempted, from its inception, to guarantee its own preeminence in the field, as well as the preeminence of a national rather than a state-by-state outlook on war relief, by convincing or compelling local associations to direct all of their supplies through its offices in the various theaters of war, for general dispensation. As one historian has argued, for some women engaged in soldiers' aid, "the idea of a large-scale plan and a relationship with a prestigious national center may have offered special appeal," but for others, the program of the USSC represented a clear threat to local control, as well as a challenge to the sovereignty of a given region, and to a more community oriented understanding of women's role in the crisis. Consequently, the "practice of ignoring Sanitary circulars and sending contributions where it was believed they could do the most good was widespread."[18] Such was certainly the case in Keokuk. In its September circular, the Keokuk Society demonstrated its resistance to USSC control and its determination to retain jurisdiction over sanitary affairs in Iowa by publicly soliciting supplies from other local organizations to be distributed at the Society's discretion.

Throughout the fall of 1861, Wittenmyer and the Society proceeded to ignore notices from the USSC and instead busied themselves with the work of coordinating state relief efforts, and with beginning the process of distributing supplies to the increasingly scattered Iowa troops.[19] In August, Wittenmyer had followed the Second Iowa south along the Mississippi through Missouri to ascertain the regiment's needs.[20] In September, she took her first official trip to bring bandages, medicines, clothing, and food to the field.[21] The trip took about ten days; she returned briefly to provide information and collect more supplies, and then left again, for another three weeks, establishing a pattern that would continue long into the war.

Some months after Wittenmyer first headed south, the Society explained the key reason behind its decision to send the female corresponding secretary rather than a male representative on such "missions of mercy": "[W]e concurred in the judgment," stated an 1862 "Report of the Ladies' Soldiers' Aid Society" printed in the *Gate City*,

> that a woman, by her wide and quick sympathies and by her life-long experience as nurse in the sick room, was far better qualified to discover at a glance the wants and necessities of the sick; and with means at her disposal, to supply them with delicate tact and discriminating judgment.[22]

The "Report" thus explicitly indicated the Society's opinion that a woman would perform the required tasks more competently than a man, given her nature and her "life-long experience" as a caretaker. The "Report" thereby addressed potential critics of Wittenmyer's abandonment of Victorian gender conventions, suggesting that even though it demanded that some individuals travel far from home and community, war relief work—just another form of charity—was still women's work. The "Report" did not explain the Society's specific choice of Wittenmyer, but undoubtedly her financial and personal independence constituted critical factors, along with her efficiency and her willingness to go.

In the wake of the September 1861 trip, forerunner of countless trips to follow, Wittenmyer expanded her title within the Society from "corresponding secretary" to "general agent." As Wittenmyer became more influential within her own organization, she also developed a broader base of recognition and support throughout the state. Wittenmyer sent home informative and emotionally stirring reports about the troops as she travelled, which state newspapers gladly published. "Mr. Editor," she wrote in October 1861 from the camp of the Second Iowa, "We are glad to know that our Iowa troops are the best officered and best drilled men in the field; they make a good impression wherever they go."[23] Wittenmyer's published letters provided welcome news about the soldiers, stimulated interest in relief activities, and enhanced her reputation. Indeed, these letters undoubtedly contributed to a growing belief in Wittenmyer's unlimited capabilities. Many women wrote to her for help in finding nursing positions.[24] Mrs. O. Amigh addressed a letter to Wittenmyer from a hospital in Quincy, Illinois, complaining fiercely about the surgeon-in-charge. "Now Mrs. W," she wrote, "do what you can for us towards removing said Doctor . . . and the 3d Iowa will bless you forever. . . ."[25] Captain J. B. Sample even thought Wittenmyer might, in her travels to the South, be able to procure for him a black servant for hire. He wrote,

I have a *personal* favor to ask *now*. I want a "contraband" . . . [and] I want to ask you to give me such information as is necessary, that I may take the p[r]oper course to secure a woman—for I very much need one. I would like a woman from 18 to 40—capable of general housework. Should she have a boy—or brother from 12 to 16—and even a young child—we will take them all. . . .[26]

There is no evidence that Wittenmyer complied with his request.

Even as Wittenmyer and the Keokuk Society were actively and successfully cultivating their stature in the field of relief to the Iowa troops, forces closer to home than the USSC prepared to undercut them. On October 13, 1861, over four months after the first meeting of the Keokuk Society, Iowa Governor Samuel J. Kirkwood created the Iowa State Army Sanitary Commission as a direct auxiliary of the USSC. There is some evidence to suggest that the Governor simply hoped thereby to "strengthen" the work of the Keokuk Society.[27] More likely, the State Sanitary Commission represented his response to pressure from the USSC to bring his state's relief efforts into line with the national organization's plan. In any case, Governor Kirkwood immediately named thirteen distinguished male citizens of the state to the Commission's leadership. He appointed the Reverend A. J. Kynett of Lyons, Iowa, to a position parallel to Wittenmyer's: "corresponding secretary and general agent."[28]

Two weeks later, on October 28, the Governor compounded what quickly came to be perceived as a direct insult to the Keokuk Society, with a brief notice in the *Gate City* describing the new Commission. As if to deny the women's effective inroads into the very public context of wartime sanitary affairs, this official notice of the Commission's establishment failed entirely to mention the relief work already in progress by the Keokuk Society or any other women's organizations throughout the state. Instead, it outlined the tasks that lay ahead of the new commissioners, which substantially overlapped with the work Wittenmyer and her colleagues had already undertaken: visiting the various Iowa regiments and reporting on the sanitary and medical conditions of their encampments, determining regimental needs, and arranging for their supply.[29]

The women's disgust with the Governor's actions, and his failure to acknowledge their organization and their months of loyal service to Iowa's soldiers poured forth in a scathing unsigned article published three weeks later, probably written by a group of women in the Society and almost certainly resonant with the opinion held by Wittenmyer, who was nevertheless far too busy—and probably too savvy—to compose it herself. (After all, an overt individual attack on the State Sanitary Commission could potentially threaten her own reputation.) This remarkably bold and lengthy complaint demonstrated the women's unwillingness to retreat from the position they had assumed in Iowa's sanitary affairs, and raised several important issues relating to the right of the Governor's men to supplant them.

In the first place, the article addressed the fact that the women's commitment to soldier relief predated by "three or four months" that of the Governor's organization, granting them an obvious seniority in the field. The article then pointed to the successes the Keokuk Society had thus far achieved in multiplying the commitment of women around the state, in forwarding needed supplies to the front, and in getting the various Iowa associations into "very fair working order," such that they "gave promise and assurance of being equal to the work they had taken in hand."[30] The women's associations in general, and the Keokuk Society in particular, the article argued, not only predated the men's Commission but also made the Commission superfluous. In short, the women were doing fine on their own.

In addition to expressing the Society's anger over the establishment of the State Sanitary Commission, the article also contained a revealing comment concerning the women's perception of the difference between their own style of working and the style they anticipated from the men. Up to now, the article asserted,

The women were all earnestly interested and were doing matters in their own way, without sounding a trumpet before them or

magnifying their efforts by eliciting the services of the Honorables
of our State in order to blazon them abroad.

Now, however, a number of Iowa's prominent male figures, the
"honorables," had come to realize that "there is a great deal of
glory running to waste in this matter," that "there is a chance
for salaries and fees in carrying out this benevolent measure
which may be parcelled out to the wealthy men of the State."[31]
These "honorables" clearly intended to avail themselves of such
advantages, at the expense not only of the women who had
preceded them into sanitary work, but also of the soldiers about
whom the men undoubtedly cared little.

Not insignificantly, the article went on to indicate that the
benevolent women of Keokuk had previously experienced precisely the same kind of interference by the state's male "honorables," in relation, it seems, to Annie Wittenmyer's free school
project less than a decade before. In the past, the article pointed
out, "a society had been formed to clothe the ragged children
of our town, and send them to school." As long as the town's
women were in charge of the project, it proved most successful.
But then, quite uninvited,

> the gentlemen pitched in, enlarged the scope of the society, elected
> a squad of honorable and reverend officers and directors, and blo-
> wed and gassed generally. A grand inauguration meeting was held,
> and one regular meeting thereafter, at which honorables and judges
> of the U. S. Court and the Supreme Court of the State, and
> Reverends and doctors, made speeches. . . .

The result of the "gentlemen's" interference on this occasion
was only chaos, neglect, and the ultimate demise of the project
as it had originally been conceived. Determined not to repeat
this experience, the women of the Keokuk Ladies' Soldiers'
Aid Society, who for months had given their time and energy
voluntarily and with great success to the cause of soldier relief,

defiantly expressed their frustration that a new commission composed entirely of prestigious male figures was about to supersede
them, capture whatever accolades were associated with war
relief, and, if the situation with the free school provided credible
evidence, undermine the work itself.

The mocking tone taken in the article with regard to "salaries," "fees," and "glory" suggested that, in contrast to the
"honorables," these good, Victorian, Protestant women did not
expect financial rewards so much as they sought the more basic
reward of simply being allowed to continue their work unim-
peded. By leaving the women alone, the article seemed to say,
the men would acknowledge the propriety of what the Keokuk
Society and other local women's organizations were doing, and
would legitimize the wartime role that women across the state
of Iowa had assumed. The article thus soundly rejected the
constraints of a prewar gender system, which characterized the
more public, administrative aspects of war relief as inappropriate
for women, and asked that Iowa's women in general, and the
Keokuk Society in particular, be allowed to continue doing
what they had already been doing, without interference. "We
trust," the article commented sarcastically, that those who

> constitute the Sanitary Commission, will "post up," roll up their
> sleeves and "pitch in," and show the women how matters ought to
> be done. We should be right glad to see them take a personal
> interest in the matter and make a personal effort, or else get out
> of the way and not stand as an obstruction in the way of the women
> of Iowa, who would do this thing up much better without them.[32]

Simply but heatedly the women demanded the right to continue
doing the patriotic work they had undertaken, in the style they
deemed most appropriate, without outside intervention. By
seeking not only to gather the supplies needed by the soldiers,
but to manage and control their distribution and to receive

credit for doing so, Keokuk's women demonstrated two key things: their aversion to perceived male pork-barrel "politics as usual," and their full determination to protect the territory they had staked out for themselves in the war effort, even if that territory exceeded the gender boundaries the Governor and his men considered appropriate.

Governor Kirkwood displayed his early anticipation of friction between the Keokuk Society and the Commission, and specifically between the organizations' leaders, by writing to Wittenmyer two weeks before the women's angry *Gate City* article appeared, praising her work and requesting her cooperation with the Commission and with her counterpart, the Reverend Kynett. "You have set an example to the women of your state," wrote Governor Kirkwood placatingly,

> which I hope will be followed. . . . Rev. Kynett . . . is corresponding secretary of our organization formed to systematize the efforts . . . in this good cause. May I request you will communicate with him and endeavor to have all efforts to this end concentrated?[33]

If he hoped to appease Wittenmyer with this letter and convince her to relinquish control over Iowa sanitary affairs and resume a more acceptable role scraping lint and rolling bandages at home, Kirkwood should have considered his sentences more carefully. His use of the phrase "our organization," in referring to the Commission, implied a contrast between "ours" (the Commission) and "yours" (the Keokuk Society), giving the former legitimate status while denying it to the latter. It was a nuance that Wittenmyer would not have missed. The Governor further insulted Wittenmyer and the Keokuk Society by suggesting that, in his mind, the new Commission now officially constituted "Iowa's organization," whereas the Keokuk Society did not. Kirkwood then compounded the offense by stating explicitly that the Commission was designed to "systematize" the presumably "unsystematic" efforts already underway by women across the state, a characterization that the Society's members certainly would not have shared.

As the women's *Gate City* article indicated, the submission of the Keokuk Society to the direction of the Iowa State Army Sanitary Commission, and even just the harmonious coordination of the two organizations' activities, required far more than a poorly worded request from the Governor. The establishment of the Iowa Commission rapidly created confusion in the broad field of the state's relief work, and aid societies across Iowa now found themselves having to choose between loyalty to the Commission, with its impressive affiliation to the USSC, and loyalty to the Society, with its prior record of efficiency and its familiar faces and ways. A substantial proportion of women's aid organizations reiterated their support of the Keokuk Society. A typical letter from A. S. Marsh of Mt. Pleasant, Iowa, reached Wittenmyer at the end of November 1861:

> Our corrisponding [sic] secretary has been in corrispondence [sic] with the Secretary of this state's Sanitary Commission [Kynett] who strongly urged all hospital goods to be sent to their care. The society however, seems favourable as far as they have expressed themselves, to sending them subject to your direction. . . .[34]

In December, Mrs. J. B. Howell, president of the Keokuk Society, wrote to Wittenmyer in the field about the receipt of more letters of support. "I have read several letters from ladies of our state," she wrote, "and from the interest they manifest I should think the zeal of our ladies is on the increase and that there is also decided preference for our organization to that of the state San. Com."[35]

Early in 1862, the Commission, finding the task of absorbing the Keokuk Society's numerous allies more difficult than anticipated, attempted to assert its dominance over state sanitary affairs by calling for the financial records of all Iowa aid associations, as if its own hegemony was a given. Secretary of the Keokuk Society Mary Strong wrote defiantly to Wittenmyer, "We have resolved not to notice it [the Commission's mandate] at all."[36] Accustomed to ignoring the demands of the USSC, the women of the Keokuk Society decided to ignore the Commission's demands as well and to continue the work of gathering and distributing relief supplies—through Wittenmyer—just as before. Still, the Commission's order provoked concern among leaders of the Society regarding the continuing confidence and loyalty of the Society's affiliates. Would the Society's failure to comply with the Commission cast a shadow over their own operations? Even as they refused to provide the Commission with financial information, Society leaders like Lucretia Knowles wrote to Wittenmyer in the hope of developing a formal account of her expenditures. "People are beginning to ask what we have done with the money we received . . . ," she wrote, and requested that Wittenmyer begin keeping more detailed records to be forwarded to the Society's treasurer.[37] As Mary Strong explained later, "our friends through the State do not know what to do, whether to send to us as heretofore or whether we have united with the Commission."[38] It was not so much that other aid associations questioned the integrity of Wittenmyer and the Keokuk Society, as that the existence of the Commission and its insistence on "systematization" under its authority made necessary a rethinking of the Society's practices. That rethinking included a formalization of procedures, suggesting that in order for the women to retain the position they had carved out for themselves in Iowa's sanitary affairs, they would have to conform, at least somewhat, to the dictates of male organizational style, at least in terms of their record-keeping standards, which had hitherto been less rigid and grounded in a simple but absolute trust in Wittenmyer's uprightness. As Strong would later publicly insist, "We are satisfied that we could not have a more economical, efficient, untiring and prudent agent to distribute our stores. Not a single box or bundle of articles has been lost that has been sent through this Society for distribution by our Agent. . . ."[39] But the need to convey and sustain this trust in public against the suspicions aroused by the Commission's demands required certain structural changes, particularly as quantities of supplies grew and systems of allotment and delivery became more complex with the war's intensification.

Like the issue of salaries and titles, the bookkeeping issue highlighted differences in style in the two organizations, differences rooted in gender. At the same time, it pinpointed stresses the Victorian gender system was undergoing on the home front as a result of the war. As long as men and women functioned within their own theoretical "spheres" of activity (men in public and women in private), questions of style did not arise. In other words, no man challenged a woman's caretaking and management techniques when she exercised them within the context of her own household or even her immediate community. By crossing over into men's "sphere," however, by taking her skills out into the larger public realm—specifically the realm of war—a woman automatically elicited criticism. The women of the Keokuk Society, and Wittenmyer in particular, had undertaken a massive project of organized caretaking in the indisputably public, traditionally male domain of war. To many observers, the undertaking was entirely inappropriate. In order to continue operating and to relieve some of the pressure their activities exerted on a stubborn Victorian gender system, the Keokuk Society's leaders increasingly felt compelled to adopt male standards of professionalism, including the keeping of much more careful, detailed accounts of the receipt and distribution of supplies than had previously been the case. Soon they would discover the benefits of salaries and titles as well.

Needless to say, the adjustment was not an altogether smooth one, and it is not surprising that Wittenmyer seems at first to have taken offense at Knowles's request for accounts. Was someone questioning her integrity? At this early stage in the war, Wittenmyer was still learning the many-faceted art of political maneuvering, in this case the art of responding tactically to one "squeaky wheel" in order to protect the operation as a whole. In a March 1862 letter to Wittenmyer, Knowles reflected Wittenmyer's irritation when she exclaimed,

> [W]hat in the world are you exercising your mind so much about your expenses for? Who suspects your honesty madam? I don[']t know of a soul under the sun that does, & if you do I wish you would name the person. . . . [T]he Society does not wish you to feel disturbed or distressed in mind on account of your expenses; & I can assure you that nobody imagines that you spend our money for oysters & mint-juleps, or Theater tickets. . . .[40]

Knowles sought to reassure the sensitive Wittenmyer that, within her Society, she had earned complete trust, and that the attempt to systematize accounts represented only a precautionary measure in light of the Commission's anticipated and real challenges. With some grumbling, Wittenmyer complied.

Although she resented the suspicion she thought implicit in the inquiries about her handling of sanitary supplies and funds, Wittenmyer had early on recognized that the Society would need to act carefully and with political shrewdness to ensure its future. In the field, therefore, she consistently matched home front attempts by Society leaders to preempt the Commission with her own efforts to monopolize the support of the military and the army medical establishment. By December 1861, Wittenmyer was writing home from St. Louis:

> I have made several important arrangements, that will secure the interests of our society here after. One is that every box of supplies

68

sent from our state, to reg[i]ments surgeons &c &c are to be turned over to our society, that is to me, or any other agent we may have out, to be used as our society may direct. All of the surgeons and many of the officers are pledged to this.[41]

In another letter, she confided to Mrs. Howell that shortly, "I shall have seen and arranged with *every surgeon* [and] then the bogus San'y Com'n of Iowa is *as dead as a door nail*, for all that they send out will be turned over to us."[42] Wittenmyer's "arrangements" in St. Louis and elsewhere aimed to ensure that control of (and also credit for) the state's relief supplies would remain with the Keokuk Society as a whole, and with Wittenmyer herself in particular.

In addition, Wittenmyer continued to press the military and the federal government for free transportation for herself and countless boxes of supplies.[43] By the spring of 1862, she had achieved her goal of a free federal government pass, presented by Secretary of War Edwin Stanton and signed by President Abraham Lincoln, allowing her to travel without restriction on all rivers and railroads across the theater of war. As the 1862 *Gate City* "Report" proudly stated, "From Generals in Departments and Divisions, besides from officers and Surgeons in Regiments and Hospitals, our Agent has met with every courtesy and necessary aid and co-operation."[44] Wittenmyer's ability to muster so much support from important men in the field represented a real coup. Her efforts to elicit public acknowledgment and endorsement of the women's organization and its dominance in Iowa's relief work had met with an important victory.

Still, a decided frustration lingered among the Society's leaders with regard to their inability to command exclusive control and loyalty at home in Iowa, and to press their claim to superior form, style, and success in providing relief to Iowa's troops.

Wittenmyer wrote privately to the Governor in March 1862, expressing her annoyance:

> The State San'y Commission are accomplishing nothing, they have received but few goods, and those goods have gone into the hands of the Western Commission and are now lying in the St. Louis Depots. Not one dollar[']s worth of goods committed to their care have reached our Iowa troops.

Expecting that Kirkwood might question her motives, Wittenmyer insisted, "I am well posted with regard to these matters and will make no statement that I can not substantiate." She went on to emphasize the Society's (and her own) competence, adding, that should Kirkwood have any doubts, "all of our Iowa officers and surgeons will bear me out in this statement."[45]

Because the women had been so quick to commit themselves to the soldiers' relief, because they had for months actively, efficiently, and voluntarily discharged their perceived duties in the war, and because they so firmly believed that the work of war relief belonged in the hands of women, they seethed over their continuing struggle to obliterate the Commission's power and influence. Appointed by the Governor and affiliated directly with the USSC, the Commission seemed to have received its legitimacy on a platter, obviating the need for it to prove its worth by actually providing sanitary relief to the soldiers as the Society, through Wittenmyer, had so diligently done for months. Even worse, not only could the Commissioners automatically pose as "legitimate" in a way that the women could not; in addition, the Commissioners received state-funded salaries, despite the uncertainty of their real contribution to the work of relief. An army chaplain loyal to the Society complained to Wittenmyer in January 1862 about the paid male commissioners' emphasis on image. He wrote,

Men coming down here and looking around a little, gathering information from Surgeons, chaplains and others, amounts to a pleasure excursion and a nice one if their expenses are paid, and they are fattened with a salary.[46]

Ironically, as much as the Society's leaders initially understood their work as an extension of women's nature and Christian responsibility and thereby necessarily an unsalaried endeavor, in truth, not all women's personal finances permitted full-time voluntary devotion to such "labors of love." Around the state of Iowa, as across the nation, individual women could only give of their time, energy, and material goods in relative proportion to their resources. At the beginning of the war, women such as Wittenmyer and the other leaders of the Keokuk Society were generally able to give a great deal, expecting little more in return than gratitude, recognition, and the satisfaction of having obeyed a "higher call." Ultimately, however, the length and brutality of the war would try both the ability and the willingness of even the wealthiest women of Iowa to continue freely committing themselves and their assets to sanitary work. Wittenmyer's determination to get the federal government to underwrite the Society's activities indicated that she knew the women could not continue indefinitely to provide relief to the soldiers without some external financial support.

Along with the women's awareness that the salaries received by the "honorable" men functioned in some way publicly to legitimize the Iowa Commission (regardless of individual need or the Commission's actual effectiveness), over time, this realization that some measure of government subsidy would be necessary simply in order for their own work to continue, accelerated the Society's revision of its originally "purely benevolent" ideals. In other words, as time passed and their control of sanitary affairs remained tenuous, the women began to appreciate the benefits of salaried status, official recognition, and professional acknowledgment, coming to realize that, in the public sphere, the granting of professional titles and the exchange of money for labor somehow served to validate, in a fashion previously unfamiliar to them, the work that a person performed. In April 1862, the Society's *Gate City* "Report" revealed this change of heart, brought on by the competition with the Commission. Mary Strong wrote pointedly that the Society—unlike the Commission—having as yet received no subsidy from the State Government (in contrast with the generosity of the Federal Government), "we cannot but think it will soon see the justice of granting us some appropriation from the public Funds to assist us in carrying out our designs; when it considers how long we have been engaged in this work, how much we have labored, and how much we have accomplished by self-sustained exertions."[47] Even more important, when Governor Kirkwood soon after sponsored a bill to appoint Wittenmyer one of two Iowa State Sanitary Agents (the other one being Kynett) and to appropriate to her $100 per month for salary and expenses, she did not refuse.[48]

It is difficult to determine precisely the reasons behind Kirkwood's decision to push the appointment of Wittenmyer through the state legislature. Possibly he believed that by formally elevating her status and the status of the Keokuk Society, he could reduce the tension between the women's organization and the Commission and elicit greater cooperation between the two. Since creating the Commission, as his November 1861 letter to Wittenmyer indicated, Kirkwood had ventured to bring the Society, and through it other Iowa women's aid organizations, under its supervision. At least initially, Kirkwood, like so many others, could not accept the independence of the Keokuk Society, either because he could not believe that the women were capable of managing their own affairs, or because he felt that to allow them to do so was somehow improper.

Correspondence between Wittenmyer and the Governor at the beginning of 1862 suggests that she made at least some superficial efforts to accede to his request that she cooperate with the Commission. "[W]e have favorably considered the proposition made by the San'y Com'n to unite with them," she wrote in January,

> and I have just communicated the [Society's] terms [for union] to Rev. Kynett. . . . We depricate [sic] the existence of *two* associations for the same purpose, as rivalry, faultfinding, and feelings of animosity are apt to follow, and we desire to sustain amicable relations with all. . . . I am exceedingly anxious for a union of the two associations, and have urged it with great zeal, as I would then be relieved of a great deal of the labor and responsibility that now necesarily [sic] falls upon me. . . .[49]

Whatever one believes about Wittenmyer's sincerity, or about the nature of the undefined "terms" that she offered to Kynett and the Commission, the negotiations ended in acrimony. Mary Strong wrote to Wittenmyer in March, "You have probably heard of the failure in regard to our uniting on honorable terms with the Sanitary Commission. . . ."[50] In the April 1862 *Gate City* "Report" Strong characterized this failure as the Society's refusal to yield its independence to an organization "whose plans had not yet been carried out with any success, whose agents had not been proved for fidelity or experience, whose executive policy was so different from that which we had found so advantageous."[51] The Governor's authorization of Wittenmyer as a State Sanitary Agent represented in part his acknowledgment that a union between the two organizations was far outside his grasp, and that his best hope for a solution to the problem lay in fostering their acceptance of parity.

There was, however, an element of even greater capitulation in the Governor's promotion of Wittenmyer. In her own March

1862 letter to Kirkwood addressing the organizations' failure to unite, Wittenmyer concluded with a request that the Governor and the state legislature now honor "our claims to public patronage," i.e., provide the Keokuk Society with some portion of the financial support that it had already extended to the Commission. She further threatened that a refusal of these claims would "oblige" the Society to expose the Commission's ineffectiveness "before the *people* of the state and *appeal to them for help*. . . ."[52] Wittenmyer was not the only Society member to hint at the possibility of publicly challenging the Commission's competence. Other members of the Society considered discrediting the Commission in order to reinforce the Society's position. "The [Iowa] Sanitary Commission is in very bad odor here," wrote Mrs. C. D. Allen of Iowa City to Mary Strong in February 1862.[53] In March, Lucretia Knowles wrote to Wittenmyer: "If they are doing *nothing* why can *we not make it public?*"[54]

In April, the Society did attack the Commission in its *Gate City* "Report." "We have . . . learned," wrote Secretary Mary Strong,

> that great quantities of stores from the Iowa State Sanitary Commission . . . were lying unused and uncalled for [in St. Louis], for a great length of time, when our troops at distant Posts were in daily need of them. . . . This detention of supplies has been noticed repeatedly. . . .

Moreover, she continued, goods that did get distributed seemed to have random destinations, a situation that Strong described as "depriving our women of Iowa of the satisfaction of providing for the comfort of those brave men who have won honor for their State."[55] Through Strong, the Society formally addressed the Commission's ineptitude, but also reemphasized the women's own understanding of wartime sanitary work—a highly organized and public form of caretaking—as a logical extension of the "natural" association of women with the home into the community writ large. From the women's perspective, it was organizations of *men* such as the Iowa Army Sanitary Commission, and implicitly, perhaps, the USSC as well, that undermined sacred notions of caretaking by distributing supplies randomly and carelessly, without women's deliberate purpose and sensitivity to need. The debate over competence and control unmasked the enormous tension in the gender system that women's intrusion into the public context of war had produced. Exerting pressure on antebellum Victorian gender constraints, Wittenmyer and her female colleagues claimed only to be doing what was proper, and what they knew best how to do.

Regardless of how he felt about Wittenmyer personally, Kirkwood knew that she commanded the loyalty of a great number of women throughout the state, without whose allegiance Iowa's relief work would come to a halt. Because he could not ignore the Society's increasingly loud and deliberate claims for official support, nor the widespread criticism of the Commission, Kirkwood sought a new solution to the conflict in his "war at home" by elevating Wittenmyer's status, making the two associations relatively equivalent, and thereby promoting, he hoped, their merger. This attempted compromise, too, failed however, as neither organization proved willing to surrender, and Wittenmyer's achievement of official stature only served her as another lesson in political tactics. She and the Keokuk Society continued for over a year to function independently of the Commission, competing vigorously with it for the state's available relief supplies.

Under the leadership of Kynett, the State Commission put up a good fight, drawing on its allegiance to the USSC and its leaders' greater experience in political maneuvering to continue rallying—or coercing—support from local women's aid associations. In March 1863, Amelia Bloomer described to Wittenmyer how the confusion produced by the existence of two major relief organizations in the state, and skillful exploitation of this confusion by the Commission, had affected the Council Bluffs Soldiers' Aid Society of which she had at one time been president and which, in its early stages, "was independent in its action," funnelling supplies largely through the Keokuk Society. "This arrangement," she wrote, "had my full sanction and approval, and for a time the other ladies interested concurred." But then, she proceeded, "the State Sanitary Commission commenced sending its circulars to us . . . [and] urged that it was best for Societies to opperate [*sic*] through the commission [as] their aid was more sure of being judiciously applied. . . ." For a while the Council Bluffs Society ignored the Commission's recommendations. Over time, however, the presence in the town of an "honorary member of the Commission" who "felt that the commission would look for him to do something here" made it difficult for the local women's group to maintain their distance. The final blow to the original women's organization came when the Commission's "honorary member" called a meeting "of ladies" explicitly for the purpose of their forming "a branch of the State Commission."

> The meeting was not very large—many did not understand the matter—those who did had in caucus fixed it all to suit themselves. . . . [T]he ladies kept still and voted as directed, by ballot. . . . I found after the meeting adjourned that many of the ladies supposed it all the same as the other society, and considered the funds &c in the Soldiers['] Aid Society as belonging to the new society. I soon set them right in the matter.

In any case, the women's organization of Council Bluffs quickly dissolved into the new, adroitly orchestrated auxiliary of the Commission, leaving leaders like Bloomer hurt and bitter. "I have never since taken an active part in labors for the soldiers," she wrote to Wittenmyer.[56] No doubt, the Council Bluffs story was not unique.

The Commission and the Keokuk Society continued to battle throughout 1863. In addition, that year saw the levelling of scandalous charges against Wittenmyer that simultaneously highlighted and threatened to erode her growing prominence. The accuser, a Reverend Emonds from Iowa City, publicly charged Wittenmyer with selling rather than simply distributing supplies, specifically eggs, butter, and sauerkraut. In response, Wittenmyer published a vehement statement of denial in the *Iowa City State Press*, in which she angrily pointed out the financial and other sacrifices she had consistently made since the start of the war in order to pursue relief work, including neglecting her "own property and business involving thousands of dollars." Emphasizing the "Christian obligation" that underlay her devotion to sanitary work, Wittenmyer recalled all the good that she had done, and the little she had requested in return. "[S]o far from ever having betrayed such a spirit of littleness and meanness" as selling supplies would imply, she wrote,

> my hands have ever been open to feed the hungry and clothe the naked; and the lowist [sic] and most degraded of Earth's fallen children who came to me for aid and sympathy have been in no wise turned away empty. Is it then probable that I would turn aside from my high mission to *peddle butter and eggs*. . . ? Such statements are not only *untrue* but *ridiculous*.[57]

The scandal never took a legal turn, remaining instead in the realm of charges and countercharges. There is also no evidence to suggest that Emonds's accusations had any foundation in fact. Rather, he seems to have twisted the details of a temporary emergency arrangement between Wittenmyer and the Gov-

ernor, in which the state furnished Wittenmyer with money to
purchase some essential supplies in the north, and ship and
resell them at cost to Iowa regiments in the south.[58]

Emonds's incentive for challenging Wittenmyer is uncertain,
although his role as a sanitary agent for the state of Iowa (by
1863 the continuing expansion of the war had caused the Governor to appoint more than two) raises some interesting possibil-
ities about an allegiance with Kynett, or perhaps just his own
resentment of a female peer.[59] Moreover, one of Wittenmyer's
correspondents identified Emonds as a "Priest of Romanism"
and linked him with the Democratic Party of Iowa and specifically with a "band of Copperheads"—Democratic opponents of
the war who were sometimes secret Confederate sympathizers
as well—suggesting that he may simply have used his own
position as a sanitary agent to take aim at the well-known
Wittenmyer, perhaps as part of a poorly conceived attempt to
undercut the Union war effort altogether.[60] Regardless, Emonds's attack on Wittenmyer implied a desire to reduce her
undeniable status in the state's sanitary affairs by undermining
her reputation for fair and honest dealing. The Governor's
assistant, N. H. Brainerd, wrote several letters of support to
Wittenmyer as the scandal unfolded, revealing his own and the
Governor's frustration with the whole affair and displaying
anger at the upheaval that further jeopardized the establishment
of harmony in Iowa sanitary affairs.[61]

Much like the earlier questions raised about her bookkeeping
procedures, Emonds's unproven charges outraged Wittenmyer's
sense of herself as both a charitable and increasingly public
figure, and her sharp response demonstrated the strength of her
determination to protect her growing reputation. In April 1861,
Wittenmyer had already been locally prominent in benevolent
activities, but her public stature two years later dwarfed her
earlier image. Gone by this time should have been any lingering

impressions of her simply as a good Protestant woman temporarily devoted to the work of supplying the troops. Wittenmyer had not only survived the threat posed by the establishment of the Iowa State Army Sanitary Commission some eighteen months before, but had also maintained her position in state sanitary affairs with such tenacity and resolve that even official support had begun to shift increasingly in her direction. Governor's Assistant Brainerd wrote to her in May 1863:

> You are becoming more widely known and appreciated in your efforts than heretofore & will soon be able to treat with silent contempt all who may oppose [you.] I think Brother Kynett has found it very u[n]profitable to fight you and will let you alone hereafter. . . .[62]

Clearly, by mid-1863, Wittenmyer had made a place for herself in Iowa sanitary affairs from which she refused to be forcibly removed. In the broad scheme of things, over the course of more than two years of relief activity, Wittenmyer had challenged prevailing expectations about the professional abilities of women such as herself, and she had held her ground until others found themselves compelled, at least temporarily, to yield and adjust their views.

Twice during the fall of 1863, representatives of various local Iowa relief organizations convened with the goal of resolving once and for all the conflict in state sanitary affairs. According to one historian, the debate revolved around the question of which organization best represented the interests of Iowa relief work, not only in its structure, philosophy, and basic practices, but in its external relationship to institutions such as the USSC. Representatives expressed concerns about the negative effect that the ongoing existence of two competing organizations and two prominent and mutually uncooperative leaders was having on the whole enterprise of sanitary relief in the state. In the end, the two conventions produced a new association, called the Iowa Sanitary Commission, which essentially became an amalgam of the two earlier associations without the formal leadership of either Kynett or Wittenmyer—although her influence remained far stronger than his—and which went on to continue Iowa's relief work until the end of the war.[63]

In December 1863, as the new organization was getting underway, Kynett officially resigned his position as "Corresponding Secretary and Gen'l Ag't of the Iowa [Army] Sanitary Commission."[64] It is tempting to interpret Kynett's resignation as a simple concession of defeat and to assume that the new Iowa Sanitary Commission abruptly yielded all loyalty to an entirely female Wittenmyer faction. Such was not, however, the case. Rather, the leadership of the new organization reflected a measure of compromise between the two previous associations—with their distinct approaches to war relief—made possible, perhaps even necessary, by Wittenmyer's refusal to crumble. Although the president of the new Commission was Justice John F. Dillon of Davenport, the leadership as a whole consisted of both men and women from around the state.[65]

Wittenmyer retained her official position as an Iowa State Sanitary Agent for some six months after Kynett's resignation, by which point her successes at home launched her into new projects in the field of war relief, this time at the national level. In her last months as an Agent, Wittenmyer faced renewed attempts to dislodge her and to limit the power she exerted over state sanitary affairs. Early in 1864, for example, opponents tried unsuccessfully to revoke the 1862 legislation that had made her an Agent in the first place, but Wittenmyer's evermore numerous defenders easily stymied this final challenge.[66] By not surrendering to defeat and by outlasting the man who symbolized opposition to her dominance of Iowa sanitary affairs, Wittenmyer ultimately won her war at home, setting the stage for her involvement in sanitary efforts on the grander, national scale. She emerged from the Civil War a nationally known figure, even as Kynett's name quickly faded from memory.

In November 1863, Nettie Sanford had written to Wittenmyer expressing her support. "I think you have too many friends to allow Mr Kynett or any other Reverend to take the Commission from your hands," she wrote. And she continued,

> It is strange, passing strange, that the charities of women must pass through the censorship of all the *pantaloons* in this state. . . . The heart that has the warm impulses of kindness and love for the soldier that woman has, generally has the head to . . . plan for concentration of action with others. . . . Believe me the whole movement against you and woman's right to dispense alms will fall to the ground. The idea is too absurd to be entertained by the intelligent people of the country. . . .[67]

In retrospect, Sanford's comments appear prescient. They also revive the discussion of the women's particular aims in the work of war relief, and of the way in which the women's determination to pursue their goals fostered tension in the midcentury, middle-class gender system. According to Sanford, war relief belonged in the hands of women, whose very nature qualified and even favored them for the work. She also addressed the issue of competence, by claiming that women had sufficient "head" to order the impulses of their hearts, thus refuting the notion that women engaged in soldier relief required some external (male) influence to systematize and control their efforts. Women, she wrote, were both emotionally and intellectually constituted for the labor of sanitary aid, and it was "absurd" for anyone to believe otherwise.

Whether Sanford would have formulated her thoughts on the subject so clearly and so adamantly without the stimulus of the struggle for command of Iowa's sanitary affairs, is a question that cannot be answered. The conflict between the two organizations certainly pushed women like Sanford to try and define a position from which to argue for the right to pursue the war work they had chosen. In any case, Sanford articulated with striking brevity the fundamentals of two years of conflict between Wittenmyer and Kynett; between the Keokuk Ladies' Soldiers' Aid Society and the Iowa State Army Sanitary Commission; between the women who believed themselves quite capable of carrying out the administrative and managerial aspects of a task for which their female hearts equipped them, and those, mostly men, who disagreed. In the end, it seemed, the women had won.[68]

After resigning her position as Iowa State Sanitary Agent in May 1864, Annie Wittenmyer moved on to a variety of other projects, none of which embroiled her again in the kind of controversy that she had experienced for the first three years of the war. In all her later work, Wittenmyer encountered far less resistance to her undertakings than she had in the early years. One explanation for this change lies in the fact that, by late 1863, she had proven her administrative skills, her fierce tenacity, and the futility of trying to thwart her. Equally important, however, Wittenmyer manifested a growing awareness of the art of the shrewd political maneuver. The Civil War saw Wittenmyer's transformation from a wealthy widow busily engaged in the benevolent affairs of her hometown, into a nationally known, politically astute leader of a broad range of war relief work. And although she displayed no explicit desire to advance the larger cause of women's rights, Wittenmyer's own personal transformation and her employment of women to assist her in her later projects foreshadowed changes in the field of professional benevolence as a whole.

At the October 1863 sanitary convention in Muscatine, Iowa—even as the new Iowa Sanitary Commission was coming into existence—Wittenmyer had presented, for the first time, her plan for the establishment of asylums for the orphans of Union soldiers, made numerous by the relentless carnage of the war. In her travels as a sanitary agent, Wittenmyer frequently met wounded and ill soldiers anxious about the futures of their children. Deeply touched by these experiences, she conceived the orphan asylum plan as a way to relieve the men's worries, and at Muscatine, her proposal was received with great enthusiasm and a promise of financial support. The Orphan Asylum Association—the first of the two major projects that occupied Wittenmyer for the remainder of the war—emerged as a result of this convention.[69]

In the early months of 1864, Wittenmyer and her associates worked hard and with much display of their new political savvy to transform endorsements and pledges of support for the asylum project into reality. In contrast with the Keokuk Ladies' Soldiers' Aid Society's independence from the state bureaucracy, for example, Wittenmyer's Orphan Asylum Association from the beginning solicited the direct backing of recently elected Governor of Iowa William Stone and the state legislature. Wittenmyer herself shrewdly urged the Association to name Governor Stone president, declining its nomination of her for that position. In addition, she took the cause of the project directly before the all-male state legislature, a step that in 1861 she not only could not, but probably would not have taken. In February, Wittenmyer's colleague Mary E. Shelton wrote excitedly to a friend,

> How I wish you had been here last night. Mrs Annie Wittenmyer *addressed* the General Assembly, hall and gallery *crowded*, a *decided success*, unrestrained enthusiasm, applause, etc. . . . [S]he could not have made a better impression, every word earnest and forcible

and it will do a great amount of good I think. . . . the gov' introduced her very nicely, and she launched out into as entertaining a
discourse as ever honored that Legislation Hall. I have teased her
unmercifully today about speaking *two hours*. She did it, and had
it been two more the interest could not have flagged. I am getting
acquainted with all the dignitaries, as they are very gracious to
Mrs. Wittenmyer. . . .[70]

In July, Wittenmyer, Shelton, and the supporters of the
Orphan Asylum project celebrated the first fruits of their labor
with the opening in Farmington, Iowa, of a home for Union
soldiers' orphaned children. Some years later, Wittenmyer
boasted that "there was no institution of the kind in all the
world" at the time the Farmington home opened its doors.[71]
She felt deeply proud of the achievement. Subsequently, the
Association oversaw the establishment of homes elsewhere in
Iowa, as the one in Farmington rapidly became overcrowded.[72]
In fact, the Association's crowning success came after the war's
end, in October 1865, with the establishment of the Davenport
home where, as a result of some particularly adroit lobbying
efforts, Wittenmyer managed to acquire from the federal government a new but vacant cavalry barracks situated on thirty
acres of land, valued at $46,000, and capable of housing over
600 children, and managed also to convince the United States
Congress to donate some $6,000 in hospital supplies to get the
home off to the right start.[73] The groundwork for such an
achievement, however, Wittenmyer and her colleagues had laid
in Muscatine.

The image of Wittenmyer smoothly and successfully lobbying
Congress for the title to a piece of U.S. Government property
contrasts sharply with that of her struggling to defend her reputation against the charge of illegally selling relief supplies to
the suffering soldiers of Iowa. Similarly, the image Shelton

presented in her letter, of Wittenmyer greeting the "dignitaries" of the state and basking in their rapt attention, contrasts with an earlier one of Wittenmyer and the Keokuk Society matching wits with Iowa's "honorables" for the control of state sanitary affairs. Clearly, by 1864, Wittenmyer had acquired critically important political skills she had lacked early in the war. Her goal in establishing the Orphan Asylum Association, she wrote, was to recruit the "ablest *men and women* of the State" (emphasis added) in order to "ensure its success."[74] Consciously or not, she had learned from her earlier struggles two crucial lessons: first, that what her friend Nettie Sanford had called "woman's right to dispense alms" was not in all cases a matter of consensus, but must instead, when extended deep into the public sphere, be carefully justified to those in power; and second, that such justification involved women like herself giving at least the impression of deference to ostensibly more official, typically male, institutions and styles, in order to avoid as much friction as possible and to allow the work to continue.[75] These lessons influenced Wittenmyer's strategy for the rest of her professional career.

Wittenmyer's orphan asylum work reflected, too, the education she had gained through her struggle to retain control of Iowa sanitary affairs, regarding the significance for women in large-scale public benevolence of taking on such attributes of professional status as salaries and titles. Before the war, Wittenmyer had devoted herself to charitable activities, primarily out of her sense of the Christian responsibility of women, particularly women whose social class "ensured" their moral superiority. But, in the face of competition for the right to continue the work she believed absolutely proper, Wittenmyer had come to advocate professional stature for herself and the women who worked with her, recognizing that salaried status elevated what might otherwise be considered the manifestations of women's caretaking "nature" to the level of "skill." Professionalization limited external competition, permitted a middle-class woman to expand the scope of her work beyond the home and the immediate community, and transformed good Christian women caring for the weak, the sick, and the less fortunate into managers, specialists, and authorities in benevolent affairs. Simply, professionalization protected the right of women in the larger public sphere to do women's work.

Wittenmyer's model for the orphan homes illustrated some of these changes in her conceptualization of women's benevolence. After a visit to the Davenport home, a journalist described the "cottage plan," the basis of the home's organization and administration. He wrote,

> The home is a model for comfort, the cottages are in perfect order, the children neatly and suitably dressed, and all clean and wholesome. . . . The children are divided into fifteen families, each under a motherly woman, the [paid] "cottage manager."[76]

The orphan homes imitated traditional homes and families, with the hired cottage managers representing the mother for each "family," and, one assumes, the financial benefactors collectively representing the father. Despite the apparent logic of such a system, it is important to note that Wittenmyer did not press for a model of orphan care in which good women of the community would voluntarily take parentless children into their own homes and raise them as part of their own families. Such a model shared with Wittenmyer's vague bookkeeping techniques of the past a certain air of formless volunteerism, lacking the qualities of traditionally male professionalism and efficiency she knew earned the respect and public support necessary for the work to thrive. Thus, Wittenmyer advocated an institutional *replica* of a real home and family, in which women with titles such as "matron" and "cottage manager" became paid professional mothers. Wittenmyer herself served as the matron of the Davenport home from 1865 until 1867, and the same journalist glowingly described her management. "We found the indefatigable Mrs. Annie Wittenmyer in command," he wrote, "bringing her powerful executive ability into play all through the institution."[77] In the exercise of her executive abilities in professional women's work, Wittenmyer created her own niche, at the same time that she provided a similar niche for middle-class women like herself.

Wittenmyer began her orphan asylum work in the fall of 1863. It was in early 1864, however, that she initiated the relief project that ultimately brought her national attention: the creation and establishment of "special diet kitchens" in military hospitals across the theater of war. In this project, Wittenmyer publicly institutionalized, in one stroke, women's traditional supervision of food preparation and the care and nurture of the sick, introducing an entirely new profession for middle-class women as paid diet-kitchen managers. Wittenmyer's final major Civil War undertaking dramatized the ongoing developments in her political savvy and in her self-understanding as a public figure. Even as the project exposed some of the limits of the flexibility in the antebellum gender system to which wartime women continued to apply pressure—for Wittenmyer and her female managers frequently encountered obstacles to their work even from those who believed in the project's fundamental value—in the end, however, the overwhelming success of the enterprise demonstrated the inability of the antebellum gender system to resist entirely the transformative force of women's wartime activities.

Wittenmyer was deeply concerned about the poor quality and the inappropriateness of the food being served to the very ill and severely wounded in the Union's military hospitals. Her anecdotes in *Under the Guns* frequently included the discussion of an item of food or drink which, when served by her to a

dying soldier, restored him to health. To one man she provided
a hearty serving of sauerkraut, to another, lemonade, to a third,
a raw onion and some salt. In each case she insisted that she
saved the soldier from certain death.[78] Perhaps the most important of these anecdotes centered on her own brother, whom
Wittenmyer found ill and starving in a Sedalia, Missouri, military hospital in the winter of 1862. In a sober tone devoid of
the joy she might otherwise have felt at seeing her brother
again, Wittenmyer wrote,

> Breakfast was being served by the attendants. Glancing down
> the room, I saw one of my own brothers, a lad of sixteen, who,
> fired with the war spirit, had gained consent to go. I had thought
> that he was a hundred miles or more away. There was a look of
> utter disgust on his face as he rejected the breakfast and waved the
> attendant away.
>
> "If you can't eat this you'll have to do without; there is nothing
> else," was the attendant's discouraging response. On a dingy-look-
> ing wooden tray was a tin cup full of black, strong coffee; beside it
> was a leaden-looking tin platter, on which was a piece of fried fat
> bacon, swimming in its own grease, and a slice of bread. Could
> anything be more disgusting and injurious to fever stricken and
> wounded patients?[79]

This encounter, compounded in her travels by countless other
similar but less personal ones, stimulated Wittenmyer's interest
in developing a comprehensive system for providing the most
gravely ill and wounded soldiers with the kind of diet she
thought proper. By late 1863, at the same time that she was
engaged in the Orphan Asylum project, Wittenmyer had begun
to turn her attention toward the issue of diet kitchens. Early in
1864, as she wound up her duties as Iowa State Sanitary Agent,
she successfully lobbied the United States Christian Commission (USCC) to underwrite the project and name her Supervi-

sory Agent for the Diet Kitchens. In addition, she made a formal request to Iowa Governor William Stone to assign her to these new duties, forestalling potential criticism that she had carelessly abandoned her responsibilities to the state of Iowa.[80]

By late 1863, the USCC, initially organized in the fall of 1861 "to promote the spiritual and temporal welfare" of the military through the distribution of religious materials and the sending of male and female religious agents into the field to succor and save, had, in addition, gradually evolved into a second, national-level source of material relief to the soldiers as well.[81] Significantly, Wittenmyer did not seek a working relationship with the United States Sanitary Commission, for reasons that undoubtedly stemmed from her conflict with its auxiliary in Iowa, as well as from her sure preference for the Christian Commission's agenda of combined spiritual and material relief, and her lingering appreciation of the more "pure" benevolence that the USCC's fewer paid agents and their generally lower salaries—in comparison with those of the USSC—seemed to reflect.[82] Wittenmyer may have learned to accept and exploit for her own purposes the increasingly standard, seemingly entrepreneurial style of institutional benevolence that the USSC—and even the Iowa State Army Sanitary Commission—represented, but she felt no need to embrace it uncritically when more familiar options were still available.

Over the course of the next eighteen months, Wittenmyer, as the USCC's national Supervising Agent, oversaw the installation of more than one hundred special diet kitchens—in which she employed about two hundred female managers—in military hospitals, beginning in the Department of the Cumberland in Nashville, Tennessee, and extending to the Departments of the Mississippi and the Potomac. According to one source, Wittenmyer's special diet kitchens issued a total of over two million rations through the end of the war.[83] Another source indicates that by the beginning of 1865 the kitchens were providing about a million rations per *month*, some of them furnishing three meals a day for up to 1800 patients.[84] Historians point out that the diet services saved the lives of thousands of soldiers, permitting them either to return home, or to rejoin their regiments at the front.[85]

In *Under the Guns*, Wittenmyer described the oft-repeated process of determining a given hospital's deficiencies and then convincing the surgeon-in-charge to permit the diet kitchen's establishment and the hiring of middle-class women to manage it. "No part of the army service was so defective," she wrote, as the military hospital kitchens during the first two years of the war. In general, the "cooks" were untrained, often convalescent soldiers assigned to inadequate facilities.[86] Of a Point of Rocks, Virginia, hospital Wittenmyer visited at the end of 1864, she wrote, "The cooking arrangements . . . were of the most primitive character," the kitchens consisting of log cabins without floors or chimneys (holes in the roof sufficed to permit the smoke to escape), in which "great black iron kettles" brewed various unappetizing concoctions. "When I saw the messes served to the sick and wounded men in the wards . . ." in "black and battered" tin cups and "rusty and greasy" platters, she recalled, "I did not wonder that the men turned away in disgust."[87]

Determined to overhaul the arrangements for food preparation, Wittenmyer confronted the apparently oblivious, but not ill-intended surgeon-in-charge, using his unguarded question, "Well, what do you think of my hospital?" as her cue. She described their subsequent conversation, in which she pressed her case with confidence. "I would begin with the kitchen," she answered:

> "I would build a kitchen with a chimney. . . . Then, I would have a floor in it, and two of the largest ranges the market affords."

"That is impossible; the government would not supply ranges."

"I will supply the ranges. The Christian Commission is ready at an hour's notice to honor any order that I am likely to give."

"The men couldn't manage them."

"No, perhaps not; but I would put in two first class women to do the managing, and the men you have could do the work."

This particular surgeon being pliable, Wittenmyer quickly got him to accept the plan and sent for two women she knew well and trusted to set it in motion. Within a week of the women managers' arrival at Point of Rocks, and under their direction, Wittenmyer reported success.

When the first meals were issued from that well-regulated kitchen in the nice white dishes and bright tinware, the sick men, many of them, cried and kissed the dishes, and said it seemed most like getting home. Instead of the slops dished out of vessels that looked like swill-buckets, there came to the beds of the very sick and severely wounded, baked potatoes, baked apples, beef-tea, broiled beefsteak (when allowed), and especially to the wounded, toasts, jellies, good soup, and everything in the best home-like preparation.[88]

Here, as elsewhere, the strong connections Wittenmyer assumed among home, home front, and women's wartime relief work in the field, were explicit.

The transformation of the Point of Rocks Hospital kitchen that Wittenmyer recalled in *Under the Guns* to some extent obscured the actual experience of making the transition from the old system to the new. One of the Point of Rocks women managers herself summarized for Wittenmyer, in January 1865, the first struggling days of the new kitchen, which saw meals, "prepared without any utensils but the stove furniture, and cooked in the stoves without any chimney, and with green pine wood,—the smoke almost blinding us." The carpenters, manager "E. W. J." explained, were still busy with the construction. Moreover, as long as everyone from the surgeon-in-charge down to the ten men assigned to assist the managers was not yet integrated into an efficient system of preparation and distribution, it was an "up-hill business all round."[89] The transition did, however, occur, the kitchen was constructed, the supplies were delivered, and the new system fell into place, such that within a short time, the new kitchen was humming with cooperation and productivity.

Wittenmyer's plan for the kitchens was relatively simple: to provide for the dietary requirements of the neediest soldiers while adhering to the dictates of strict military discipline, so as to permit special care while avoiding any untoward disruption of military hospital life.[90] Each hospital was to construct a separate facility for the preparation of special diets, and each kitchen was to function under the general authority of Wittenmyer, the local authority of the hospital's surgeon-in-charge, and the immediate authority of two or three women managers Wittenmyer hired herself.[91] In any given hospital, ward surgeons were expected to present the women managers with special food orders for the patients under their care—a "bill of fare" with the patient's name, location, and dietary needs and desires; ward masters consolidated these orders for the women managers to enable them to judge how much of what foods must be prepared; and the women would then supervise the "homelike" preparation of the food by the male kitchen staff (up to thirty men, in the largest hospitals), and its distribution to the bedside of each patient.[92]

The salaried employment of middle-class women as kitchen managers ("These dietary nurses were *not cooks*," Wittenmyer insisted[93]) was a critically important feature of the basic plan for the special diet-kitchen project—a reflection of Wittenmyer's determination to guarantee women's continuing, very public involvement in war relief, and of her growing concern with the legitimating effects professional status on this wartime "women's work." Kitchen managers thus earned $20 per month with expenses paid—$8 more per month than women nurses, but a modest salary by mid-nineteenth-century standards.[94] The money provided a living for some of the managers, but its true importance, as Wittenmyer knew, lay in the legitimacy and professional stature it gave to the work they were doing.[95]

Wittenmyer, not unlike Dorothea Dix with her nurses, furnished the women managers with explicit instructions regarding their conduct with the soldiers, their adherence to military regulations, and their performance of duty. Like Dix, who feared that women nurses' access to the military hospitals would be cut off instantly should rumors of immorality surface, Wittenmyer knew that no amount of political maneuvering on her part could counteract the kind of criticism women kitchen managers would provoke if accused of impropriety or insubordination, endangering the diet-kitchen project as a whole. As she explained, only "competent women were needed to take the management of this important work," women of "culture and social standing" capable of commanding the "respect and confidence of officers and surgeons in charge."[96] A manager's deportment, Wittenmyer wrote, must show that she had "been with Jesus, and learned of Him, who is meek and lowly in heart."[97] Wittenmyer selected each manager carefully, to ensure the woman's character and dedication. "Your work," she reminded the female managers, recalling her own reasons for becoming involved in war relief in the first place, "has its foundation in Christian self-sacrifice. The only possible sufficient motive for you, is a desire to do good to the suffering."[98] Admonitions like this reflected Wittenmyer's personal religious philosophy, as well as her recognition of and adherence to class-based gender expectations, and her appreciation of the ways in which such expectations could be exploited for the sake of her larger goals. Wittenmyer knew she had to hire women who presented her opponents with the fewest possible points of attack. The diet-kitchen project, and Wittenmyer's own success as a public figure, depended on the subtlety with which the women she employed could make inroads into professional territory previously guarded by men.[99]

To a great extent, her tactics were successful. By commanding the two hundred women she hired for diet-kitchen work to conform to all military dictates, by reminding her managers that their job was in all cases to assist and obey surgeons, by surrendering a portion of her managers' autonomy, Wittenmyer limited the potential backlash the women evoked from the military men who surrounded them. By compelling the female managers to adhere to military discipline, Wittenmyer protected them from the charges of insubordination that fully independent movement might have elicited, charges that might easily have undermined the diet-kitchen project altogether. Along with the undeniable value of the special diet kitchens to the health of the Union military, Wittenmyer's deliberate attention to military protocol, her prudence in hiring and, of course, her repeatedly proven dedication to the welfare of the soldiers, together preempted virtually all opposition to the special diet-kitchen plan's implementation. As Wittenmyer wrote once the project had gotten underway,

> The kitchens have come to be regarded, not merely as an important adjunct to a hospital, to be tolerated, but as a source of benefit to the sick, and service to the surgeon—indispensable where they can be obtained. They have the endorsement of the highest medical authorities—the grateful blessing of thousands, to whose restoration to health they have directly contributed—the good wishes and earnest prayers of the humane, who have witnessed their beneficent operations.[100]

The simplicity and clarity of the chain of command served to discourage much practical opposition, but by no means all.

After the war, postwar historians claimed that "So effective were the orders under which the [diet kitchen] department was conducted . . . not the least difficulty or misunderstanding occurred. . . ."[101] But such a characterization masked the day-to-day conflicts that arose between women managers and their male medical colleagues over matters of status, control, and power. The experiences of Julia A. Clark and her daughter Catharine, employed by Wittenmyer to oversee the establishment of the special diet kitchen at the Brown Hospital in Louisville, Kentucky, illustrated some of these sorts of problems that women encountered in the diet-kitchen work.

Julia and Catharine Clark reached the Brown Hospital in June 1864. Julia's first letter home to Chicago displayed enthusiasm and optimism about the enterprise. She wrote of their arrival,

> [A] ward surgeon received us most politely . . . [and] expressed himself quite delighted with our coming[,] said that Ladies are very much needed, that they do a vast amount of good &c. The boys all look at us as if we were friends and we shall be before long. . . . We are now waiting for the Surgeon in charge who is . . . to give directions for us and to us—we are subject entirely to his orders—a la militair [sic].[102]

Julia's only apparent concern at this point was the possibility of competition for a kitchen site. As she explained, "There is a good building . . . which the cook suggested I should ask for to use as a special diet kitchen—*but* a contract surgeon it is said wishes it with his wife. . . . Thus you can see difficulties which may arise."[103] In fact, the surgeon-in-charge did initially refuse Julia's request for the building, but subsequently changed his mind upon learning of the sudden death of the contract surgeon's wife. "How mysterious are the dealings of providence," wrote Julia.[104] Catharine described the situation to her father in a letter two days later:

> The building we occupy is a separate one, it is like a shed built of rough boards contains four rooms in a row partitioned with rough boards and the whole is white-washed. One room we occupy as a kitchen, one as a store-room and one as our bed room and the other will be occupied by the men who are detailed to work for us. . . .[105]

Once the surgeon-in-charge allocated a building for their use, both mother and daughter hoped that things would go smoothly. Other difficulties arose, however, which Julia summed up in a letter toward the end of June. "The establishment of these kitchens is rather an experiment and a very important one," she wrote.

> It is said here tho' of course I do not wish it repeated, that I am the only one who could have done it. . . . [F]irst we could not have the building, next we could not have lumber [to refit the building for the new kitchen], next we could not have men [detailed to work there]. . . .[106]

Julia did not name the source of these obstacles, but one suspects the surgeon-in-charge, who in all military hospitals was the single person most able to threaten the success of any undertaking, and who at the Brown Hospital may have continued to be ambivalent about the Clark women's presence. Soon, however, Julia was able to write home with renewed optimism about the results of their persistence: "[N]ow we have all," she wrote, including "the entire confidence of the Surgeon in charge, the chaplains, the respect of the asst surgeon. . . ." Best of all, she added, "[I] am daily growing in control over the men [under her supervision], tho' I must confess owing to some circumstances it has been rather a task. . . ." Julia urged her husband not to summon her home until she had completed her assignment to her own satisfaction. "Should I leave [now] the lady next in charge to me would vary the plans so much and often, that disorder would soon follow I think," she fretted. Nonetheless, she wrote placatingly and with "proper" feminine deference to her husband, "if you still wish me to come home immediately write to me or telegraph to me otherwise I should like to stay till the kitchen is in order which I hope will be soon."[107] Apparently, the summons from Chicago did not come.

The impression that the Clark women had managed, by the end of June, to develop the rapport with the hospital staff necessary to the completion of their assignment, was shaken by a letter Julia addressed on the first of July to Assistant Surgeon B. E. Fryer, revealing continuing tensions between herself and, it appears, the male hospital staff. "Sir," she wrote,

> I regret being under the necessity of saying that I must now resign the place which your humanity and courtesy have given me unless I receive the assurances from *yourself* that we shall not again be subjected to the annoyances of the last night. . . .[108]

The particulars of the "annoyances" are unclear, although Julia's letter suggested some form of sexual impropriety. Julia remained evasive even in a letter written the same day to her husband: "There have been some peculiar circumstances occurring lately," she wrote.

> I cannot detail them now—but be assured you will not be ashamed of your wife and daughter—perhaps may think more highly of them than ever—you will be amused and angry by turns, but I think quite satisfied at the last. . . .[109]

Apparently, Julia found unconvincing such "assurances" (if any) as the assistant surgeon chose to make, for on that very day she resigned, leaving a Mrs. Underwood in her place as the special diet-kitchen manager.[110] The two women subsequently returned to Chicago to rejoin their family and continue their sanitary work on the home front.

Although Catharine accompanied her mother home, within six months she found her way back into the diet-kitchen service, under Wittenmyer's authority. Whatever unpleasant experiences had occurred at the Brown Hospital, Catharine was not discouraged entirely from the work. In January 1865, she wrote home to her mother from Mt. Pleasant Hospital in Washington, D. C., "The hospitals here are managed differently from those we saw last spring, there is much more military order & discipline."[111] To her sister she described her quarters—"comfortable," with a "warm coal stove and bright lamp on the table"— and the kitchen—about thirty by forty feet in size, with six windows and with two "very large ranges one at each end. . . ."[112] In another letter she noted, "There is nothing at all unpleasant about our situation. . . ." Although, as she wrote, "the carpenters are very slow in furnishing our room, and our quarters are rather circumscribed, and we have no storeroom," Catharine acknowledged the presence of the critical factor in the smooth functioning of the diet kitchens: "Neither [Surgeon in Charge] Dr. Allen nor any of the surgeons intrude themselves upon us."[113]

That the rest of the hospital staff in general, and the surgeons in particular, should not "intrude themselves" upon the establishment and supervision of the diet kitchens surely constituted the common hope of the women managers. Just as the members of the Keokuk Society believed that, as women, they knew best how to accomplish the great task of providing relief to the soldiers, so too the women of the diet kitchens typically believed that their knowledge of household management should permit them a free hand in their work. At the same time that they enjoyed the status, and the adventure, of being subject, at least in theory, to military discipline, they also ironically perceived themselves as somewhat autonomous, not drones or drudges, but morally upstanding middle-class ladies who had simply and properly transferred their caretaking and household management skills from the home front to the battle front. Wittenmyer's managers understood themselves to be professional administrators in the familiar, yet new, context of the military hospital kitchen, and under the steady pressure of their active wartime extension from the home to the war front of the role of household manager, the midcentury Victorian gender system yielded them some ground.

Still, some medical men persisted in their firm conviction that the front was no place for women, resisting as long as possible attempts by Wittenmyer and the Christian Commission to establish special diet kitchens in their hospitals. Others allowed that women had a role to play in the military hospital context, but as nurses, cooks, or laundresses, certainly not as kitchen managers. The surgeon in charge of the Adams General Hospital in Memphis, Tennessee, for example, reported angrily to Wittenmyer in July 1864,

> That there has been a material misunderstanding between you and the ladies you have sent to this house can not be doubted. They say that they did not come here to do cooking, with the exception of a few delicacies, such as making puddings, corn starch, and such little niceties. . . . They think they came here to act as supervisors superintendents and inspectors. I want no one in that capacity for no good could result. In short I want practical and working cooks and no other kind and you need not put yourself to any further trouble as I have no doubt but that I can get along better without them.[114]

"This is not what we agreed upon," he claimed.[115] Obviously, his image of the work Wittenmyer's managers were to perform differed sharply from hers.[116]

In a more cooperative tone, but exhibiting the same inability
to conceive of women in a managerial role, the surgeon-in-
charge of a Parkersburg, West Virginia, army hospital wrote:

> There is a special Diet Kitchen at this Hospital, in which I wish
> to employ Female cooks. . . . Please inform me at your earliest
> convenience how many female cooks would be allowed for this
> hospital . . . [and] also your pleasure in refference [sic] to the
> particular females to serve.[117]

Wittenmyer later noted at the bottom of this letter: "I answered
that I employ no cooks, only superintendents of special Diet
Kitchens, and sent him all the conditions on which I would
supply. He accepted but no doubt to the day of his death will
call them *cooks*."

As the special diet kitchens became a regular feature of the
military hospitals, and as the women managers proved their
worth, lingering resistance to their presence faded, and friction
between them and the rest of the hospital staff decreased
sharply. In February 1865, Catharine Clark wrote home about
staff relations at the Mt. Pleasant Hospital:

> We have a very good set of men in the kitchen, eleven in all, but
> I did not know until I heard them talking tonight how intelligent
> they were and how much feeling they had. Soldiers have such a
> way of controlling and repressing themselves. . . .[118]

Clearly, the women managers needed to learn to appreciate
men's contributions to the diet-kitchen service as well.

Pockets of tension remained, of course, in part because a
number of Wittenmyer's women took more seriously than others
the notion that their high moral character and their Christian
faith permitted them, even compelled them, to function also

as crusaders against sin in the workplace. The diet-kitchen manager of a large military hospital in Madison, Indiana, discovered that the surgeon-in-charge was tampering with the hospital coffee supply, having kitchen workers dry and reuse the grounds, which they occasionally mixed with logwood.[119] Wittenmyer appointed a woman colleague from the USCC, S. E. Vance, to the task of determining whether the kitchen manager's charges were true. Vance installed herself at the hospital and observed affairs there until she felt absolutely certain that she could corroborate the initial allegations in a formal way. After some weeks, she wrote to Wittenmyer, "The evidence is nowhere wanting in any part—I have not given you a single item which cannot be proved by more than 2 or 3 witnesses."[120] Vance recognized the delicacy of the investigations and the controversy inherent in such a serious challenge to a man in authority. "So far as I am aware," she wrote, "I am yet on good terms with [the surgeon]. . . . I think he is perfectly ignorant of my knowledg[e] of the matter or at least the extent of my information."[121] Ultimately, the investigation resulted in the surgeon's resignation, demonstrating the force of Wittenmyer's influence as well as the vigor of her subordinates. The surgeon and others like him undoubtedly perceived such conflicts as stemming directly from the presence of intrusive women in a context where they did not belong. Resentment was unavoidable.[122]

By the end of the war, however, the overall image of the special diet kitchens, the women who managed them, and the woman who had general supervision over the whole operation, was profoundly positive. As historians later noted, the kitchens "commanded the respect of officers and men, and proved a powerful instrument of good."[123] Needless to say, Wittenmyer's achievements in carrying forth this well-received project were not coincidental. Rather, they represented her firm grasp of the lessons she had learned from the struggles of her first three years in the field of soldiers' aid.

The success of the special diet-kitchen project, the professionalization of the individual women who ran it, and Wittenmyer's own elevation to the stature of a public administrator of national repute, were above all a result of her refusal to be confined or limited by antebellum gender expectations, and her determination to master the political tactics necessary to allow her—and women like her—to move more freely in the world of men and war. Supported—even vindicated—by the conscious or unconscious assistance of countless women across the north, who responded effectively to the upheaval of the Civil War in a variety of war relief projects and goals, Wittenmyer demanded wartime adjustments in the mid-nineteenth-century, middle-class gender system that advanced the status of women in benevolent work and established a place for them in the public arena from which they later would not retreat.[124]

After the war, the same Reverend Henry Bellows who had so highly praised the Civil War nurses, offered accolades to Union women on the home front who had contributed significantly and efficiently to the war effort through their local aid societies. "Men did not take to the musket," he wrote, "more commonly than women took to the needle."[125] Women, having surrendered to the military "their husbands and sons, their brothers and lovers," had devoted themselves to the business of soldier relief, and they had done so, "not in the spasmodic and sentimental way, which has been common elsewhere, but with a self-controlled and rational consideration of the wisest and best means of accomplishing their purpose." Women had acted systematically, with "business-like thoroughness in details," "sturdy persistency," and, most importantly, in "thorough cooperativeness with the other sex." Bellows proffered his supreme compliment to the women of the ten thousand soldiers' aid societies across the Union, when he wrote that they had "proved by their own experience that men can devise nothing too precise, too systematic or too complicated for women to understand, apply and improve upon, where there is any sufficient motive for it."[126]

Bellows enthusiastically celebrated women's wartime efforts in soldiers' aid. By characterizing war relief as a field of endeavor in which men led the way and women—as men's subordinates—cheerfully followed their example, however, he glossed over the possibility that women in Civil War relief work had created their own systems and developed their own tactics in contrast and often in conflict with those of men, and in so doing had displayed qualities and behaviors that betrayed the Victorian stereotypes of woman's "nature." In fact, for four years, Wittenmyer, the women who worked with her, and other women across the Union, had challenged prevailing notions about the propriety of middle-class women serving in public caretaking roles, and about the idea of such women's incapacity for professional work and public leadership, by becoming leaders and administrators of work they initiated on their own, in ways they themselves devised, and with vigor, determination, and efficiency that caught off guard men who considered themselves the masters of such endeavors. In so doing, Wittenmyer and women like her provoked concern among some observers about possible long-term postwar changes in Victorian gender arrangements. By laying this emphasis on the harmony, no doubt also experienced, among women and between women and men in aid society work, Bellows left little room for the consideration of the sort of struggles in war relief that Wittenmyer's story reveals.

Photo courtesy of the Oswego County Historical Society,
Oswego, New York.

CHAPTER THREE

"A Thing that Nothing but the Depraved Yankee Nation Could Produce"

Mary Walker, M.D., and the Limits of Tolerance

Because of her determination to wear male attire, Dr. Walker has been made the subject of abuse and ridicule by persons of narrow minds. The fact that she persists in wearing the attire in which she did a man's service in the army blinds the thoughtless to her great achievements and to her right to justice from our government.

—Mary S. Logan, *The Part Taken by Women in American History*

Few people have ridiculed Dr. Mary to her face . . . just why it would be hard to say. Perhaps it was because she had a sort of dignity, and because about her essential "goodness" there has never been any question.

—The New York Times, 25 March 1912

In April 1861, as the first shots were fired at Fort Sumter, Mary Edwards Walker was twenty-nine years of age and a doctor of medicine (M.D., Syracuse Medical College, 1855), who had been in practice in her home state for approximately six years.[1] The daughter of reform-oriented parents, Walker was raised in Oswego, New York—a frontier boom-town in the heart of the Second Great Awakening's "burned over district"—in an atmosphere charged with the ideas of abolitionism and sexual egalitarianism spread by the evangelists as they passed rapidly through the region in the 1820s and 1830s. Like their brother, the Walker daughters were encouraged in their intellectual pursuits even as they were required to participate fully in the countless arduous chores of farm life.[2] This early experience of equal treatment from her family shaped Walker's ambitions and her irrepressible determination to demand the same from the world beyond her door. Her decision at age twenty to undertake a medical education and seek work as a physician (her father was a self-taught local doctor as well as a farmer) was to her one of pure logic. It was what she wanted to do, and she had learned at the family hearth that she had the capacity to do it. Who, then, could oppose her?

In fact, when she got her degree in 1855, Walker was one of only a handful of women doctors in the United States, which included Dr. Elizabeth Blackwell, who had received her degree six years before Walker, and who would later spearhead the Woman's Central Relief Association's attempts to recruit nurses for the Union army.[3] Blackwell's success in school and in her career, however, had not led to a generalized acceptance of women in medicine. Geneva Medical College itself turned away Blackwell's sister, Emily (and all other women applicants), only two years after the elder sister's graduation.[4]

At midcentury, most doors simply remained closed to women

interested in studying and practicing medicine. Despite their intense involvement in colonial-era health care, especially in midwifery, women, over the course of the last half of the eighteenth and the first half of the nineteenth century, had experienced a gradual exclusion from the increasingly professionalized field of medicine in the United States, in which formal institutional education leading to a degree was becoming standard, replacing the apprenticeship and licensing system more common in the past.[5] As the higher education of women in general was still a matter of bitter debate involving concerns about capability and propriety—women's colleges would not be founded in any numbers in the United States until after the Civil War—it is no wonder that the notion of formally and regularly educating women for the medical profession met broad opposition. By 1858, only about three hundred women physicians had graduated from medical schools across the country, whereas 18,000 men could make the same claim.[6]

Women's gradual isolation from the field of medicine by the mid-nineteenth century reflected the ascension of a gender system that broadly identified the professional care of the sick and the public stature of the physician with maleness, that regarded the "revolting details of everyday medical practice as being totally incompatible with true femininity," and the necessary education "clearly beyond woman's capacity."[7] Some midcentury medical schools, however, demonstrated a willingness to accept and graduate women students. Ironically, if perhaps predictably, most such institutions were deemed "nonregular" (or "sectarian") in the struggle for philosophical and procedural hegemony that accompanied medical professionalization and led to the establishment in 1847 of the American Medical Association by a group of self-proclaimed "regular" or "orthodox" men.[8] Victorian America witnessed sustained and vicious competition between regulars—the ideological descendents of Benjamin Rush, whose medical practices emphasized dramatic (or "heroic") intervention (bloodletting, blistering, the prescription of mercury and calomel)—and a growing number of non-regular practitioners, whose increasing popularity derived from their advocacy of milder forms of treatment, including homeopathy (which discouraged the use of massive doses of medicine), hydropathy (which focused on various forms of water-therapy), Thomasonianism (which promoted dietary reform and herbal remedies), and eclecticism (which combined the teachings of the other three in its opposition to orthodoxy).[9]

Not surprisingly, the non-regular schools' dedication to the reform of orthodox medicine and the supression of its excesses was, in many cases, paired with a rejection of other social conventions such as women's exclusion from the medical profession. Walker's alma mater, which adhered to the principles of eclecticism, demonstrated its full commitment to American medical reform by allowing three women to join its entering class in 1849, the same year Blackwell graduated and Geneva Medical College restricted entrance once again to men.[10] The more ready acceptance by non-regular schools of women students, however, although it allowed women like Walker to pursue their personal ambitions, contributed grist to the general mill of hostility toward women in professional medicine. Female graduates of such schools, far more so than the few Elizabeth Blackwells of the antebellum era, typically found themselves ostracized and treated as "quacks" by male regulars.[11] Years before the Civil War began, therefore, when she determined to attend Syracuse Medical College, Mary Walker inescapably embroiled herself in this controversy. At her graduation in 1855, as one of two speakers in her class, Walker displayed an uncertainty distinct from the early optimism that had led her into the medical field. "As graduates," said Walker to the gathered faculty of the College, we are soon to leave and perform the active duties of the profession, and we trust you will never be pained by hearing that any have failed to be successful in, and respected by the community where we may chance to reside.[12]

In fact, throughout her life Mary Walker would confront repeated challenges to her right to practice medicine, on the basis of her gender[13] and her non-regular training.[14]

In addition, she would suffer disdain, and occasionally even arrest, for her choice of clothing, for, as the young Walker had rejected gender constraints in her choice of professions, she had also rejected popular standards of middle-class women's dress.[15] As a child, Walker had been taught by her parents to consider corsets and other tight-fitting items of women's clothing unhealthy,[16] and in medical school, she began to experiment—for practical as well as philosophical reasons—with various models of the "reform dress" commonly and somewhat disparagingly known as "bloomers," after Amelia Bloomer, a key advocate of women's dress reform.[17] Walker's efforts to discover a comfortable, utilitarian mode of dress, however, elicited mostly disapproval and derision. "They said she was too lazy to wash her clothes," wrote one biographer, "that she wanted to display her legs, that she was seeking publicity. . . ."[18]

In fact, Walker believed strongly that conventional clothing imperiled a woman's health to the point of threatening her sanity. "The greatest sorrows from which women suffer to-day," she wrote in 1871, "are those physical, moral, and mental ones, that are caused by their unhygienic manner of dressing!"[19] Walker objected to the layers and yards of fabric with which middle-class women of her day typically draped their bodies, noting that the weight of so much material alone constituted an unbearable burden. She urged women to abandon their long, heavy skirts and petticoats, which collected dirt and grime as they swept along the ground and the floor, for lighter, shorter, and more sanitary clothing.[20] In 1861, Walker's own chosen garb consisted of a one-piece linen "undersuit," slacks "made like men's" and "buttoned to the waist of the undersuit or . . . arranged with the usual suspenders," and an upper garment resembling a knee-length dress, cinched in at the waist and with long sleeves, a high neck, and a full skirt.[21]

Walker argued for women's dress reform as a way to "protect" the wearer and to "allow freedom of motion and circulation." Liberating the physical body, she wrote, simply improved a woman's "mental strength."[22] And yet, elaborating on ideas she had first learned at home, Walker noted that practical reform dress also provided women with a particular kind of physical independence, a kind of independence unfortunately provocative of opposition.[23] For midcentury, middle-class Americans, trousers represented maleness, and maleness in turn represented independence and freedom. For herself and for others, Walker recognized that the assumption by middle-class women of the centerpiece of male clothing (like the assumption of a place in the male profession of medicine) implied a renunciation of certain limitations on women's behavior. A woman who donned bloomers (or sought to practice medicine)—a woman such as Walker herself—embodied a threat to the "natural" social order.

Imbued with the reform mentality that had been central to her upbringing, however, Mary Walker was not afraid to call the prevailing Victorian social order into question for the sake of her ideals and the personal goals she adopted early on. "It is my motto," she wrote in a letter to the radical woman's rights reform journal *The Sibyl: A Review of the Tastes, Errors, and Fashions of Society* in 1862, "to live my principles. . . ."[24] By the time the war began, therefore, in her profession and her clothing, Walker had already begun to lay firm foundations for a lifetime of (to her mind) quite reasonable engagement in nineteenth-century conflicts over what she perceived to be unconscionable restrictions upon her sex.

To focus only on Walker's nonconformism, however, is to forget that she was in many ways also a child of midcentury Victorian culture, a woman who, for example, although she challenged convention by attending medical school, acquiesced to convention by falling in love with and marrying a fellow student—Albert Miller—with whom she set up a joint practice shortly after graduation in 1855.[25] Although the marriage did not last (Miller appears to have been shamelessly disloyal), and she did not remarry or even, it appears, seriously pursue another intimate relationship—not entirely for a lack of offers[26]—divorce did not prevent Walker from echoing contemporary cultural sentiment to the effect that a "[t]rue conjugal companionship is the greatest blessing of which mortals can conceive in this life—to know that there is supreme interest in *one* individual, and that it is reciprocated." Although rare, she wrote, "there *can* be a beautiful confidence, where soul reads soul, appreciatingly, and neither tries to deceive the other."[27] An iconoclast by breeding and training, Walker nevertheless had some deep roots in Victorian ideology.

In any case, it was the same combination of courage and almost naïve ardor manifest in her enthusiasm for love despite personal disappointment, her drive to practice medicine despite the hostility that confronted her as a woman and an eclectic, and her eagerness to rescue middle-class women from the confines of their apparel despite persistent criticism that she was merely a "crank" seeking the public eye,[28] that led Walker to Washington, D.C., following the outbreak of fighting between the north and the south in April 1861. Deeply patriotic, Walker yearned to serve the Union at the same time that she firmly believed that the chaos and the carnage of war might provide precisely the necessary conditions for a woman physician to achieve recognition and success and thereby widen the path for other women to enter the medical profession.[29] Apparently without consideration or concern for the opposition she would engender, Walker headed for the Capital with more than one letter of recommendation in hand.[30] In Washington, she promptly began her unprecedented pursuit of an official commission as a surgeon in the Union Army.

In proposing to persuade the Army's Medical Department to grant her a commission as a military surgeon, Mary Walker set for herself a profoundly difficult task. As we have already seen, if female nurses early in the war repeatedly heard the adage that the war front was no place for women, they managed, as time passed, to overcome much of this prejudice by arguing that the work of nursing was "natural" to women, and that military nursing simply represented an unusual application of a woman's "natural" abilities in the context of emergency circumstances. Female nurses demonstrated that by employing women in military hospitals, the army could return more quickly to the front those convalescent soldiers who had hitherto performed the work.

Such arguments, along with indisputable proof in action of their usefulness, allowed women nurses, such as Sophronia Bucklin, to make considerable headway in the military medical establishment. Mary Walker, however, had no such arguments to muster, for few among those who proved themselves susceptible to the argument about women's "natural" nursing abilities found anything "natural" at all in the idea of a woman performing surgery or even performing a physical exam, especially if the patient were a soldier and a man. Any attempt by Walker to suggest that as a woman she was more suited than a man to perform the duties of an army surgeon would have fallen flat, as would any attempt to argue that her employment could potentially free a male surgeon for battle duty. Walker's only hope, therefore, lay in convincing officials to honor her credentials, to ignore her gender, and to accept her as an equal applicant for a surgeon's commission. In addition to challenging Victorian gender standards, she challenged the foundations of the whole gender system and the system of power and authority that was its corollary.

It is not surprising, then, that even the chaos of the first months of the war failed to afford Walker easy access to an official position with the Union Army's Medical Department. In theory, one possible avenue for Walker's entry into the service would have been through the volunteer regiments called for in the aftermath of the attack on Fort Sumter, who selected their own surgeons, in many cases "without reference to Federal regulations" regarding competence and licensing.[31] Walker did not take this route in the latter half of April, perhaps because she did not have the necessary personal connection with an individual who was putting a regiment together, or because she had not yet closed down her practice. Indeed, in April and early May, she may have believed with the bulk of the Union that the war would be relatively short and bloodless and that her services would be unnecessary. Additionally, there is no evidence to suggest that the regiments' willingness to commission non-regular physicians was matched by a willingness to commission women. In any case, within a month of the outbreak of war, the Army Medical Department had altered the regulations for regimental surgeons and assistant surgeons to require that they be appointed by their state governors,[32] further narrowing the access to a commission of a female non-regular such as Walker. By the time she headed to the front, she must have thought that her best chance for a surgeon's commission lay in approaching the Medical Department at its headquarters in Washington and personally convincing officials there of her merits.

In fact, already by the fall of 1861, the obstacles to Walker's successful pursuit of a commission, *especially* in the Capital, were mounting. Just before the war began, the Medical Department for an army of 16,000 men consisted only of the superannuated Surgeon General Thomas Lawson (soon to be replaced by Clement A. Finley), about thirty surgeons, and about sixty assistant surgeons.[33] By the time of Walker's fall arrival in Washington, the bloody first Battle of Bull Run had shattered any hopes that the war would end quickly, and the need for a rapid expansion of the Medical Department had become obvious. That expansion, however, was to occur under the watchful eye of the newly formed United States Sanitary Commission (opposed by Finley, and ultimately the cause of *his* demise as Surgeon General in April 1862), which had plans to reform and radically upgrade the Department by encouraging the recruitment and commissioning of younger and better-qualified (from the USSC's perspective), regularly trained medical personnel, along with the elimination of precisely the sort of questionably competent doctors that the regiments had been attracting on their own. Of course, all doctors trained in non-regular schools quickly came under suspicion.[34] Thus, by the time she reached Washington in the fall of 1861, Walker's ambition to serve officially as an army surgeon would likely have met with resistance, regardless of her gender.

There is no doubt, however, that being a woman further complicated the situation. The elimination of male "quacks" (as defined by the Medical Department's reformers, whose ascent to hegemony, much like that of medical "orthodoxy" itself, was at least as much a matter of skilled political maneuvering as it was of superior education, training, and philosophy[35]) constituted a problem to be solved—or not—according to the dictates of the supply and demand of physicians overall as the war progressed. To be perceived as a female "quack" added a whole new wrinkle. Nevertheless, Walker persisted, undaunted by, perhaps not even recognizing, the complexity of the situation and the extent and the vehemence of the combined opposition to women and non-regulars in the government's medical establishment.

Her persistence paid off, at least to some degree. Against all odds, in November 1861, Walker wrote home to her family in Oswego, on stationery displaying a picture of the Indiana Hospital, which occupied a crowded portion of the United States Patent Office in Washington, and which primarily housed wounded and sick Indiana troops. "I supposed you all expected me to go to war," she wrote with humor, "and I thought it would be too cruel to disapoint [sic] you, and have accordingly made my way to 'Dixie Land'. . . ." She continued:

> I am Assistant Physician & Surgeon in this Hospital. We have about 80 patients now. We have 5 very nice lady nurses, and a number of gentlemen nurses. We have several cooks; and a dispenser to put up and prepare the medicine, after our orders.
>
> Every soul in the Hospital has to abide by my orders as much as though Dr. [J. N.] Green gave them. & not a soldier can go out of the building after stated hours, without a pass from him or myself. . . .[36]

After the war, Walker described the circumstances that had led to her establishment at the Indiana Hospital in what was in fact a temporary, voluntary, and noncommissioned position under surgeon J. N. Green's authority.[37] Having arrived in Washington, Walker proceeded to visit a number of military hospitals hoping to find a vacancy she might convince authorities to let her fill, as a first step toward a permanent commission. At the Indiana Hospital, she introduced herself to Dr. Green, whom she found working alone, his predecessor having "died from overwork" some time before. Dr. Green had been unable to replace his former assistant, due to the general confusion and the shortage of medical volunteers, and Walker, learning of this situation, perceived what she considered a perfect opportunity to maneuver her way into the official medical structure, while simultaneously providing genuine service to the soldiers. Carrying a letter from Dr. Green, in which he specifically requested her assignment to the Indiana Hospital under his authority, Walker approached Surgeon General Finley for an appointment. Dr. Green had written,

> Miss Dr. Walker from N. Y. has come on to Washington seeking a position as Asst[.] Surgeon in some of the hospitals or regiments.
>
> I need and desire her assistance here very much believing as I do that she is well qualified for the position. She is a graduate of a regular [sic] Medical College, and has had a number of years extensive experience, and comes highly recommended.
>
> If there is any way of securing to her compensation, you would confer a favor by lending her your influence.[38]

Despite Dr. Green's obvious confidence in Walker, and even his incorrect attribution to her of a regular medical degree— Dr. Green may well have intentionally chosen to gloss over Walker's non-regular education in order to limit as much as possible the obstacles to her appointment[39]—Finley refused the request, bluntly stating "that he could not appoint a woman." Not disheartened, Walker turned to Assistant Surgeon General R. C. Wood, who had been Acting Surgeon General prior to Finley's replacement of Lawson in June, and who thus seemed to have a measure of seniority,[40] hoping he could and would overturn his superior's decision. He did not, although, as his later support of her would suggest, perhaps more out of concern for proper military procedures than as a result of any qualms about women doctors or any doubts about Walker's particular qualifications. "After Dr. Wood had read my credentials," Walker wrote,

> he said to me that if the surgeon general had been out and he had been acting [in the surgeon general's place] that day he would have appointed me, and he expressed his regrets that the surgeon general had not been delayed beyond that hour.

Following this meeting, Walker returned to the Indiana Hospital, described her encounter with Finley and Wood, and then told Dr. Green she would serve as his assistant anyway, at least for the time being. "This [I] did," she added, "and entered upon my duties just the same as though regularly appointed."[41]

Walker remained at the Indiana Hospital for about two months, during which time, according to Dr. Green's own testimony in a letter of introduction written weeks after she began her voluntary service, she rendered "valuable assistance . . . as Assistent [sic]" and proved herself "an intelligent and judicious Physician."[42] Later, Walker wrote of attending day and night to approximately a hundred patients, who were "very much pleased" to discover a new physician in their midst. She evaluated their cases (including diagnosing smallpox for purposes of quarantine), prescribed treatment, and assisted in operations. As a woman, too, she frequently responded to requests for services that the female nurses also performed, such as writing letters for wounded and sick soldiers, or just sitting at their bedsides talking of the home front. But the bulk of her time Walker spent doing work that simultaneously exercised her medical skills and alleviated some of the pressure on her colleague. "It was a great relief to Dr. Green," she wrote, "because such had been his constant duties . . . that he was very much worn. . . ." Some days, Dr. Green delegated to her the full responsibility of examining and prescribing medication and diet for all of the hospital's patients, at which times, Walker later noted,

> the hospital steward accompanied me with the book to write down the condition of the cases . . . and the prescription that was given to each individual case, as [must] be done in a large hospital, as it is impossible for a physician to remember every individual case where there are a hundred to be seen every day.[43]

Clearly, Walker took great pride in her *ad hoc* position at the Indiana Hospital. She described, with obvious pleasure, an incident in which a guard in town stopped a soldier carrying a pass bearing her signature. The guard threatened to arrest the soldier on the charge that such a pass could not be legitimate, as "there are no women surgeons in the army." The soldier smugly reported his response to Walker: "Yes there is," he told the guard, "and you go right with me to the Patent Office hospital and you will see her." The guard did not arrest him.[44]

Her love for the work aside, the fact that Walker had so quickly cultivated the support of a male colleague and established herself as even a noncommissioned volunteer physician in a military hospital, represented a remarkable achievement. It is true that in one sense Dr. Green could not afford to turn her away, given his own exhaustion and the number of patients under his care. But in his high praise of her work, Dr. Green also demonstrated a willingness to see past her clothing, her controversial medical degree, and her "gender-inappropriate" demand for recognition as a female military surgeon, to the very real contribution Walker was able and determined to make to the war effort.

Nevertheless, neither Dr. Green's support nor Walker's love of her work and of the authority and power that came with her position could permanently sustain her in Washington. Without a military surgeon's commission or a civilian surgeon's contract, Walker had no dependable income, something that she frankly needed, being, like Sophronia Bucklin, a woman accustomed to supporting herself. The Union Army's Medical Department paid $169 per month to the more than two thousand full surgeons (ranked as majors), and between $100 and $130 per month to each of the almost four thousand assistant surgeons (ranked as captains or first lieutenants) it commissioned over the course of the war.[45] The army also ultimately employed over 5,500 contract surgons who remained civilians and held no formal military commissions, but who received the pay of first lieutenants (between $80 and $100 per month) and bore the title of "Acting Assistant Surgeons."[46] Given that army nurses earned only $12 per month for their less secure, lower status jobs, one can imagine the appeal for this independent woman of any one of these military physician's positions with its regular monthly income and status.

Still, throughout the fall of 1861, Walker served without pay at the Indiana Hospital—bedding down in a hospital alcove and sharing hospital rations[47]—in part, one suspects, because she hoped thereby to convince the Surgeon General of her seriousness, her practical qualifications, and the wisdom of granting her official paid status. Her decision to remain also reflected Walker's personal generosity and her rootedness in the Victorian gender system's dictates of female self-sacrifice. Indeed, when Dr. Green offered to give her a part of his salary, she refused him on the grounds that he "needed all that he had for his wife and children."[48] Single and without dependents, Walker was willing to survive without a steady income as long as she was able to do so.

By the beginning of 1862, however, Walker no longer worked at the Indiana Hospital. Most likely, her two months of voluntary labor had left her anxious about her long-term financial situation, and also discouraged about her chances for a commission. She left Washington in January for New York City, where she took one term of courses at the Hygeia Therapeutic College in March and received an additional medical certificate that she undoubtedly hoped would augment her credentials. October found her back in her hometown of Oswego, New York—probably lodging with her family—where she delivered one of perhaps a series of lectures on her experiences in Washington, almost certainly for some fee.[49] Walker could not be kept from the war, however, especially as the spring and summer of 1862 brought increased fighting in both the western and eastern theaters.[50] By the end of the year, she had returned to the Capital, and in the months to follow, she dedicated herself with fresh enthusiasm to her professional and patriotic goals.

Back in Washington, aware that she could not compel the army to grant her a commission, and unwilling to leave the possibility of a commission purely to chance, Walker revived, on a geographically wider scale, the strategy that had led to her position at the Indiana Hospital, travelling independently to sites where the numbers of sick and wounded soldiers were so great that military officials could not turn away her emergency assistance. Late in the fall, Walker headed for the Warrenton, Virginia, encampment of the Army of the Potomac, commanded since November 7 by General Ambrose Burnside (replacing General George McClellan), where a typhoid fever epidemic raged. The troops under Burnside's command were brutally worn down and therefore more susceptible than ever to camp diseases, as a result of the Second Battle of Bull Run in August, which produced 16,000 Union casualties and was later characterized as a "very complete smashing" of the Union's Army of Virginia (whose remnants were subsequently united with the Army of the Potomac),[51] and the Battle of Antietam in September, strategically the Union's first major success despite some 13,000 federal casualties.[52] Walker travelled to Warrenton and, with permission from the medical director at the camp, tended the sickest of Burnside's soldiers over the course of several days, using her own nightgown, she later wrote, to wash and cool their feverish faces. In addition, she repeatedly pressured officials to have the sickest soldiers removed to Washington, where she believed more abundant medicines and medical personnel would permit them to receive better care.[53] That she actually convinced the authorities to transfer the soldiers to the Capital is no less astonishing than the fact that she herself received orders to assure the soldiers' safe passage there. On November 15, General Burnside personally signed a formal request that Walker escort the sick troops north:

> The General Commanding directs that Dr. Mary E. Walker be authorized to accompany and assist in caring for, from Warrenton Virginia to Washington D. C., the sick and wounded soldiers now at the former post. The Surgeon in Charge there will afford every facility to Dr. Walker for that purpose. Dr. Walker is entitled to transportation to Washington. . . .[54]

Permission received, Walker boarded the northbound train with Burnside's troops under her care. In her own account, she wrote with some humor of the train engineer's confusion. "I stepped up to the engineer," she wrote,

> and asked why he didn't start. "I have no authority," said he. "Then I will give you orders," I replied. "Start at once for Washington. Oh yes, I have the authority," and I waved at him my letter from General Burnside.[55]

As in the fall of 1861 at the Indiana Hospital, at Warrenton, Walker had convinced a key male figure to recognize her commitment to the Union army, to acknowledge the value of her medical contributions, and to grant her temporary unofficial status equivalent to that of a commissioned army surgeon.

Shortly after she delivered Burnside's troops to Washington, Walker headed south again, this time to Fredericksburg, Virginia, where the mid-December battle—part of the Union's poorly coordinated drive to take the Confederate capital at Richmond—had taken a toll on the federal forces roughly equivalent to that at Antietam three months before, or approximately 13,000 casualties.[56] Once again, amidst a "carpet of bodies" including "corpses . . . 'swollen to twice their natural size' "[57] Walker cared for the survivors. "I was directed by the managing surgeons," she wrote later, "to take any cases I chose and dress them preparitory [sic] to sending them to Washington." She described one case in which an exploding shell had ripped a silver dollar-sized hole in a soldier's skull and left his pulsating brain visible to her view. And she wrote of overseeing the proper loading of sick and wounded—foot rather than head first—onto a transport boat headed north.[58] At Fredericksburg, as at Warrenton, Walker's devotion to the wounded was welcome, but was compensated only with rations and a tent. Recognizing this injustice, in January 1863, Dr. Preston King—who had been with her at Fredericksburg—presented to the federal government an account of Walker's work with the troops there, favoring her with the description "physician and surgeon," and requesting that she receive some financial compensation for all she had done. "I presented to the Secretary of War," wrote Dr. King to Walker in January 1863,

a statement of your services . . . in the Hospitals and in attendance upon the sick & wounded of the volunteers [at Fredericksburg], and of expenses and disbursements paid out of your own funds for their relief, and the justice & propriety of your having compensation. . . .

Unfortunately, he noted, "there is no authority of law for making allowance to you," and hence no compensation (and certainly no commission) would be forthcoming.[59]

It was undoubtedly during her trips to the south, where she encountered first hand the hideous consequences of battle as well as the frighteningly brutal forms that emergency medical triage and battlesite treatment could take, that Walker developed the same repulsion for unnecessary amputations that many female army nurses shared. Her formal medical training at Syracuse, which had deemphasized heroic interventions of any sort, laid the foundation for convictions that came full-blown in the context of thousands of real casualties. Ironically, those who later diminished Walker's contributions to the care of the sick and wounded by arguing that they more closely resembled those of a nurse than a surgeon, may well have depended for their evaluations on the evidence of Walker's own resistance to performing surgery she considered unnecessary or dangerous.[60] In fact, a friendly June 1863 newspaper article published in her home town of Oswego, New York, but originally written for the New York *Tribune*, described Walker as "a legitimate daughter of Esculapius" who was known to be able to "amputate a limb with the skill of an old surgeon and administer medicine equally as well."[61] Yet it is clear that Walker generally took what came to be known as the "conservative" position with respect to amputations, seeking instead the restoration of the injured limb whenever possible.[62] "I made it my business . . . ," she wrote,

whenever I found that there were contemplated operations, and a complaint from a soldier that a decision had been made to remove a limb, I casually asked to see it, and in almost every instance I saw amputation was not only unnecessary, but to me it seemed wickedly cruel. I would then swear the soldier not to repeat anything that I told him, and then I would tell him that no one was obliged to submit to an amputation unless he chose to do so, that his limbs belonged to himself. I then instructed him to protest against amputation, and that if the physicians insisted upon it that if he had never used a swearing word to swear and declare that if they forced him to have an operation that he would never rest after his recovery until he had shot them dead. I need not say that secrecy regarding what I had told to the soldier was kept and that my advice was followed and that many a man today has for it the perfect and good use of his limbs who would not have had but for my advice, to say nothing about the millions of dollars in pensions that would have been paid without all the suffering, had I not decided it my solemn duty to the soldiers instead of carrying out etiquette towards my medical and surgical brothers.[63]

Walker's comments reflected not only her negative attitude toward amputation as a cure-all, but also her awareness that she could only effectively subvert avidly pro-amputation surgeons by acting quietly rather than confronting them head on. Naïve at times, but certainly no fool, Walker knew her position was consistently tenuous, and that she was vulnerable to ouster whenever the need for her services lapsed—as an intruder on the field of wartime medicine by virtue of both her gender and her rejection of certain standard medical procedures. To protest amputations too boldly would only have further limited her chances of gaining a commission.

Walker's ability to gain the welcome support of army men such as Drs. Green and King and General Burnside, reflected more than just her own medical and political skill. It reflected as well a certain tentative yielding of official resistance in the face of Walker's steadfastness in seeking to prove herself worthy as a female army physician. Nevertheless, as 1862 drew to a close, a true capitulation on the part of the government—in the form of a surgeon's commission—continued to elude her. Indeed, a dynamic fluctuation characterized Walker's Civil War medical career to this point and, really, through war's end in April 1865, between moments of crisis in which emergency conditions permitted her to stretch the limits of gender tolerance, and periods of relative stability and calm in which the boundaries of acceptable behavior snapped taut in front of her once more. Without the Medical Department's official recognition in the form of a surgeon's commission or even a civilian physician's contract, Walker returned from each emergency to confront what amounted to denial of the contributions she and those who had worked closely with her knew she had made, and could continue to make, to the health of the Union soldiers.

Yet, she remained undaunted. In 1862, Walker had left Washington after her separation from the Indiana Hospital. But, in 1863, following her working sojourns in Warrenton and Fredericksburg, and despite her continuing inability to obtain a commission, she decided to stay on in Washington and turn her energies toward the pursuit of various benevolent projects brought to her mind by the exigencies of war. Through these projects, Walker provided valuable services to the community as well as a degree of financial sustenance for herself, at the same time that she kept her name and purpose before both the public and the officials whom she hoped to impress. Had she been able to maintain even an informal but steady connection with a military hospital, her lack of a commission would not have prevented Walker from receiving lodging and food. Instead, she struggled to survive on her own while pursuing her professional ambitions.

As one of her first projects, Walker enlisted the financial help of a woman suffrage group in the city to establish a home where "respectable" women could stay while visiting Washington. Walker had encountered more than one woman who had come to the Capital, desperately seeking a sick or wounded soldier, and who, unable to locate her loved one quickly, had then found herself compelled to remain. Contemporary popular opinion assumed that a "proper" woman never travelled without a male escort. Walker took it upon herself to act upon general concerns for the many women who arrived in Washington alone and with little baggage, and whose transient appearance typically caused hotels and boarding houses to turn them away as women of suspect character. She approached the local suffrage group and received pledges and funds that enabled her to rent a house, hire a matron for it, and turn it into a women's lodging house where she could live as well.[64] Later, she extended her women's housing project into a portion of a second residence. In addition, she organized a service to assist women in finding their relatives around the city, so familiar, by this time, had she become with Washington's medical facilities.[65] "One of these days," wrote soldier and admirer Edwin DeFoe to Walker when he learned of her efforts,

> when some enterprising individual undertakes to write the history of this rebellion [you will] figure very conspicuously, as one who has done much good for the wives and widows of the soldiers; that is if I can credit what I hear.[66]

Walker's own accounts suggest that she also attempted to establish a private medical practice in the Capital during this time. After the war, Walker wrote that, with the exception of Dr. Lydia Sayer Hasbrouck (who was also the editor of the reform journal *The Sibyl*, to which Walker occasionally submitted articles even during the war), there had never been a woman physician in Washington "previous to my coming . . . [and] there was not for several years another woman physician who practiced medicine in Washington except myself."[67] For a variety of reasons, however, no doubt including both continuing strong local prejudice against women in medicine and also Walker's own distraction by her many other activities, the practice seems not to have been particularly stable or economically successful. Indeed, a September 1863 article about her in *The Sibyl* called for assistance for her from its reform minded readers: "If she needs pecuniary aid," the article noted, "we are sure that every reader who loves the faith and truths we are contending for, or hates the wrongs that law and custom have heaped upon our sex . . . would feel they were helping their own cause in aiding one so worthy and capable of doing a great and good work."[68] Overall, it is difficult to determine precisely how Walker managed on her own for such a long time without a steady source of income. But she did manage, remaining in Washington where she figured she had the best chance of ultimately gaining employment with the army.

By late 1863, her high profile, her active involvement in so many projects, and her repeated intervention (often unsolicited and always unofficial) on behalf of the health and welfare of the soldiers she encountered in her travels, had spread Mary Walker's name so widely that, much like Annie Wittenmyer in Iowa, she began to receive letters from a range of sources asking her assistance in all sorts of matters, some only tangentially connected with her primary status as a physician. As so often occurred with female nurses and ladies' aid society workers generally, soldiers had begun to see her as an independent advocate of sorts, and they frequently requested that she act as a liaison between themselves and the military establishment. Late in September, for example, Fitzhough McChesney wrote to Walker,

although aware of your many dutys [*sic*] I make so bold as to intrude on them by asking you to assist one who has lost health and the use of a limb while in the service. I do not wish a discharge but would like to be placed on detached duty of some kind. . . .[69]

How McChesney's case settled is unknown. In November, Walker approached the Medical Director of the Army of the Potomac in reference to another soldier, "the only son of an aged and widowed mother" who "has a wife and two sisters, all of which, are in a measure dependent upon him. . . ."[70] For this man she requested a furlough, later noting on the back of her own copy of the letter that the Medical Director had indeed granted the request. Also in November, Captain Alex Springsteen wrote for help in filling a "special requisition" for his troops. "They need mittens," he wrote, "and I know of no one except you on whom to make [this request] and expect it to be filled."[71] That same autumn, Walker helped gain the release of "a number of men" held at a military prison in Georgetown on false charges of desertion.[72] Over the course of the year, Walker had established herself as a friend to the soldiers in and around Washington, by presenting herself as someone who simultaneously cared about their welfare and could and would do something to promote it.

Out of her many projects, Walker developed a new idea for achieving her goal of gaining an official surgeon's commission, which entailed organizing her own regiment and having herself named its surgeon. In early November 1863, she wrote to Secretary of War Edwin Stanton:

> Will you give me authority to get up a regiment of men, to be called *Walker's U.S. Patriots*, subject to all general orders, in Vol. Regts.?
>
> I would like the authority to enlist them in any loyal states, & also authority to tell them that I will act as first Assistant Surgeon.[73]

Walker felt certain that she could come up with a regiment, "having been so long the friend of soldiers."[74] Not surprisingly, however, Stanton refused her request. Again, Walker confronted the military's resistance to granting her official status, despite an obvious and growing willingness to make *unofficial* use of her numerous skills. Even as Stanton was turning her down, Walker headed to Chattanooga in Tennessee, to provide medical aid to the 7,500 wounded survivors of the Battle of Chickamauga, the "bloodiest battle in the western theater," which found the western Army of the Cumberland's local medical facilities woefully inadequate.[75] This time, Walker bore a letter recommending her employment in a hospital there, signed by Assistant Surgeon General R. C. Wood—who back in the fall of 1861, had regretted his inability to overturn Surgeon General Finley's decision regarding her initial request for a commission. The letter notwithstanding, the surgeon-in-charge at Chattanooga refused to employ her as anything but a nurse, an arrangement that Walker found unsatisfactory.[76] Still, this new thwarting of her desire for a surgeon's commission (or even a civilian contract) did not confound her fundamental dedication to the soldiers' medical needs, and she remained in Tennessee at least long enough for her efforts on their behalf to garner the respect of General George H. Thomas, Commander of the Army of the Cumberland, who soon became her champion.

Early in January 1864, no doubt emboldened by her ongoing contacts—for good and ill—with men in power, Walker addressed a sharply worded letter to President Abraham Lincoln, venting her frustration with a military system that continued to take advantage of her voluntary services but refused to legitimize her. She wrote,

Whereas, The undersigned has rendered much of valuable service in her efforts to promote the cause of the Union . . . she begs to say to his Excellency that she has been denied a commission, solely on the ground of sex, when her services have been tested and appreciated without a commission and without compensation and she fully believes that had a man been as useful to our country as she modestly claims to have been, a star would have been taken from the National Heavens and placed upon his shoulder.[77]

She requested from the President himself an assignment to duty in the "female ward" of the Douglas Hospital in Washington, "as there cannot possibly be any objection urged on account of sex," admitting, nonetheless, that she still preferred a "surgeon's commission with orders to go whenever and wherever there is a battle. . . ."[78]

Five days later, Lincoln refused Walker's request, in a letter that seemed to express his own basic neutrality about the issue of women doctors, even in the military. His refusal, he assured her, represented only his concern to preserve the loyalty of the Medical Department hierarchy. The Department, he wrote, was "an organized system in the hands of men supposed to be learned in that profession and I am sure it would injure the service for me, with strong hand, to thrust among them anyone, male or female, against their consent."[79] Even Walker's daring attempt to convince the President himself failed to bring her the official recognition she desired.

Not long after the exchange of letters with Lincoln, however, a variety of factors, including her dedication and determination, the army's desperate need for more medical personnel, and the accumulated evidence of her service to the army, contributed to Walker receiving an assignment to a specific regiment.[80] On January 6, 1864, Assistant Surgeon A. J. Rosa of the 52nd Ohio Volunteers (Army of the Cumberland) died suddenly, and over the course of the next three weeks General Thomas, who had witnessed Walker's service at Chattanooga, oversaw her official appointment, as a civilian contract surgeon, to become Rosa's successor. Thomas's orders called for Walker to report early in

February to Colonel Dan McCook of the 52nd Ohio, stationed at Gordon's Mills near Chattanooga.[81]

Unfortunately, the personal satisfaction that Walker must have felt as a result of this formal legitimation of her more than two years' service to the Union Army, was tempered by an unpleasant—and later extremely significant—confrontation, prior to her departure for Gordon's Mills, with a group of male doctors staunchly opposed to her contract. Like most of the 5,500 civilian doctors who ultimately spent time as noncommissioned army contract surgeons, Walker faced a precontract examination of her medical abilities by a board of military doctors selected by the Medical Department.[82] After the war, she discussed the examination with obvious distaste in a September 1865 grievance letter to President Andrew Johnson, in which she argued that the men who sat in judgment in January 1864 did not take her seriously and never intended to declare her qualified, regardless of her professional and practical training and experience. Even prior to the exam, she wrote, Acting Medical Director of the Army of the Cumberland Dr. George E. Cooper had treated her with disdain and informed her in no uncertain terms that he did not "want any female surgeons." This was only the first of many indications, to Walker's mind, that "it *mattered not what my qualifications were*, he would not have the 'dignity of the profession' so trampled upon as to have a *female* invasion in the *Military* Department." She went on to describe the examination, which she claimed to have approached initially with the confidence that the " 'board' would do what was right." Within moments she knew she had been mistaken.

> I had scarcely entered the room before I felt the *Cooper influence* and was almost *dumb*.
> I felt that the examination was intended to be a *farce*, & *more*

than half the time was consumed in questions regarding subjects that were *exclusively feminine* and had no sort of relation to the diseases & wounds of *soldiers*.

I saw through the whole, and without *seeming* to comprehend them, asked them to "give a favorable report to Dr. Cooper,['] & the examination ended.[83]

Among the members of the examining board was Roberts Bartholow, himself an assistant surgeon and captain in the army, who shortly after the war provided his own assessment of the examination in an extended letter to the editor of the *New York Medical Journal*, which seems to have taken particular note of the Walker case. Like Walker's letter to President Johnson, Bartholow's account reverberated with anger and exasperation. Bartholow, too, believed the examination to be a farce, but for reasons different than Walker's. For Bartholow, the absurdity of the United States Army offering a surgeon's contract to such a "medical monstrosity," particularly one "dressed in that hybrid costume," was manifest. As he described the scene, Walker

presented herself for examination, with a little feminine tremor and confusion, and before settling down to the graver business of the medical examination, tried to propitiate us and secure a favorable report, so that we might take it for granted she possessed the requisite knowledge. She betrayed such utter ignorance of any subject in the whole range of medical science, that we found it a difficult matter to conduct an examination. The Board unanimously reported that she had no more medical knowledge than an ordinary housewife, that she was, of course, entirely unfit for the position of medical officer, and that she might be made useful as a nurse in one of the hospitals.[84]

And he added, "She had never been, so far as we could learn, within the walls of a medical college or hospital, for the purpose of obtaining a medical education."[85] As Walker certainly would have laid all of her credentials—including her diploma—proudly before the board, Bartholow can only have meant to deny Syracuse Medical College's stature as an institution of "real" medical education.

On only one point regarding the examination did Bartholow and Walker agree: that the board of doctors, rightly or wrongly, found her incompetent. However, given that the bulk of the Union Army's commissioned surgeons and assistant surgeons—and therefore probably the entire examining board—by this time were coming from regular medical schools,[86] it is worth noting that the strong condemnation of Walker's professional credentials expressed in Bartholow's account undoubtedly stemmed in part from the persistent antipathy between practitioners of regular and non-regular medicine. In other words, the board that examined Walker would probably also have dismissed as unfit for government service any man holding a degree from the eclectic Syracuse Medical College.

And yet Bartholow's focus on Walker's gender in his account (her "feminine tremor," her "hybrid costume," and the equation of her medical knowledge with that of an "ordinary housewife") suggests strongly that he—and probably the entire board of examiners—was blinded from the start by discomfort with the notion of women, particularly women in trousers, in the medical profession. Clearly, Walker's gender and her appearance exacerbated the wrath Bartholow already felt with respect to her education and training. Bartholow's claims about Walker's medical incapacity and her behavior at the examination were colored by his hostility toward her dress and her professional ambitions, which he perceived as a betrayal of her womanhood as well as an encroachment on Victorian manhood.[87]

In any case, the great disparity between the two conflicting accounts of the examination process illustrates the intensity of feeling that Walker's ambitions and actions aroused in many of her observers, as well as the strength of her own commitment to achieving her goal, a commitment that seems, on occasion at least, to have overwhelmed her strategic sense, her political savvy. In Bartholow's case, one suspects that no evidence, not even the preliminary approval of Assistant Surgeon General Wood or the endorsement of Commander of the Army of the Cumberland General Thomas, could suffice to convince him of the medical competence of this woman, or any woman. In Walker's case, one suspects that her ongoing struggle for recognition and legitimation over time evoked a fierce and uncompromising defensiveness toward those who gave even the appearance of questioning her abilities.

Regardless, the board's proclamations about Walker's ignorance and ineptitude failed to alter the willingness of two crucial authorities—Thomas and Wood—to assign her as an assistant surgeon to the 52nd Ohio, a move they would have been unlikely to make had they ascribed much weight to the board's evaluation. In her letter to President Johnson after the war, Walker gratefully referred to Thomas in particular as the "noble Gen'l" who displayed welcome "encouragement that I should have all the opportunities . . . that I wished."[88] Indeed, Thomas's steady support of Walker for the duration of the war contrasted sharply with the animosity of figures like Bartholow and Cooper.[89] Similarly strong attitudes, both positive and negative, shadowed Walker throughout the war and throughout her life, a consequence of the pressure she applied to the limits of gender tolerance in her era.

In camp with the 52nd Ohio, Walker received no less conflicted a welcome than she should have expected on the basis of the mixed responses she had experienced across the theater of war since the fall of 1861. Her later account of this period in the war indicates that her relationship with Colonel McCook himself was good: She described him as a "man of great sympathy and a large sense of justice," and noted that he demonstrated more than mere tolerance of her presence with the regiment, on at least one occasion asking her to review the troops in his absence. "This is the only instance in the war," she wrote, "as far as I am aware, where a woman made a revue."[90]

But, when the Rev. Nixon B. Stewart (presumably the regiment's chaplain) published his history of the 52nd Ohio in 1900, his portrayal of the soldiers' reactions to Walker's appointment recalled instead the sentiments of her opponents, Drs. Cooper and Bartholow. "How she got her commission [sic]," he wrote, "no one seemed to know." After describing her background and her appearance—"She wore curls, so that everybody would know she was a woman. . . . In form she was slender and rather frail looking in body. . . ."—Stewart commented that "The men seemed to hate her and she did little or nothing for the sick of the regiment."[91]

This stark statement veiled the deeper ambivalence towards Walker that Stewart expressed elsewhere, as when he explained that he and his fellow soldiers simply did not know what to do with a woman in their midst. "We thought of our mothers and sisters as our dearest friends," he wrote, "and could not bear the thought of having them share with us the rude usages of camp life." Perhaps in spite of himself he added, "We believe[d] she [Walker] was honest and sincere in her views . . . yet the majority of the men in the regiment believed she was out of her place in the army. . . ."[92] Stewart, like many others, found the presence of a woman doctor at the front both incongruous and troubling.

In fact, Stewart's observation that Walker ultimately provided little in the way of medical services to the men of the 52nd Ohio seems accurate. The troops were in winter quarters in and around the miller's (Gordon's) home, and were in relatively good health at the time of her February arrival.[93] In contrast, civilians in the surrounding area—proximate to Chattanooga—had suffered intensely as a consequence of the battles of the last several months of 1863. As Walker wrote,

> The people in that country were in a pitiable condition. Both armies had been upon the ground . . . but the Confederate army had been all through there pressing every man into service, even those that were too young . . . and it left the women, as they said to me, "To root hog or die. . . ."[94]

Like most civilians in conquered areas, those near to Gordon's Mills learned not only to "live under their new rulers,"[95] but also to expect from them a measure of compassion. Walker, with Col. McCook's permission, readily responded, leaving her cramped quarters in the miller's kitchen—which she shared with his large family—to spend a great deal of her time carrying supplies out into the community and treating medical cases as they arose. "I cannot tell how sincerely I pitied those people," she later wrote. She treated patients with typhoid fever, delivered babies, pulled teeth, and generally attended to the civilians' medical needs, in most cases refusing payment, and more than once remaining away from camp all night.[96]

Among the troops of the 52nd Ohio, Walker's service to the surrounding community raised serious doubts about the true nature of her assignment. "Many of the boys," wrote Nixon Stewart, "believed her to be a spy,"[97] and indeed there is evidence to suggest that Walker had from the start been told by her superiors to use any access to the civilian community as a means of gaining whatever information she could about Confederate military maneuvers. Some time after Walker's separation from the regiment, General Thomas himself indicated to Assistant Adjutant General E. D. Townsend that her original assignment, "[a]s I now remember," had in fact included an element of spying. Walker, he wrote, had approached him with a proposal to join the 52nd Ohio as a contract surgeon "so that she might get through our lines and get information of the enemy."[98]

Months before her departure to Gordon's Mills, a September 1863 article about her in *The Sibyl* noted that Walker, having been denied a formal position as an army surgeon, had for some time attempted to convince various officials of the wisdom of her acting as a spy for the Union. According to the writer for *The Sibyl*, sometime during the winter of 1862–1863, perhaps in the wake of caring for his typhoid-ridden troops, Walker had proposed to General Burnside "a well-digested plan of entering and returning from the enemy's lines. . . ." Believing her plan too dangerous, Burnside refused to entertain it. Later, no doubt following Burnside's release from command of the Army of the Potomac in late January 1863, Walker discussed her ideas with two other generals, Winfield Scott Hancock and Darius Couch. As the article described these men's responses, "The latter approved her design, and the former, kindled by the nobleness which found a response in his own breast, also acquiesced." With their permission, Walker's plan "was to be carried out in case a renewed conflict, at one time expected, should take place after the battle of Chancellorsville[, Virginia, in early May 1863]."[99] Unfortunately, the article continued, by the time circumstances seemed right to implement Walker's plan, General George Meade, who became Commander of the Army of the Potomac in June 1863, refused to allow it. "Alas!," the writer commented. "If a woman is proved competent for a duty, and anxious to perform it, why restrain her?"[100]

If, by February 1864, Walker had for some time harbored intentions to become a Union spy, she did not leave much evidence to that effect in her own writings. Even in her description of her time with the 52nd Ohio, Walker made no overt

reference to espionage activities, focusing instead on her provision of medical care to the community beyond the camp.[101]
Clearly, throughout the course of her wartime service, Walker
valued most highly, and felt the greatest pride in connection
with, her role as a military physician. For Walker, legitimation
as an army surgeon was the crucial goal, and any spying activities
she planned, or in which she may in fact have been engaged—
although they undoubtedly held a certain allure for this adventurous, seemingly fearless female patriot—were of secondary
importance.

Just as well, too, for if she indeed had espionage in mind as
she rode about the countryside surrounding Gordon's Mills, she
cannot have experienced much satisfaction with her results. In
her first weeks with the regiment, Walker travelled beyond the
lines only in the company of "two of the officers and two
orderlies" (and with "two revolvers in my saddle as well").
Under such conditions, little spying would have been possible.
Once Walker began to travel alone and unarmed, however, it
was only a short time before she went too deep into enemy
territory.[102] Riding far from camp on April 10, 1864, Walker
came upon a Confederate sentry, who refused to believe her
claim to be delivering letters.[103] Only two months after her
assignment to the 52nd Ohio, Walker found herself a prisoner
of the Confederacy.

Once in Confederate hands, Walker provoked substantial
confusion and commotion among her captors, who determined
to transport her from Tennessee to Richmond, Virginia, where
military authorities could decide her case. A horseback ride of
several days under military escort brought her to the Confederate capital, where she met with a combination of exasperation
and hostility. Straining to account for what seemed a sharp
discrepancy between her gender and her profession (as doctor,
spy, *or* soldier), Captain B. J. Semmes lapsed into mockery as
he described her arrival. "This morning," he wrote in a letter,

we were all amused and disgusted too at the sight of a *thing* that nothing but the debased and the depraved Yankee nation could produce—"a female doctor"—. . . brought in by the pickets this morning. She was dressed in the full uniform of a Federal Surgeon, looks hat & all, & wore a cloak. . . . [She is] fair, but not good looking and of course had tongue enough for a regiment of men. I was in hopes the General [Joseph E. Johnston] would have had her dressed in a homespun frock and bonnet and sent back to the Yankee lines, or put in a lunatic asylum. . . .[104]

C. S. A. Brigadier-General William M. Gardner, the administrator of Walker's case at Richmond, had another plan in mind, however—to accomplish a formal exchange as soon as possible—as there existed no "prison accommodations fit for a woman's occupation in Richmond." But he felt duty-bound first to give her a "fatherly lecture," in which he pointed out, among other things, that Walker would have avoided a good deal of suspicion and been more successful (as a spy) had she dressed herself in more "feminine garb." Furthermore, he sought to explain to this "anomaly"—whom he described as a "the most personable and gentlemanly looking young woman I ever saw," a woman who showed evidence of "good birth and refinement as well as superior intellect"—the foolishness of her participating in war at all, war being, of course, "no place for a woman." Gardner noted with unmistakable satisfaction that whether or not he had managed to convince her that he was right, he "must have impressed her with some comprehension of the indignities she had invited, for her composure finally gave way, and she got to crying, just as an ordinary woman might have done."[105] Pleased with what he interpreted as his ability to force Walker back within the proper constraints of her gender, Gardner did not consider the possibility that the sheer terror of capture had provoked her tears.

Although Gardner had hoped for a rapid resolution of the

Walker case, by 1864 the process of arranging prisoner-of-war exchanges had become exceedingly difficult, with authorities on both sides feuding over conditions.[106] As a result, Walker was consigned to Castle Thunder Prison in Richmond, a converted tobacco warehouse that housed some three hundred and fifty prisoners,[107] where she remained until August. There she endured, in addition to the unavoidable loneliness and anxiety, also filth, vermin, and foul rations, as well as daily threats to her safety by guards playfully shooting their guns near the prisoners' cells. Although she wrote home cheerfully to her worried family of having an abundance of food, a clean bed, and a pleasant roommate from Corinth, Mississippi,[108] if Castle Thunder was anything like the Confederate prison in Andersonville, Georgia—considered only the "most extreme example" of southern prisons—it was an overcrowded deathcamp in which exposure, starvation, and other sorts of "savage and barbarous treatment" were the common fare.[109] A niece later claimed that Walker, who was about five feet tall and whose normal weight was probably close to 120 pounds,[110] returned from prison weighing "only about sixty pounds,"[111] a dramatic (probably somewhat exaggerated) drop that would have represented a serious health threat. (And, indeed, Walker later cited the conditions at Castle Thunder as the source of the complicated health problems she experienced for the rest of her life, particularly with her eyes and vision, which impaired her ability to practice medicine in the postwar years.[112]) The four months she spent in Richmond undoubtedly cost Walker dearly in physical and mental anguish. Even so, Walker's courage and resolve remained strong.

Finally, on August 12, 1864, Walker received her release from Castle Thunder in exchange for a six-foot tall "Southern officer with the rank of major," a man whose rank and impressive height remained for the rest of her life a source of enormous gratification.[113] In her own mind, the fact that she, a woman of diminutive stature, had been deemed worthy by the federal government of exchange for such an imposing figure, brought with it a sorely lacked sense of vindication. Neither the imprisonment nor the exchange, however, brought about an end to Walker's struggles to make a legitimate place for herself in the military medical establishment. Those who may have believed that at Castle Thunder she had gotten what she deserved for overstepping the bounds of her gender, and may have expected her time there to have convinced her of the wrongheadedness of pursuing a career in the military, would soon discover that they had given her too little credit and had underestimated the strength of her resolve and her sense of purpose. Upon her release, far from retreating meekly to her home in Oswego, Walker returned to Washington to recover her health and consider her next avenue of endeavor.

At the beginning of September, Walker made a brief visit to the 52nd Ohio.[114] Shortly thereafter, she wrote directly to Major General William T. Sherman, now Commander of the Union's western armies, with a new proposal for official service. "Having acted in various capacities, since the commencement of the rebellion," she wrote,

> without a Commission from Government & three years of service having Expired, I now most respectfully ask that a Commission be given me, with the rank of Major, & that I be assigned to duty as surgeon of the female prisoners & the female refugees at Louisville Ky.[115]

The very next day, longtime ally General George Thomas personally penned a letter of support. He wrote,

> Approved & respectfully forwarded, heartily recommending that the rank of Major as requested by Miss Walker MD may be con-

ferred upon her. Her services have no doubt been valuable to the government & her efforts have been earnest & untiring, & have been exerted in a variety of ways. I would suggest that she be ordered to report to Col [R. C.] Wood Asst Surg. Gen at Louisville Ky where she could very properly be assigned as surgeon in charge of the Hospital for Female Prisoners & Female Refugees.[116]

Although his statement that Walker might "very properly be assigned" to a women's hospital reveals the limits of his own gender tolerance, more important is the fact that General Thomas supported Walker's attempt to take her employment with the army to a new level, making her a ranked, commissioned army surgeon rather than an unranked civilian contract surgeon, as she had been with the 52nd Ohio.

Apparently, Walker's capture and imprisonment by the Confederate forces had softened the hearts of some officials who had previously opposed her, or had at least caused them to recognize her tenacity and her utility. Perhaps, too, Thomas's stock with the army was by now so high, as a result of his many military successes, that his recommendation could not totally be ignored. In any case, in September 1864, the Union Army not only paid Walker the $432.36 due for services rendered between the time of her assignment to the 52nd Ohio and the time of her release from Castle Thunder, but also—instead of settling their accounts with her permanently—acceded to her request and posted her at the Louisville Female Military Prison, which primarily housed Confederate women arrested for spying and other anti-Union activities.[117] In contrast to her own and General Thomas's wishes, however, Walker still did not receive a military commission. Rather she remained a contract surgeon, but now with the somewhat confusing title "Surgeon in Charge" that led many to believe—at the time and also subsequently— that she had, indeed, like other full surgeons in the army, been commissioned with the rank of major. (To the end of her life, many addressed her accordingly as "Major Dr. Walker.") Walker's contract, signed by Assistant Surgeon General Wood, stipulated a salary of between $100 and $113.83 per month, depending on her responsibilities at any given time.[118]

In theory, the assignment at Louisville represented a far less controversial position than Walker had held as a regimental contract surgeon attending to the physical welfare of male soldiers. As a woman friend and nurse shrewdly pointed out in a letter to Walker from her own wartime post at a hospital in Chattanooga, "Who could object to the *propriety* of your position now?"[119] Unfortunately, despite her many demonstrated contributions to the war effort and despite the unflagging endorsement of her prominent supporters—now including General Sherman—the same issues that had dogged Walker for the past three years regarding her qualifications to serve the Union as a physician, let alone a woman physician (wearing trousers!) in a position of authority, followed her to Louisville. Less than two weeks after her arrival, Assistant Surgeon General Wood received a letter from Dr. E. O. Brown, who had been relegated by Walker's appointment to the position of surgeon-in-charge of the Male Military Prison only, although he had previously supervised the building in which women prisoners were housed as well. "I have the honor," wrote Dr. Brown with some irony,

> to state that I regard Dr. M. E. Walker as incompetent to prescribe for the sick in the Female Prison, and would further state that her tyranical [sic] conduct has been intolerable not only to the inmates of the Prison, but to myself.[120]

Dr. Brown's comment regarding Walker's "tyranical conduct" was revealing. To him, the instruction that he step aside and allow a woman to take up the reins of power can only have constituted an unacceptable defiance of gender hierarchy. But, perhaps even more important, his comment about her conduct spoke volumes about the general conditions at the female prison, which, by the time Walker arrived, had undergone a long period of careless, even frivolous management by Dr. Brown and others. So bad was the situation at Louisville that Lieutenant Colonel J. H. Hammond, Post Commandant, characterized the women's prison as "no better than a brothel," in a letter to Wood expressing his conviction that should Walker be given "control of her own building & its inmates," and should Dr. Brown be prevented from any further interference, "I will consider it a decided improvement." In response to a request from Walker that "some measures be taken" to ensure her authority and prevent Dr. Brown from "visiting and prescribing" at the Female Military Prison and encouraging the inmates "not to obey any of the orders of any Surgeon but those given by himself,"[121] Hammond implored Wood to "Pray let Miss Walker straighten it out & tell Dr. Brown to stick to his own building & patients."[122] By his description of the Female Military Prison before Walker's arrival, Hammond evoked an image of general moral disarray, which he believed a woman in charge might be able to overcome more effectively than Dr. Brown had done. Hammond drew upon midcentury popular notions about the moral authority of middle-class women, notions that Walker herself believed to a great extent.[123] Wood returned Hammond's letter with the note: "An order has been issued placing Dr Mary E. Walker in charge."[124]

Over the months at Louisville, Walker struggled with Dr. Brown's attempts to supersede her at her post, as well as the resentment and hostility of other male hospital employees. Years later, in connection with Walker's request for a government pension, two orderlies who had worked with her at Louisville testified in notarized statements to Walker's constant harassment by the male lieutenant in command of the guards at the Female Military Prison. According to Charles Griswald, on one occasion, the lieutenant challenged Walker's right to take a prisoner out of the building for a walk, and proceeded to send both Walker and the prisoner under guard to the office of the Post Medical Director, E. E. Phelps. Phelps promptly allowed the women to leave and sent the guards home with instructions to tell the lieutenant that he

> had no business to interfere with the Medical Dept. of the Prison, and further that if the Officer in Charge of that Dept. [Walker] chose to take her patients to *Canada* he should not in any way interfere in her business, as she alone was responsible.[125]

The second orderly, Cary Conklin, wrote of the lieutenant that he "seemed to take every opportunity, and study to do whatever he thought would annoy and make the position of the Surgeon in Charge a very trying one."[126]

Proud of her appointment as surgeon-in-charge, however, Walker aimed to bring order out of the chaos that surrounded her, but in so doing she fell quickly "out of sympathy with what she considered to be the ungrateful demands of her patients,"[127] who had grown accustomed to Dr. Brown's laxity. Late in October, barely a month after she had assumed responsibility, a number of alienated inmates communicated their complaints about her in a letter to the Military Commander of the 26th Kentucky Volunteers, Colonel Fairleigh. They wrote,

> We the inmates of the Female Military Prison do hereby ask and request of you that you will remove Dr. Walker as none of the inmates will receive her Medicine, and that you will give us another Surgeon, if not let us remain without any Surgeon. Most of the Prisoners are in favor of Dr. Brown if you can let him return as we have had him once and all like him.[128]

The inmates' expression of discontent reflected their own basic distrust of a woman doctor, particularly one in a supervisory position, but also their frustration with her attempts to "improve" them as part of her program to upgrade prison conditions. On October 7, Walker had written to Hammond to enlist his help in sending a number of young women home, where she hoped they would "do better" than the cramped, degraded prison conditions allowed. "Please give me an order for their transportation," she entreated him, "& I will see them start at *different* times to their respective places."[129] Walker, supported by Hammond, understood her role at the prison to encompass care for the prisoners' moral as well as their physical well-being; the prisoners, unaccustomed to such a watchful eye and, with Dr. Brown, unwilling to submit to the unfamiliar authority of a woman, persisted in demonstrating their resistance. As for Colonel Fairleigh, he forwarded the inmates' letter to Assistant Surgeon General Wood who expressed his reluctance to "disregard the wishes and official request of Major General Sherman" embodied in Walker's original assignment to that post.[130] Walker remained on the job.

The conflict in Louisville continued to escalate, however, and on January 15, 1865, Walker wrote an angry letter to Hammond's successor as Post Commandant, a Lieutenant Colonel Coyle, who seemed far less supportive than his predecessor of her appointment. "I thought you a man of sufficient discretion and judgement [sic]," she scolded Coyle, "to comprehend things as they exist, and then I thought you had sufficient moral courage to pursue a course consistent with an enlightened conscience." She outlined for him her versions of certain actions she had taken at the prison that had aroused criticism, citing in particular her refusal to permit the women to sing rebel songs or engage in "disloyal talk"; her censure of familiarity among the guards, the male cooks, and the prisoners; her replacement of four of the male cooks with female ones; her emphasis on the prisoners' cleanliness and good behavior toward one another and their small children who were imprisoned with them; her careful observation of the interaction between rebel visitors and inmates; and her willingness to exact punishment for insubordination.[131] All of Walker's actions fell safely within the limits of her responsibilities as surgeon-in-charge. She was, after all, dealing with rebel prisoners, not just debilitated Union soldiers, and the rigor of her approach to the task at hand grew out of her wholehearted attempt to accomplish it, in a situation compounded by the unreliability of both the internal and the external support she had hoped to receive.

A few days after sending her letter to Coyle, rather than a message of reassurance, Walker received orders from C. C. Gray of the Assistant Surgeon General's office to confine her work at the Female Military Prison to "strictly professional," presumably medical affairs. Gray wrote: "you will exercise no other authority than that of a physician and inflict no punishments."[132] It is uncertain whether Walker complied with Gray's order. Undoubtedly, she understood the order to imply a sharp constriction of her administrative powers, powers she had worked hard to achieve and was reluctant to surrender. Ironically, Gray's order specifically challenged Walker's right to perform what he might otherwise have considered the "gender-appropriate" work among the female prisoners of reconstructing their moral selves. Such an order highlighted the confusion that Walker provoked as a female doctor seeking a full acceptance for herself as a legitimate representative of the military medical establishment.

By March, the situation at Louisville was reaching its final flashpoint. At least one contemporary critic attributed the constant friction at Louisville to Walker's personality. Colonel Daniel Dill of the 30th Wisconsin Volunteers stationed in Louisville wrote to Phelps, "It is *perfectly impossible* for *anyone* to get along with her."[133] Certainly nothing in the record suggests

that Walker had an irresistibly sunny disposition. But the fundamental problem for Walker's opponents was not her personality.
Had she just dressed "properly," or had she been willing to
exercise her independence and strength of character in the
increasingly acceptable position of a military nurse, she might
have enjoyed the popular accolades granted to women such as
Clara Barton and Mary Ann ("Mother") Bickerdyke.[134] But
Walker's refusal—perhaps better described as a personal, constitutional incapacity—to be confined within even the expanded
wartime constraints of her gender, lodged her between a number
of ardent friends, some in high places, and countless enemies,
who remained dedicated to the idea of ousting her entirely from
the service. Put another way, the constellation of Walker's
gender, her profession, her clothing, and her relentless pursuit
of her goals—her determination to "live her principles"—con-
founded all efforts to fit her into a single, simple category. By
acknowledging for themselves her sincerity and the actual good
she had already performed, observers such as Dr. Green of the
Indiana Hospital, Dr. King from Fredericksburg, and Generals
Burnside, Thomas, and Sherman, were able to respond to
Walker with tolerance and even genuine good will. Others,
however—and they were more numerous—found Walker too
disruptive of sociocultural assumptions about gender, specifically the relationship between gender and authority, and responded instead by dismissing her.

In March 1865, ground down by her apparently thankless
labor at the Female Military Prison, Walker requested a transfer
to what must have by now seemed a less taxing environment—
the battle front. "It is six months today since I was assigned
here," she wrote to Post Medical Director Phelps,

and it has been an untold task to keep this institution in a good
condition *morally* & I am weary of the task & would much prefer

to be where my services can be appreciated & I [can] do more good *directly* for the Cause.[135]

Phelps, noting the lack of "harmonious action between the medical and military officers" at Louisville, relieved Walker of her position.[136] Personally, Phelps supported her, and he subsequently acknowledged her "superior talents and acquirements," commended her for her performance of the "complicated and difficult duties" at Louisville, and praised the "active energetic & persevering spirit which . . . characterised [sic] her in her whole military career and which . . . enable[d] her to render even more service to her country than many of our efficient officers bearing full commissions."[137] Faced with Walker's own discontent and his desire to ease the tension at Louisville, however, he chose a solution fundamentally satisfying to all parties concerned.

Despite her subsequent request that she be sent as a surgeon to the front, Walker spent the final weeks of the war in Clarksville, Tennessee, having accepted a brief assignment to take charge of an orphan asylum and refugee home there.[138] On May 5, her long time opponent in the Medical Department, Dr. George Cooper, relieved her of duty there in a letter indicating that her connection with the army had been terminated altogether. "Madam," he wrote,

I am informed that your services are not needed at the Refugee home in Clarksville, Tenn, inasmuch as the Medical Officer in Charge can do all the work required of him. You can present yourself at either this office or that of the Asst Surgeon General as your services are no longer required in this Dept.[139]

The war had ended, and Walker had received her final orders. As was the case following her release from Castle Thunder, and no doubt in large part because she could not bear to ex-change her wartime experiences amidst the hustle-bustle of Washington or her adventures with the army in the field, for a rural life in Oswego, Walker chose not to head home. Instead, she turned to the immediate task of transforming the work she had done for the army into capital for her future, which meant pursuing a commission as a peacetime military surgeon on the basis of her contributions during the war. With much of the same naïve enthusiasm and faith that had brought her to Wash-ington in the first place, Walker refused to acknowledge that any allowances made for her under the extreme circumstances of war would only be sharply curtailed after peace was declared. To her opponents, in wartime an irritating but occasionally useful phenomenon, Walker became in peace—in a manner she failed to understand or accept—an unpleasant problem to be handled and finally dropped.

Walker began her pursuit of a postwar commission as an army surgeon within weeks of the war's end, enlisting the help of none other than the new President, Andrew Johnson. Initially, she set her sights on the Bureau of Refugees and Freedmen, where she hoped to receive an appointment as a medical inspec-tor, perhaps sensing rightly that questions about propriety and competence arose far less frequently in the context of medical care for blacks than for whites, especially white men and sol-diers.[140] Beyond this, she also aimed to convince the govern-ment officially to substitute her now expired civilian contract with a commission retroactive to the date of her appointment as surgeon-in-charge at the Female Military Prison in Louis-ville—an action she hoped would certify beyond any doubt her wartime status as a female army physician.

Throughout the summer of 1865, President Johnson received letters from Walker's supporters, men whose work with her at some point during the war or whose knowledge of her dedication to the Union effort, led them to sponsor her as a candidate for a commission with the Freedmen's Bureau. "I have the honor," wrote W. H. De Motte of the Indiana Military Agency to President Johnson in June,

> to add my endorsement . . . of the character, qualifications, and services of Miss Maj.[sic] Mary E. Walker; and respectfully to express the wish that you, as the Chief Executive of a Government in which merit is held as the true ground of promotion, will see fit to recognize and suitably reward those services.[141]

In the same vein, the Michigan Military Agency's D. E. Millard wrote,

> It gives me great pleasure to add my testimony to the character and services of Maj.[sic] Mary E. Walker, rendered in so many ways during the long and bloody ordeal through which we have just passed. I certainly feel that her services deserve proper and honorable recompense and I trust she will receive from your Excellency the consideration which is so justly her due.[142]

W. A. Benedict, the Connecticut State Agent for the Freedmen's Bureau, urged President Johnson to assign her as a medical inspector to his organization, arguing that her appointment "could not fail to give satisfaction to those who best know her worth, especially to the officers and soldiers of our noble Army."[143]

The cumulative evidence found in these and other letters in favor of Walker's appointment moved Johnson to consider the issue carefully. "It would seem . . . ," he wrote to Secretary of War Edwin Stanton in August,

> that she has performed service deserving the recognition of the Govt.—which I desire to give—if there is any way in which—or precedent by which this may be done.[144]

But a note on the return letter signed by the new Surgeon General, M. B. Ames, restrained Johnson's potentially generous hand. Ames reminded Johnson of Walker's "failure" before Dr. George Cooper's board of examiners prior to her attachment to the 52nd Ohio, and advised that even "were recognition of her services, other than payment of them desirable, there is no manner in which it could be accomplished consistently with law and regulations."[145] Ostensibly concerned with such "law and regulations," Ames betrayed his desire to pay Walker off and let the military be done with her.

President Johnson, however, continued to consider the merits of Walker's case, influenced no doubt by the arrival of more letters of support. At the end of August, Secretary of War Stanton referred to Johnson a letter from Dr. J. Collamer, himself a surgeon in the army, who admitted that, although Walker's requests were "novel in character," they were still worthy of attention.[146] A week later, F. E. Spinner of the United States Treasury testified to Walker's qualifications for a commission "as a Surgeon in the Army," and encouraged the President to make the commission retroactive to 1864, as Walker had desired.[147] At the end of September, Walker herself sent Johnson a lengthy document outlining her experience with the army and presenting her case against Cooper's examining board.[148]

In October, the government attempted to bring the deliberations to a close. On October 30, Judge Advocate General J. Holt of the War Department's Bureau of Military Justice addressed a long letter to the President in which he presented his analysis of all the information gathered in connection with Walker's application "to receive an appointment in the medical department of the army, or some similar recognition of her public services."[149] Holt began with a discussion of Walker's request for a formal acknowledgment of the value of her services, possibly "in the nature of a commission." He pointed out that, in the case of a retroactive commission, Walker had already assured the government that she would "not apply for any *pay* as an officer," and would in fact "*resign* her commission upon its being once duly granted and accepted." Clearly, the issues of "acknowledgment" and "recognition" held the greatest significance for Walker, who no doubt now felt herself under pressure to disappear from view and from memory. In response to this demand, Holt only echoed Surgeon General Ames's advice about the lack of precedent "within the knowledge of this bureau for her appointment," casting his vote with Walker's opposition.[150]

Moving on to a brief discussion of Walker's sex as possibly an "*insuperable* obstacle to her receiving the officicial [sic] recognition she asks," Holt admitted that, although the War Department had never considered this precise question before, other departments had been known to select women for "public offices of trust and importance." Instead of considering her sex specifically, Holt advised a focus on her merits, "presented as they are by numerous testimonials from general officers, army surgeons, civil officials, and citizens."

Holt then proceeded to review a range of "testimonials" in Walker's favor, including the many letters of support from army doctors familiar with Walker's work, other letters confirming her graduation from Syracuse Medical College and her work as a practicing physician in Rome, New York, a collection of military documents and orders demonstrating the validity and the skillful execution of her various assignments, as well as documents characterizing her imprisonment in Richmond as a result of her dedication to the Union. After addressing eight categories of "testimonials" in support of Walker's demands for recognition, however, Holt recalled what for him represented the conclusive argument against her. Referring to her confrontation with Dr. Cooper's board of examiners in January 1864, he wrote,

> notwithstanding all this evidence as to her merit and efficiency in the public service, Miss Walker has not succeeded in satisfying the requirements of the medical department of the army. . . .[151]

Perhaps Holt's final position reflected postwar attempts to purge the Medical Department of all vestiges of non-regular medical practice that had been manifest during the wartime emergency. It is impossible, however, to ignore the ease with which Holt assigned a greater weight to the conclusions of Dr. Cooper's board than he did to the testimony of so many others equally qualified to judge Walker's abilities. Surely, Holt must have been aware of the ongoing struggle between regular and non-regular physicians in American medicine, as well as the particular antipathy of the regulars to women entering the medical field. As an official of the Department of Justice, he might well have been expected to factor these considerations into his own judgment concerning the examining board's decision in the Walker case. That he does not seem to have done so suggests that Holt's promise to consider fairly the "merits" of Walker's case and bypass the issue of her sex was little more than a pretense for bringing forth a predetermined ruling.

Having decided to recommend against Walker's request, but acknowledging his awareness that the President had "been so far impressed by the testimony in regard to [Walker's] service" to consider awarding to her "such formal and honorable recognition of those services as may not be in conflict with law," Holt presented a possible solution. Although Walker's "failure" before Cooper's board should, he believed, preclude her from *future* employment with the army, it need not therefore necessarily rule out a reward in the form of some "commendatory acknowledgment" for services indisputably rendered on behalf of the Union in the *past*.[152]

And so, in line with Holt's recommendations, on November 2, 1865, Assistant Adjutant General E. D. Townsend addressed a short letter to Walker containing the War Department's final decision regarding her request. He wrote simply,

> Your application for a commission in the military service of the United States has been considered by the Secretary of War, and decided adversely.
>
> There is no law or precedent which would authorize it.[153]

This letter was followed, on November 11, by President Johnson's signing of a bill to present Walker with the Congressional Medal of Honor for Meritorious Service.[154] The bill read, in full,

> Whereas it appears from official reports that Dr. Mary E. Walker, a graduate of medicine, "has rendered valuable service to the Government, and her efforts have been earnest and untiring in a variety of ways," and that she was assigned to duty and served as an assistant surgeon in charge of female prisoners at Louisville, Ky., upon the recommendation of Major-Generals Sherman and Thomas, and faithfully served as contract surgeon in the service of the United States, and has devoted herself with much patriotic zeal to the sick and wounded soldiers, both in the field and hospitals, to the detriment of her own health, and has endured hardships as a prisoner of war four months in a southern prison while acting as a contract surgeon; and
>
> Whereas by reason of her not being a commissioned officer in the military services a brevet or honorary rank can not, under existing laws, be conferred upon her; and
>
> Whereas in the opinion of the President an honorable recognition of her services and sufferings should be made;

It is ordered. That a testimonial thereof shall be hereby made and given to the said Dr. Mary E. Walker, and that the usual medal of honor for meritorious services be given her.

Given under my hand in the city of Washington, D. C., this 11th day of November, A. D. 1865.[155]

On the one hand, the Medal of Honor was a physical token of the government's recognition of Walker's contributions to the Union Army during the war, and Walker displayed her delight and her pride in the honor by pinning the medal to her lapel daily throughout the rest of her life, even after a 1918 revision of the conditions under which the medal could be presented resulted in its revocation from 910 former recipients, of whom Walker was one.[156] On the other hand, the Medal of Honor symbolized the government's final rejection of Walker as an official—certainly a permanent—part of the military medical establishment. The Medal of Honor attested to her unique expression during the war of loyalty and patriotism, but it did not unequivocally concede the legitimacy of her claim to have been a surgeon in the Union Army.

Although her name and her exploits had become well-known by 1865, thanks to the unending curiosity she aroused, Walker's story does not appear in any of the early histories of women in the war. Not even the Reverend Henry Bellows, who evinced such unbridled praise for female nurses, women on the home front, and women engaged in soldier relief, reserved a word of approbation for Walker's wartime adventures, contributions, and accomplishments.[157] To explain this exclusion from the early postwar record, however, requires only that one consider how much Walker's own perception of her rightful place in the Civil War context differed from the dominant image of the

Victorian woman, how much social dissonance was produced by her unconventional desire, as a woman, to become a military surgeon, compounded by her rejection of accepted styles of middle-class women's dress. One imagines the early postwar writers' speculations: Should one acknowledge and thank such a troubling, troublesome character, even if her devotion to the Union was irrefutable? How to retell Walker's complicated wartime story to make it fit within the confines of Victorian conventions of womanhood?

For Walker was no ordinary woman, not even when the exigencies of war meant that a Bucklin or a Wittenmyer altered the standard of who might be considered "ordinary" among mid-nineteenth-century, middle-class women. Like Bucklin and Wittenmyer and thousands of others in the Civil War, Walker was a bright and talented female patriot who determined to serve her country as she saw fit, and struggled to gain approval for doing so. But Walker, unlike the others, exceeded the limits of gender tolerance for her era, and early historians, conceiving of no reputable place for her in the official record of women in the war, instead allowed her very real contributions to the defense of the Union to fade in the bright light of unexplained controversy. In May 1931, a woman who, as a child, had met Mary Walker when Walker visited her school and lectured on her Civil War experiences, noted in a letter to biographer Lida Poynter, who was at work on a manuscript about Walker's life, her conviction that Walker "was a very brave woman, I am sure. We are apt to forget that and remember only her peculiarities."[158] How very right she was.

CHAPTER FOUR

THE WOMEN AND THE STORYTELLERS AFTER THE WAR

[W]e feel assured that our record [of women in the Civil War] is far more full and complete, than any other which has been, or is likely to be prepared, and that the number of prominent and active laborers in the national cause who have escaped our notice is comparatively small.

—LINUS P. BROCKETT AND MARY C. VAUGHAN,
WOMAN'S WORK IN THE CIVIL WAR

As the United States descended into war in the spring of 1861, few Americans could have foreseen the ensuing conflict as an occasion for middle-class women to redefine, perhaps permanently, popular standards of behavior considered appropriate for their sex. And yet, by their words and actions during the Civil War, northern, middle-class women such as Sophronia Bucklin, Annie Wittenmyer, and Mary Edwards Walker consciously and unconsciously transgressed certain antebellum Victorian boundaries separating them from men. Moreover, they propelled both sexes into a postwar context in which popular enthusiasm about women's wartime contributions competed with the desire among many for a return to a perceived prewar social equilibrium, an equilibrium grounded in precisely those "proper" gender roles and relations that the war had allowed to lapse.

As some women struggled, after the war's end, to consolidate their often unanticipated wartime advances into the predominantly male world of public life, action, and status, war historians worked furiously to construct an image of women in the war that would encourage women's silent retreat to their homes and communities. To do so, however, they would have to deny or at least obscure crucial aspects of women's wartime experience, and ultimately, their efforts to return middle-class women to the confines of Victorian gender ideology would meet with only limited success.

Of the three women whose stories have been presented here, Sophronia Bucklin was the only one whose wartime service to the Union—with its challenges to prewar ideals about woman's place and nature—seems to have represented a unique, relatively untransformative moment in her life. Bucklin's precise postwar activities are difficult to trace, but she seems to have retired from her three years as an army nurse to the private, modest life that she had left behind in September 1862—a life, in other words, that manifested no visible extension of her wartime confrontation with Victorian gender constraints.

As there were few if any peacetime opportunities for women in nursing in 1865, Bucklin could not easily have fulfilled any hopes she might have had of pursuing a postwar nursing career. Instead, she resumed her work as a seamstress, most likely living with various family members—perhaps as a roving "maiden aunt"—until she reached an age at which living alone could be considered respectable, and until the passage of the nurses' pension bill in 1892, granting former Union Army nurses who could document their service a monthly pension of $12, made living alone more feasible.[1] A January 1865 letter from her sister Almira, written while Bucklin was still at the front, indicates that she may at that point have had plans to marry a former soldier after the war. "[T]ell me all about it," Almira wrote enthusiastically,

> his name and ware he livs wen at home and wat his occopation is wen at home i hope you will hav better luck then the rest of us has had in a companion i never had much pleasure with mine. . . .[2]

Without access to Bucklin's reply, it is impossible to determine whether the marriage plans fell through, or Almira conjured the whole affair in her own mind. In any case, Bucklin never married.[3] Between 1870 and 1890, she received letters at various locations around central New York: in Rochester (1871); "West Pwy" (1877); and McGranville (1884).[4] The year the pension bill passed, Bucklin settled quietly in Ithaca, New York, where she remained until her death ten years later.[5]

In addition to her work as a seamstress, Bucklin set aside time after the war to compose her own frank account of her army service, *In Hospital and Camp*, which appeared in 1869.[6] Undoubtedly, Bucklin hoped that her book not only would serve as a "record of thrilling incidents" in the life of an army nurse, but also would augment her postwar income. In fact, *In Hospital and Camp* seems to have experienced only limited commercial success in the years following its publication, perhaps in part because of the book's private printing.[7] In addition to writing her memoir, Bucklin kept her Civil War service alive in her own memory by joining the Woman's Relief Corps of the Grand Army of the Republic (WRC)—the only national organization for female Civil War veterans—not long after its establishment in 1873. She remained a member of the WRC until her death in 1902.[8]

Despite her apparent retreat to a prewar lifestyle, Bucklin's long association with the WRC, together with the writing of *In Hospital and Camp*, suggests strongly the enduring centrality to her self-understanding of her wartime experiences, even over the course of the transient decades following Appomattox. Undoubtedly, Bucklin's Civil War service as an army nurse had enhanced her self-reliance, even if it had not ostensibly changed her life. Certainly, her years as a nurse had inspired her to seek a connection with other women whose lives had similarly passed through the storm of war.[9] At the end of her memoir, Bucklin had wistfully written,

> Among the sad memories of these years . . . there remain some pleasant ones—the cherished of my life. In the silent watches of the night and the peaceful hours of the day they come to me as ministering angels to soothe my soul, when troubled with life's many little perplexities, and awaken in me a charitable view of earthly affairs.[10]

In the years after the war, in the quiet life she had taken up once more, Bucklin surely found a rich source of personal courage and confidence—as well as solace and tranquility—in those memories from her years at the front.

In contrast with Bucklin, once peace had been restored, the now nationally known Annie Wittenmyer set about recasting her Civil War activities—apparently without taking a breath—into a profoundly public career that lasted for the rest of her life. In the immediate postwar period, Wittenmyer's name came to be closely linked with the emerging women's temperance movement. Less than a decade after war's end, in 1874, the Woman's Christian Temperance Union (WCTU)—the first national women's organization in the United States—elected Wittenmyer as its founding president. She held that position for the next five years, travelling extensively, speaking at temperance meetings around the country, attending large temperance conventions, and helping to organize twenty-three state auxiliaries to the national Union. In 1882, she published a massive work on the movement, entitled *The History of the Woman's Temperance Crusade.*[11]

This was not Wittenmyer's first book. The year before her election as WCTU president, she had published *Woman's Work for Jesus*, a lengthy discourse on the role of women in the benevolent and missionary work of the Christian Church, and a summons to action. "[T]here is no higher manifestation of the Divine love," she wrote, "than that exhibited by Christian women in their efforts to relieve the needy and rescue the fallen."[12] The book reflected Wittenmyer's postwar involvement, under the auspices of the Methodist Episcopal Church and the Bishop Matthew Simpson, in what came to be known as the "home missionary movement"—the multilayered outreach of middle-class and elite women to the nation's underprivileged, outreach of the sort for which Wittenmyer's earlier free school had provided one example. In connection with this movement, too, Wittenmyer travelled extensively and gave a great number of public speeches to audiences of all sizes.[13]

Nor was *The History of the Woman's Temperance Crusade* Wittenmyer's last book. In 1885, she also published *The Women of the Reformation*, a series of sketches about women active in the sixteenth-century Protestant movement. Ten years later, she published *Under the Guns*, an account of her activities during the Civil War. In the interim, she served as an associate editor for the New York-based magazine *Home and Country*, edited two newspapers of her own, *The Christian Woman* and *The Christian Child*, and wrote a regular column in New York's *Weekly Tribune*. Wittenmyer contributed articles to a variety of other periodicals as well.[14] Moreover, she remained in active public service long after her departure from the presidency of the WCTU in 1879. A founding member of the Woman's Relief Corps, Wittenmyer rose to its presidency in 1889.[15] In 1892, at the age of sixty-five, Wittenmyer's work with the WRC took her to Washington, D.C., where she spent five months lobbying successfully for the nurses' pension bill.[16] By the end of her life, Wittenmyer's leadership in various postwar benevolent enterprises had only heightened her public and professional status and enhanced the national reputation she had initially garnered during the war. In 1898, as if to declare its own approval of her, the federal government passed a bill granting her a $25 per month pension. Until her death, two years later in 1900, Wittenmyer received more than twice the monthly pension granted to army nurses such as Bucklin.

In spite of her own very public, very prominent postwar life, Annie Wittenmyer always maintained a vision of the role of middle-class women that was essentially conservative. As Frances Willard, Wittenmyer's successor to the WCTU presidency, later wrote, Wittenmyer believed firmly that "the vast amount of talent and energy brought into activity by the philanthropies of the war should be maintained on a Christian basis in the Church,"[17] rather than in what would soon become the postwar woman's rights/suffrage movement, as others would argue. Wittenmyer's own experiences in the war told her that a woman's political influence could be achieved without the exercise of the vote, and she eventually broke with the WCTU over that very issue, making way for the leadership of Willard, who supported—and believed that the WCTU itself should endorse—woman suffrage.[18] "Much has been said and written, of late," Wittenmyer wrote, "on the home duties of women, their social disabilities, and their claims to political preferment. . . ." In the context of a battle between those who would fight to overcome women's "social disabilities" and stake women's "claims to political preferment," and those who would commit themselves totally to the protection of "woman's sphere," for the balance of her life, Wittenmyer herself "entered into the broad, unculti-vated field lying between the two."[19]

As for Mary Walker, in the months immediately following the war, she embarked on a lecture tour of the United States and Great Britain, giving speeches that dramatically recounted the details of her extraordinary Civil War career.[20] After the tour, like Annie Wittenmyer, Walker dedicated herself whole-heartedly to a range of public concerns—including the nurses' pension bill[21]—simultaneously writing and travelling exten-sively and producing two books and several pamphlets, before her death in 1919.[22]

Although both Wittenmyer and Walker steadily pursued goals they had identified long before Sumter, for Wittenmyer those goals lay primarily in Christian, institutional benevo-lence, whereas for Walker they lay in the quest for permanent changes in the Victorian gender system, marked by increases in women's access to political power (woman suffrage), profes-sional power (the admission of women to medical schools and the development of legitimate paid positions for them in the medical-surgical field), and social power (the right of women to dress in a practical rather than an ornamental style). A complex figure who relentlessly defied Victorian gender stereo-types, Walker—in contrast with the *postwar* Wittenmyer at least—disturbed and irritated more observers than she charmed, including many whose reformist causes she ostensibly shared. In the face of the protracted struggle by Elizabeth Cady Stanton, Susan B. Anthony, and others for a constitutional amendment granting women the vote, for example, Walker argued that no such amendment was necessary, as the franchise was not, in fact, "a creation of the United States Constitution . . . [but rather a] Birthright" for all Americans. For Walker, this meant that women should simply proceed to vote without waiting for a law to permit them to do so. Mainstream suffragists, such as Stanton and Anthony, increasingly distanced themselves from Walker for fear that her "extremism" (not to mention her insistence on wearing the controversial reform dress—and, later, more traditionally masculine clothing—that many of them had quickly abandoned) would draw negative attention to the suffrage movement and place its goals in jeopardy.[23]

In the postwar period, Walker's ever-bolder repudiation of Victorian gender guidelines prompted much public ridicule and dismissal. The fame she had earned as a result of her dedicated wartime service turned quickly to notoriety in light of her militant advocacy of woman's rights and other political causes. Long after her death, a man who had known her during his childhood in Oswego told an interviewer that, in later life, Walker "was practically ignored by the general public" of the town. Asked why he thought that might be so, he answered,

> I guess she was a little bit queer. People thought she was more of a rabble rouser than anything else, but she wasn't. That was just her way. She didn't have any close friends to back her up or anything so she just battled it out. . . .[24]

Walker died alone and virtually penniless at the age of eighty-seven.[25]

Even as Bucklin, Wittenmyer, and Walker were beginning to work out the directions and the details of their postwar lives—indeed, even before General Robert E. Lee's surrender of his troops at Appomattox, Virginia, in April 1865, marked the defeat of the Confederacy and the virtual end of the Civil War, northern historians began eagerly to record the Union's indebtedness to women's dynamic participation and to develop an image of the "real" woman in the war. In 1864, writer Mary Eastman published a poem about a young woman who died in the course of her service to the Union soldiers.[26] "Jenny Wade of Gettysburg," apparently based on a true story, reflected a particular configuration of the symbols of northern women's commitment to the Union, in which a woman unselfishly dedicated her virtuous and generous nature to the care of the Union soldiers. Shortly before the battle of Gettysburg, Jenny Wade ignored warnings from soldiers on both sides about her safety in order to continue baking bread for the Union troops in the home she shared with her ten-year-old brother, whom she had sent away under Union protection. To a rebel soldier's plea that she abandon her home, Eastman's Jenny responded with pure patriotic fervor:

> "Until the battle's o'er I wait;
> My hand shall bathe the aching brow,—
>   My hand the gushing wound shall bind,—
> And the limbs, pain-disturbéd now,
>   From me shall death's composure find;
> The icy drops, from yon bright spring,
>   I'll bring to quench the hero's thirst;
> And I shall find some soothing thing,
>   Let pain and fever do their worst;
> and I shall give the hungry bread,—
> For sweet and light my loaves shall be
> To those who soon will come to me,
> Singing the song of victory."[27]

Later that day, Union soldiers found Jenny dead amidst her perfectly baked loaves:

> "For you poured out her bosom's tide,—
> For you, for her dear land, she died!
> Well may you weep!

> But her loved name
> Will every patriot heart inflame, —
> Will every coward bosom shame!
> Ne'er from this country's altars fade
> The memory of Jenny Wade."[28]

Jenny Wade, baker of bread and martyr, was shot dead in service to the Union, performing a woman's task, which had been transformed into a patriotic duty in her own eyes and in the eyes of the men for whom she gave her life. Jenny Wade, brave and true to the cause of the Union and to the dictates of Victorian womanhood, gave her own life to save her brother, Harry, and to feed her Brother, Billy Yank.[29] Jenny Wade was a popular hero, and a splendid example of Yankee womanhood.[30]

So, too, was Barbara Frietchie, eighty-year-old resident of Frederick, Maryland, who, in September 1862, refused to join her townsfolk in taking down their Union flags upon the arrival of General Thomas J. ("Stonewall") Jackson's troops. Instead, as John Greenleaf Whittier retold the story in a poem widely quoted after the war, Frietchie imperiled her life by defiantly waving her flag from the upper window of her home.

> In her attic-window the staff she set,
> To show that one heart was loyal yet,
>
> Up the street came the rebel tread
> Stonewall Jackson riding ahead.
>
> Under his slouched hat left and right
> He glanced; the old flag met his sight.
>
> "Halt!"—the dust-brown ranks stood fast,
> "Fire!"—out blazed the rifle-blast.
>
> It shivered the window, pane and sash:
> It rent the banner with seam and gash.

Quick, as it fell, from the broken staff
Dame Barbara snatched the silken scarf;

she leaned far out on the window-sill,
And shook it forth with a royal will.

"Shoot, if you must, this old gray head,
But spare your country's flag," she said.

Jackson, blushing with shame at the sight of the elderly patriot, called his troops not to harm "a hair of yon gray head," and allowed her flag to wave throughout the day.[31] Barbara Frietchie, a real woman elevated to the status of a poetic symbol of "light and law," became an emblem of Union women's intransigence in the face of the rebel battery. Like Jenny Wade, she was an early symbol of the ideal Union woman: patriotic, devoted, unafraid, sacrificing even life itself, but doing so in a role understood to be female. Certainly, no man, except perhaps a very old or infirm one, could have received praise for baking bread for the troops or for brandishing a Union flag from his upperstory window. By their glowing depictions of Jenny Wade and Barbara Frietchie, Eastman and Whittier helped to lay the foundation for popular postwar images of northern women's Civil War service.

In the immediate postwar period, two massive volumes, Frank Moore's *Women of the War* (1866) and Linus P. Brockett and Mary C. Vaughan's *Woman's Work in the Civil War* (1867), quickly became the central commemorative histories of northern women's participation in the Civil War. It is difficult to overstate the significance of these two histories in continuing to construct what rapidly became the culturally dominant postAppomattox images of women—and of women's interaction with men—in the war. Although the two works shared a great deal in terms of their style, format, and outlook, there were differences. Most significantly, although Moore wrote as an independent historian,[32] Brockett and Vaughan—by means of a lengthy introduction by the Reverend Henry Bellows—proudly revealed their affiliation with the United States Sanitary Commission (USSC), of which Bellows was President.[33] Brockett and Vaughan's affiliation with the USSC, and therefore the federal government, gave *Woman's Work in the Civil War* a somewhat enhanced stature as the first *official* version of women's Civil War history. In any case, however, in both books the critical and heroic aspects of northern women's wartime commitment lay in their courageous self-sacrifice for the soldiers and for the war effort as a whole (as Moore's subtitle, *Their Heroism and Self-Sacrifice*, illustrated) and in their unflagging cooperation with men in the business of civilian war support.[34]

Noting in his introduction to *Women of the War* that, "we may safely say that there is scarcely a loyal woman in the North who did not do something in aid of the cause—who did not contribute, of time, or labor, or money, to the comfort of our soldiers and the success of our arms . . . ,"[35] Frank Moore devoted the bulk of his book to the wartime stories of thirty-eight women of "fine and adventurous spirits" who had poured "a steady stream of beneficence down to our troops in the field." Among others, Moore wrote of Mrs. Fanny Ricketts, wife of a Union Army captain who, upon learning of her husband being wounded, passed through the rebel lines, "at all hazards and despite all obstacles," to reach and tend to him. He wrote of Margaret E. Breckinridge, a hospital and transport service nurse who temporarily overcame her own delicate health in order to "do what she could, and all that she could, to aid in the fierce struggle against the rebellion . . . ," and who eventually died in the service. And he wrote of Mrs. John Harris, the secretary of the Philadelphia Ladies' Aid Society, a "pallid and low-voiced lady, who, when the brazen trumpet of war rang across the continent, glided from her sick chamber, and entered upon a self-imposed and self-directed career of Christian and sanitary labors."[36] Overall, the women who drew Moore's most rapt attention were those readily recognizable, by Victorian standards, as feminine "angels of mercy."[37] Such women—rather than those who strayed from their appropriate gender roles—deserved Moore's, and America's, praise, for their "shining deeds have honored their country, and wherever they are known, the nation holds them in equal honor with its brave men."[38]

The same emphasis on the glorious self-sacrifice of middle-class and elite women that Moore displayed in *Women of the War*, dominated *Woman's Work in the Civil War*, although Brockett and Vaughan dedicated their commemorative to those nameless and faceless multitudes of "loyal women of America," whose "patient endurance of privation," most notably when they were "called to give up their beloved ones for the nation's defense," enabled others to "minister relief and consolation to our wounded and suffering heroes."[39] But, as if to say that the common woman's surrender of her loved ones to the enemy's sword and musket represented a sacrifice so basic to her nature as to require only the briefest passing mention, Brockett and Vaughan then turned their attention to the stories of more conspicuous women in the war, many of whom were recognizable by name or description from Moore's earlier work. Like Moore, Brockett and Vaughan wrote of Mrs. John Harris, a "pale, quiet, delicate woman, often an invalid for months, and almost always a sufferer," who nonetheless possessed a "firm and dauntless spirit." Moore's ethereal, selfless Margaret Breckinridge, too, recurred in their work as a "true heroine of the war. . . . Patient, courageous, self-forgetting, steady of purpose and cheerful in spirit. . . . With her slight form [and] her bright face. . . ."[40]

Chapter after chapter in both early postwar works described the dedication of individual women nurses—Moore's delicate but persistent "angels of mercy"—but for whom the Union cause might well have faltered. As symbols of the life left behind, and of home, family, and community, female nurses eased the soldiers' loneliness as well as their physical pain, reminded them of the things for which they fought. Civil War nurses, wrote Bellows, were "an exceptional class . . . [of] women with a mighty love and earnestness in their hearts . . . and an ability to show it forth."[41] Early writers also remembered individually some of the thousands of women who supported the Union through their work in soldiers' aid societies across the north, women who, the writers explained, played an important role during the war by transmitting the memories and influence of the home front to the battlefield, acting as conservators of both the physical welfare and the moral character of the soldiers. These women, like the nurses, discharged culturally significant and gender-specific duties, for which they deserved lavish praise.

If both *Women of the War* and *Woman's Work in the Civil War* reverberated with praise of northern women's selflessness and generosity,[42] both similarly rang with adulation for women's superior ability to mesh, virtually seamlessly, their own efforts on behalf of the Union with the efforts of men. Just as woman's peacetime "sphere" theoretically complemented that of man, in wartime, as men took up their functions as soldiers, warriors, and heroes in the thick of the fight, women at home and at the front did what *they* knew best how to do: dressing, cleaning, feeding, supplying, and simply loving the soldiers, without complaint and without hesitation. Like men's, women's patriotism rose naturally from deep within them to meet the soldiers' needs and the needs of the nation. "Men," wrote Bellows in his introduction to *Woman's Work in the Civil War*,

> usually jealous of woman's extending the sphere of her life and labors, welcomed in this case her assistance in a public work, and

felt how vain men's toil and sacrifices would be without woman's steady sympathy and patient ministry of mercy, her more delicate and persistent pity, her willingness to endure monotonous details of labor for the sake of charity. . . . .

Rivalries between men and women that one might have expected to arise, he insisted, had passed wordlessly into oblivion as both sexes adjusted easily—and women, selflessly—to the new circumstances of war.[43] In this depiction, shared by both commemoratives, of the flawlessly complementary response of the sexes to the outbreak of war, there was no pressure exerted on the Victorian gender system. There was only the logical, natural progression of events.

Given all this, it is, perhaps, not surprising that the early writers dedicated very little time to the discussion of more than four hundred women who blazed individual trails for themselves by spending the years between 1861 and 1865 armed and riding with the troops.[44] To ignore this group of women entirely would have defied the public's awareness of figures such as Kady Brownell, Bridget Divers, and Annie Etheridge, whose fame was widespread. Instead, the early historians granted such women a degree of recognition they considered proportional to their numbers and their actual contributions to the war effort, on the one hand, and their representativeness of "true" Yankee womanhood on the other: a short chapter for each of one or two individuals, and a few pages collectively for the lot.[45]

To Moore, such women represented bizarre aberrations, indeed in many cases they were women overwrought with passion (against a backdrop of "passionless" Victorian womanhood), women who

went to avoid separation from those who were dearer to them than ease, or life itself; others, from a pure love of romance and adventure; and others, from a mental hallucination that victory

173

and deliverance would come to the war-burdened land only by the sacrifice of their lives.[46]

Unlike male enlistees, such women did not go clearheaded into the service but, instead, failed to heed the dictates of reason and thus slipped over some vaguely defined edge of decorum, if not sanity.

More significantly, perhaps, they were women who typically came from *non*-middle-class origins. "No less praiseworthy and admirable," wrote Moore at the beginning of his section on Irish Bridget Divers, who had spent much of the war riding with the First Michigan Cavalry,

> have been the devotion and self-sacrifice of those who were born in less favored circles, and brought with them to the work, if not the elegance of the boudoir, the hearty good will, the vigorous sense, and the unwearied industry of the laboring class.[47]

By introducing Divers this way, Moore indicated that the propriety of the wartime activities of women of the "laboring class" simply could not be gauged by the same measure applied to the "ladies," and he thereby swiftly diffused any discomfort middle- or upper-class readers might experience in response to the notion of the woman soldier. Such a thing, he seemed to say, was virtually unimaginable for a "lady," confined as she was—in the popular mind at least—to the "elegance of the boudoir." A working-class woman, on the other hand, revealed her "hearty good will," "vigorous sense," and "unwearied industry" when she attached herself to a regiment and took up the duties of a soldier.

Even so, Moore assured his readers that the *de facto* wartime activities of regimental women were fundamentally domestic and self-sacrificial in nature. Divers, he wrote, gave her "whole soul" to the work of "aiding and sustaining the soldier." Annie Etheridge, who spent time with each of the Second, Third, and Fifth Michigan Regiments, "when not actively engaged on the field or in hospital, . . . superintended the cooking at brigade headquarters." When her brigade moved, he added, Etheridge "would mount her horse and march with the ambulances and the surgeons, administering to the wants of the sick and wounded."[48] Such descriptions cleansed Divers and Etheridge of unseemly masculine characteristics and behavior while back-handedly recognizing them as military heroines who traveled armed, and remained in the field throughout the war. In memory, they became exceptionally courageous nurses and dietary aides rather than female soldiers.

Brockett and Vaughan also wrote about Annie Etheridge, and, like Moore, they emphasized those manifestations of Etheridge's "courage" that were visible in her work of caring for the health of the men in her company. "So fully convinced were the officers from the corps commander down, of her use-fulness and faithfulness in care of the wounded," they wrote,

> that at a time when a peremptory order was issued from the head-quarters of the army that all women, whatever their position or services should leave the camp, all the principal field officers of the corps to which her regiment was attached united in a petition to the general-in-chief, that an exception might be made in her favor.[49]

Brockett and Vaughan lauded Etheridge for her uniqueness, but tempered their judgment by focusing on her feminine healing abilities. They pointedly ignored the possibility that there may have been other factors in Etheridge's performance, such as her courage in battle, which contributed to the regiments' urgent desire to retain her.

Moore placed his material on "Women as Soldiers" at the very end of the book. There is no indication that he did so in order to save the best for last; instead, the material appears almost tacked on, a compromise, perhaps, between the need to acknowledge women in uniform and a fervent desire to ignore them. Brockett and Vaughan, however, displaying a general discomfort with the notion of women in actual military service in such things as their caveats about Etheridge's true role in her regiment, elsewhere abruptly unmasked what amounted to a harshly critical judgment of such creatures. "The number of women who actually bore arms in the war," they admitted with apparent neutrality in their short chapter on "Military Heroines,"

> or who, though generally attending a regiment as nurses and vivan-
> diéres [sic] [daughters of the regiment], at times engaged in the
> actual conflict was much larger than is generally supposed, and
> embraces persons of all ranks of society.[50]

But words of acknowledgment yielded quickly to a surprisingly vivid statement of conscious, punitive denial.

> Those who from whatever cause, whether romance, love or patrio-
> tism, and all these had their influence, donned the male attire and
> concealed their sex, are hardly entitled to a place in our record,
> since they did not seek to be known as women, but preferred to
> pass for men. . . .[51]

"[A]side from these," they added, "there were not a few who, without abandoning the dress or prerogatives of their sex, yet performed skillfully and well the duties of the other."[52]

For the early postwar writers, the willingness of women to "abandon the dress or prerogatives of their sex," even for the sake of the Union's war effort, presented a serious problem. Women who temporarily overstepped the bounds of "their sex" might be forgiven and even, possibly, celebrated, provided they showed no signs of "preferring to pass for men," or of forgetting or denying the basic limits imposed on them by their gender. Brockett and Vaughan could not ignore the fact that the war had made vulnerable some of middle-class American society's stricter gender guidelines and had upset the perceived equilibrium of the prewar gender system. That did not mean, however, that they must sanction such changes in any way, or lend their influence to a postwar redefinition—or worse, a rejection—of antebellum social rules and gender constraints. A woman's "abandonment of the dress or prerogatives of her sex" represented an unnecessary transgression under any circumstances; and a woman who transgressed in this manner was simply *not* "entitled to a place in the record."

One is not surprised, therefore, that Mary Walker found no place in Brockett and Vaughan's work, or the work of others who wrote immediately after the war to commemorate women's loyalty, devotion, and active service to the Union.[53] Mary Walker outraged the sensibilities even of those who believed themselves tolerant and progressive and who proposed to celebrate the many and varied works of Union women during the war. In a manner unparalleled by other women in the war, by her clothing, by her personal and professional ambitions, and, perhaps, most of all by her refusal to surrender to prevailing intolerance, Walker violated even the most flexible of wartime gender standards and pushed the extremes of admissible female behavior past their already attenuated wartime limits. Postwar historians such as Brockett and Vaughan, who candidly expressed their disapproval of women who "from whatever cause . . . donned the male attire and concealed their sex," must have been confused, disturbed, perhaps even repelled by this woman who not only "donned male attire" (albeit without ever actively seeking to "conceal her sex"), but also expected to have the full freedom of physical movement, abundance of professional and economic opportunities, and independence of personal character of a man, *as a woman*. In the eyes of her contemporaries, Mary Walker defied the very basis of the Victorian gender system: the distinctive and complementary nature of maleness and femaleness. She went far beyond applying temporary wartime pressure to certain aspects of the system, virtually threatening to destroy it entirely.

Surely, one way to discourage other women from heeding her example and following in her footsteps lay in erasing the footsteps she left behind. Alternately, given that Walker's wartime experiences and contributions had already claimed for her a considerable amount of fame, one could, as the postwar historians did, leave her story to an eager, sensationalist press to tell. In the wake of the early commemorators' silence on Walker's service to the Union army, from the 1860s to her death in 1919, *The New York Times* published almost fifty articles about Mary Walker—many of which distorted the facts of her war years as they did the rest of the details of her life and her endeavors, and most of which displayed a harsh, judgmental tone often tinged with mockery.[54] These articles, in the absence of more even-handed contemporary accounts, allowed for the construction of a popular postwar image of Mary Walker as an eccentric, perhaps megalomaniacal, perhaps mentally unstable, seeker of the public spotlight, best dismissed as a "freak" and a "crank," or at the very least a silly "little lady in pants."[55]

By choice, early postwar writers concentrated instead on those women's stories that could, more easily than Mary Walker's, be tailored to fit prewar Victorian stereotypes of womanhood. Influenced by their own underlying, socially conservative motives, early historians thus projected for popular postwar consumption a very particular image in which Yankee women during the war expressed only the finest, most feminine qualities and instincts—selflessness, "womanly" courage, devotion to family and community—all within the context of perfect working relationships with men, and all for the sake of resurrecting a stable world temporarily battered by strife, a prewar Victorian world to which they would happily return once peace was declared.

Significantly, the demands of such an image required not only the exclusion of someone so bold as Mary Walker, but the reconfiguration of the story of the also famous—if differently so—Annie Wittenmyer, as well. Indeed, although the early commemoratives spoke kindly of Wittenmyer, it is noteworthy that they highlighted not so much her work with the Keokuk Ladies' Soldiers' Aid Society, but rather her inauguration and supervision of the Special Diet Kitchen project.[56] Although it seems reasonable that the early writers should focus on the diet-kitchen work that ultimately brought her national recognition, it is, nonetheless, worth noting that they had nothing whatsoever to say about her bitter fight, long before her engagement in the diet-kitchen project, to preserve her own and the Keokuk Society's status and hegemony in Iowa sanitary affairs against the all-male, USSC-affiliated Iowa State Army Sanitary Commission. Early historians clearly recognized that an account of the details of Wittenmyer's war at home against a male, state-sanctioned bureaucracy did not square with their preferred image of women's wartime cooperation, subordination, and self-sacrifice, whereas a discussion of the diet-kitchen project might allow readers to perceive the now-famous Wittenmyer in a more maternal, pseudodomestic, noncombative light. Frank Moore subsumed his account of Wittenmyer's war years into a chapter about her assistant in the Orphan Asylum and Diet Kitchen projects, Mary E. Shelton.[57] Brockett and Vaughan opted for a portrayal that, rather than discussing her abundant prewar benevolent work as a logical precursor to her vigorous service to the Union, implied that Wittenmyer had emerged from the serene isolation of her drawing room only for the duration of the war, after which she disappeared back into a middle-class widow's oblivion. Brockett and Vaughan's Wittenmyer was one whom the war found "residing in quiet seclusion at Keokuk," who nevertheless "[w]ith the menace of armed treason to the safety of her country's institutions . . . felt all her patriotic instincts and sentiments arousing to activity." So urged on by patriotic fervor, Wittenmyer "laid aside her favorite intellectual pursuits, and prepared herself to do what a woman might in the emergency. . . ."[58] After the war, they wrote, Wittenmyer returned home to Keokuk "to resume the quiet life she had abandoned, and to gain needed repose, after her four years' effort in behalf of our suffering defenders."[59] Such a portrayal— which her pre- and postwar charitable activism belies—isolated Wittenmyer's wartime activities from any enduring political context or meaning, minimized her story's potential impact on postwar gender relations, and contained her image within the antebellum gender system's ideal of middle-class womanhood.

And what of Sophronia Bucklin? Although the early postwar historians wrote glowingly of the service provided by numerous individual Civil War nurses, Bucklin was not one who claimed their attention. Moore did not mention Bucklin at all. Brockett and Vaughan devoted a single line to her: "Miss Sophronia Bucklin, of Auburn, N. Y.," they wrote, "an untiring and patient worker among the soldiers of the Army of the Potomac, also deserves a place in our record."[60] Clearly, neither of the early commemorative histories could possibly have included a full chapter on each of the thousands of women in the north who gave years of their lives to the Union cause. True, Bucklin's story lacked the romance of a woman who had devotedly followed her beloved husband into battle, or had sacrificed the great comforts of an elite lifestyle in order to enter the nursing service, or who had "glide[d] from her sick chamber" when the "brazen trumpet of war rang across the continent" to serve the boys in blue.[61] Nor, indeed, did Bucklin ride off to the front on horseback, the immigrant, working-class daughter of a regiment. Her story was plainer and less dramatic than others, perhaps worthy of mention but not of elaboration.

Even if her virtual exclusion from the postwar record was simply a matter of her being among the lesser known women nurses of the Union—though Brockett and Vaughan's mention of her tends to undercut this notion—one wonders if perhaps other things than Bucklin's ordinariness might ultimately have tainted her image in the eyes of historians who demanded, at least retrospectively, pure self-sacrifice as the only legitimate motive, and pure (submissive) cooperation as the only legitimate style, for women active in the nursing service. After all, the fervor of Bucklin's patriotism had failed to overshadow completely her consciousness of her need and right to receive financial compensation for her labor.[62] Moreover, throughout the war, she had retained a sharply critical eye toward the military medical establishment, and had, on more than one occasion, gone beyond mere observation to vigorous confrontation with the various obstacles—both human and institutional—to the work she had set out to do. Although, in general, the historians generously praised female Civil War nurses, none of the nurses they praised demonstrated such attributes. Surely, the less compromising, less self-sacrificial aspects of Bucklin's wartime service conflicted with the early writers' image and representation of Victorian womanhood, excluding her from laudatory treatment. Instead, their focus rested on nurses whose wartime service to the Union was not (at least not so clearly) tainted by matters of money or of open conflict with male superiors and coworkers, and whose behavior in hospitals and on the field seemed to conform more readily to a carefully constructed postwar image of Yankee womanhood designed to circumscribe the social and political consequences of wartime stresses on the gender system that women such as Bucklin exerted.

By virtue of their crafted portrayal (or exclusion) of the individual women's Civil War stories, early postwar historians set the tone for popular understanding of northern middle-class women in the war, and of the war's long-term meaning for American women as a whole and for postwar gender relations.[63] In chapter after chapter, they denied the war's function as a crucible of change for the interrelationship of men, women, and power—the war as a context in which enormous friction and pressure provoked grinding adjustments to the Victorian gender system. In his own introductory chapter to *Woman's Work in the Civil War* addressing the revealing question of whether or not women who had been active during the war would, in the postwar period, revert precisely to their prewar roles and activities, Linus Brockett had indeed answered "no," agreeing that women's wartime experiences had changed them. War, Brockett conceded, had allowed "the gay and fashionable woman" to rise from the "emptiness and frivolity" of her life into a new life of action "of which, a month before, she would have considered herself incapable"—a new "life of action" which, for many, even the end of the war should not bring to a halt.[64]

But, although he acknowledged that their participation in the Civil War would have permanent consequences for some American women, Brockett was not advocating women's postwar political activism on their own behalf. Rather, he was encouraging their devotion to a "higher and holier" calling in the realm of voluntary philanthropy.[65] Surely, Brockett did not

mean to disregard the depth of antebellum women's involvement in benevolent activities.[66] Instead, his statement served
a prescriptive purpose, redefining middle-class women's postwar
social position to counteract any (temporary) changes allowed
by the unusual circumstances of wartime. Brockett's words reflected the sentiment of many of his peers, that the outpouring
of middle-class female energy between 1861 and 1865 now
required redirection. Indeed, two years later, Brockett under-
scored his postwar vision for middle-class women in an argument
against woman suffrage. Woman's powerfully "affectional and
emotional nature," he explained, disqualified her for an
involvement in politics. "Downward, and still downward she
would plunge, till she would astonish and confound her male
associates by her daring and reckless audacity in the contrivance
of party schemes." Instead, the middle-class woman's nature
called her to "a greater ministry," providing for

> the practical education of the humbler classes of their own sex, to
> elevate them from the slough of poverty and despondency, in which
> so many of them are sunk, not by the gifts of an indiscriminate
> charity, but by kindly sympathy, encouragement, and coun-
> sel. . . .[67]

In the gender-appropriate work of charity and benevolence,
Brockett argued, the women whose stories filled the pages of
Woman's Work in the Civil War could expend their newly found
talents and energies. This would be their "higher and holier"
calling in the postwar world, providing them with the "greatest
joy and the highest honor."[68]

Although they managed to cast a long shadow in terms of
popular perceptions of individual wartime women and Yankee
womanhood as a whole, in the end, early postwar writers such
as Brockett could not entirely contain the actual consequences

for American culture, and Victorian gender ideology, of women's participation in the Civil War. Even Annie Wittenmyer's postwar life, although devoted to conservative philanthropic activities and antisuffrage, went beyond the bounds of Brockett's expectations, what with her fundamental independence from male control (in such organizations as the WCTU, especially), her regular assumption of high-status positions, her extensive travelling, and her extremely public profile. Wittenmyer's unique postwar experience aside, however, middle-class women's wartime successes in soldier relief in general—especially at the leadership level (local, state, or national)—induced changes in the business of public charity after the war, including an increase in women's paid professional opportunities as well as a revision of power relations between men and women in the field. Brockett and the other early writers of women's history in the war, did not foresee such changes, and would not have approved.

Early histories of the sanitary commissions emphasizing men's role consistently paid tribute to women's diligent efforts in the production, collection, and distribution of food, clothing, medicine, and other supplies to the Union troops.[69] Indeed, according to these accounts, middle-class women's labor on behalf of the soldiers represented the great bulk of the ground- and footwork of all the "umbrella" relief commissions. Early histories underestimated, however, the degree to which the countless women who transformed their church groups, sewing circles, and local charitable societies into wartime powerhouses of relief developed, over the course of the war, effective tactics and methods for accomplishing on a previously inconceivable scale the otherwise familiar activity of caring for those in need. These accounts entirely denied the postwar implications of middle-class women's new organizational skills and strategies.

In reality, women in the leadership of war relief at any

level—women such as Annie Wittenmyer—found themselves steeped in competition and in political conflict with men as a result of their disavowal of antebellum perceptions regarding their inability to function professionally and institutionally in a context larger than the immediate community. They confronted, for the first time, the argument that they should collaborate with and be subsumed by male-dominated local, state, and national organizations in order for them to fulfill their goal of bringing the moral and practical influences of the home out onto the battlefield. In the face of this argument, women in soldier relief developed strategies to protect and extend the work they believed, somewhat ironically, to be little more than a practical manifestation of that most salient feature of the proper Victorian woman's character, her virtue. In turn, their various efforts after the war to cooperate with, to imitate, and to assume paid, professional positions within male-run organizations of public benevolence, typically displayed as a common motive the preservation of (1) a critical aspect of the prewar definition of woman's "nature"; (2) the lessons in strategy and political maneuvering that they had learned during the war; and (3) the desire to continue the expansion of women's "sphere" of social and moral influence that the war had begun.

With considerable difficulty, women in war relief had fought to retain control over their own organizations and projects, to demonstrate their capacity for professional leadership, and to cultivate the political skills and acumen necessary for success. By their persistence and their conscious development of new styles, female leaders, in many cases, learned to work effectively with the men's organizations and even earned their male colleagues' respect and cooperation. In so doing, they forced men not only to concede the value of women's relief work at the local level, but also to loosen their grip on the reins of power and to make room for women, as paid professionals, within the bureaucracies and the leadership of first wartime and then postwar national organizations. Despite any efforts to the contrary on the part of the early postwar historians, the pressure exerted on the antebellum gender system by middle-class women's skillful execution of war relief, in the long term, altered perceptions of women's suitability for such work and generated opportunities for them, after the war, in large-scale institutional leadership. As one recent historian has written, "The end of the war did not, for these women, signal a reprieve from wartime rhetoric, fervor, or responsibility. They carried the war and its lessons with them in embarking on new benevolent endeavors,"[70] of which the Woman's Christian Temperance Union (WCTU) and the Woman's Relief Corps were prime examples. The enhanced scope and elevated status of middle-class women's postwar charity work undoubtedly exceeded what Brockett had prescribed for them as agents of a "higher and holier" philanthropic calling, derived directly from their prior achievements in soldiers' aid.[71]

The postwar period also saw gradual changes for middle-class women in terms of their access to paid work in nursing. In December 1899, Sophronia Bucklin received a letter from her niece, Erva, from Chicago, in which Erva spoke with frustration about her attempt to obtain a paid nursing position at a hospital in the city. "When I applied and was accepted at the Baptist Hospital," she wrote,

> they were paying nurses eight dollars a month for their work. . . . After I got here, the other nurses told me that I had been deceived—that the hospital had quit paying nurses and I should have been told of it.[72]

Erva remained at the Baptist Hospital for a month, and then took a position as a private nurse. Still, she insisted, "[I] am going to enter another hospital as soon as I can get into one that pays wages."[73]

That Erva in 1899 addressed concerns about her nursing career to her Aunt Sophronia was not a random event. Surely, any member of Bucklin's extended family who corresponded with her knew of her Civil War service, and Erva's determination to be paid for her work as a nurse echoed sentiments that Bucklin expressed in her memoir and that she may have explicitly articulated to Erva at one time. Above all, Erva's letter proclaimed a link between Bucklin's life and her own.

A critical aspect of this link lay in the appearance of independent nurses' training programs in the United States, beginning in 1873, eight years after the war's end. These first programs closely followed the model of Florence Nightingale's schools in England, emphasizing the training of "young, educated," presumably middle-class "women of upstanding morals" for "paid, skilled" hospital service. In the wake of the Civil War, American doctors increasingly acknowledged a need for "skilled support staff" in their hospitals, just as "British doctors had been clamoring for higher quality, literate nurses since Florence Nightingale had demonstrated women's suitability for the job in Crimea." In both countries, the postwar desire for "quality, literate" nurses translated into the gradual development of a paid profession for middle-class women in health care.[74]

Thus, despite conservative backlash, Civil War nurses such as Sophronia Bucklin initiated a process in the United States that the creation of training programs less than ten years after Appomattox furthered: the establishment of nursing as a permanent and legitimate profession for middle-class women. The development of the idea of formally training women as medical attendants signified perceptual changes regarding the nature of hospital medicine itself—i.e., that good care required more than the periodic attention of a male physician—and also regarding the mental and physical capacities of middle-class women, and their ability to learn, understand, and carry out the rigors of patient care in a public setting. The existence of nurse training programs further implied the existence of hospital nursing positions for graduates to fill.

Erva's letter, then, together with the development of nurse training programs, demonstrates that the postwar period witnessed permanent adjustments to the Victorian idealization of the middle-class "angel of the household," with its assumptions about her unsuitability for the work of public caretaking, and its restriction to men of any and all access to paid positions in the medical field—a shift, in other words, in middle-class gender boundaries. Such a shift undoubtedly alarmed those who had hoped to restrain the transformative social consequences of women's involvement in the war, and who would have celebrated Bucklin's postwar return to private life. There is more than a hint of irony in the fact that the very same class of women whose presence at the war front had, in 1861, elicited male medical officials' fierce resentment and stern disapproval, by 1873, emerged as the new nursing schools' preferred trainees. Clearly, the commemorators' delicately contoured descriptions of Civil War nurses, which doggedly adhered to prewar stereotypes of fragile, self-sacrificial, middle-class womanhood, ultimately could not overshadow public and professional awareness of either the gruesome nature of Civil War hospital work, or the stamina, dignity, self-confidence, and skill of the women who had performed it and had sought to be paid for it.

Of course, the process of gender system readjustment is slow and never without friction or resistance, and social conservatives always joust with advocates of change. Hence, Bucklin's niece continued to encounter obstacles in her efforts to find a paid nursing position some twenty years after the first professional nursing schools had opened. Nevertheless, the roots of

Erva's expectations about her nursing career lay in the wartime labor of her aunt "Phrone" and women like her. Through their participation in Civil War nursing, women like Bucklin created new opportunities for themselves and for their daughters and granddaughters, who, in turn, continued to question and confront popular definitions of womanhood, of women's role and position in the public realm, and of the relative status and the proper interaction of women and men.[75]

Civil War nurses and middle-class women involved in soldier relief during the war trespassed *en masse* into the "public sphere," claiming for themselves new professional territory in wartime relief and nursing, including titles and wages and, in so doing, became wielders of a kind of institutional power previously hoarded by men. Revised perceptions about women's strengths, intelligence, and talents, and the emergence in the postwar period of professional opportunities for women in fields reminiscent of women's largest areas of Civil War activity, revealed that shifts in the gender system had indeed occurred and that middle-class men, as a result of women's pressure during the war, had found themselves forced to surrender ground in matters of character, personhood, and professional stature. Without a doubt, then, the return to the status quo antebellum that key postwar writers envisioned was no longer possible; too much had changed during the war. Civil War women had undermined the perceived equilibrium of the system that prevailed before Sumter, and a new equilibrium based on wartime and postwar reevaluations of the genders had to be sought. Pressure exerted at any point in a system demands some kind of response. To a great extent during and after the Civil War, as women pushed against the constraints of the Victorian gender system, men yielded a degree of control and territory, indirectly expanding the "natural" boundaries of women's "proper" sphere of action and, to some extent, contracting their own.

The stories of Sophronia Bucklin and Annie Wittenmyer open windows on the sort of boundary redefinition between the genders—the unbalancing and rebalancing of the Victorian gender system in response to women's pressure and despite all efforts to the contrary—that Civil War nurses and women in war relief brought about. In contrast, Mary Walker's story is a lonely one of an unusually radical, bold, and "masculine" woman doctor in a society unprepared for women doctors at all. In conjunction with the stories of Bucklin and Wittenmyer that of Mary Walker demonstrates that, although thousands of women's wartime pressure against the constraints of the Victorian gender system yielded real results, in truth some types of pressure were more effective than others, and some parts of the system were more easily maneuvered than others.

Walker sought and finally achieved employment through the Union Army's Medical Department as the military's sole female surgeon, only to have her achievements effectively dismissed as soon as the war had ended. The Medal of Honor Walker treasured until her death was at once a small token of recognition by the federal government for her wartime service and the only evidence of her significant personal victories.[76] Clearly, the story of Walker's solitary struggle of determination and frustration reveals a great deal about the *limits* of Civil War era tolerance for gender system change—for its exposes the impressive resilience of the foundations on which the Victorian gender system rested and which, in turn, limited the sort and the degree of the changes and adjustments it was possible for women at midcentury to elicit. Walker's inability at the end of the war to convince the federal government to grant her either a retroactive or a future surgeon's commission, while it did not undercut her wartime accomplishments, nonetheless signified the impermanence and fragility of such an achievement. Moreover, the results of Walker's defeat were not confined to her own life. She had hoped by her Civil War service to increase opportunities for other middle-class women in the medical profession, but she did not succeed. Although both women and blacks became slightly more numerous in medicine following the war, "prevailing social prejudices" kept their numbers small until the middle of the twentieth century.[77] Mary Walker's Civil War service did little or nothing to lower the barriers for women, not because she was a bad doctor, but because by virtue of her singularity and her notoriety she became a lightning rod for nineteenth-century anxieties about gender identity.

Antebellum Victorian America, with its rigid guidelines for men's and women's "appropriate" characteristics, appearances, behaviors, and social positions, produced few women who shared with Walker such complete and unabashed disregard for gender conventions. Large numbers of women like her simply did not exist at the time the Civil War began, or at any other time in the nineteenth century. One might attribute her ultimate ineffectiveness in overturning the system to the fact that she stood virtually alone against it, except that she was clearly not isolated or hidden from view. Rather, she was a veritable magnet for popular attention at the same time that she engaged the entire federal government, and many of the Union's most prominent military leaders, in her struggle. Indeed, it seems that the existence of even *one* such woman, so utterly defiant of the gender system as a whole, was more unsettling to many than the thousands of other women who, during the war, variously challenged traditional gender boundaries. And, thus, even a medical and cultural crisis of enormous magnitude such as the Civil War did not generate for her a permanent, socially acceptable niche in middle-class America. Mary Walker's startling ambitions, her uncompromising attitude, and her unorthodox (if practical) choice of clothing, provoked far more uneasiness among her observers than thousands of women in dark, hoopless dresses seeking nursing positions at the front, or bearing supplies from home to soldiers in the field, could possibly have done.

Nothing Walker did in the aftermath of the war eased the way for long-term popular acceptance of her person or her goals. By remaining visible (not least of all in the nation's Capital), and by pressing relentlessly for various personal and "feminist" political causes, Walker paradoxically and tragically provided ample ammunition to her conservative foes. Not satisfied with a larger but still limited portion, Walker wanted the same freedom she believed men possessed to sample at will and in whatever manner she saw fit from the entire pie of social opportunity. It was a desire that evoked great distress in her class peers, male and female alike, progressive as well as conservative, because it so utterly threatened time-honored perceptions about the need for gender boundaries, though those boundaries might under certain circumstances change.

In his presidential address before the American Medical Association (AMA) in 1871, Dr. Alfred Stillé seemed to have Walker in mind when he discussed the phenomenon of the woman doctor:

> Certain women seek to rival men in manly sports . . . and the strong-minded ape them in all things, even in dress. In doing so, they may command a sort of admiration such as all monstrous productions inspire, especially when they tend toward a higher type than their own.[78]

Stillé clearly abhorred the sort of woman Walker represented, who refused to be contained within standard descriptive gender categories that contradicted her own desires and ambitions. His status as AMA president in 1871, combined with the AMA's refusal to accept women members until 1915, fully sixty years after Walker had received her degree from Syracuse Medical College (and sixty-six years after Elizabeth Blackwell graduated from Geneva Medical College), displays the endurance and the pervasiveness of his attitude within that esteemed organization. According to one medical historian, as late as 1910, "there was a popular impression that medical women could be recognized on the streets by dress and bearing."[79]

Those who adjusted to the presence of female nurses at the front and female aid society workers in the field could, to a great extent, rationalize such things in terms of the wartime extension of women's peacetime responsibilities in the home. After the war, it was possible for those seeking change to point to such women's wartime contributions as evidence in favor of what amounted to permanent gender system modification— the creation of a formal nursing profession for women and the broadening of paid leadership positions (sometimes at the national level) for women in institutional benevolence.

It was not possible to employ the same strategies in Walker's case, so profoundly and boldly did she challenge fundamental ideas about the cultural domain men and women might occupy in the middle of the nineteenth century, and in Walker's case the Victorian gender system's resistance to change in its fundamental structure prevailed. In the final analysis, this resistance stemmed not from the fact that Walker pushed so much harder and so much more bluntly than Bucklin, Wittenmyer, and thousands of other women like them—although she did; nor from the fact that Walker's demands on the surface were more outrageous—although they were. A woman surgeon in the army? Wearing trousers? Even Bucklin and Wittenmyer would have found the notion shocking. Still, the gender system's resistance to Walker ultimately reflected her rejection, at the deepest level, of even *redefined* gender boundaries, and her repudiation of any notion of middle-class womanhood that still permitted some sacred territory to be occupied only by middle-class manhood. Walker rejected gender boundaries, even altered boundaries, on principle. She wanted unrestricted access to the full territory of being human, and a system based on balance, complementarity, and harmony between two distinct (if constantly revised) genders simply held no place for her.

And so, despite her brief enjoyment of the fulfillment of her goals in the nation's emergency, and although she lived to be eighty-seven years old and saw women in the United States Army in World War I wearing slacks and jackets, Walker alone and with all her contradictory qualities was unable to achieve her ultimate goal, the subversion of the gender system altogether. Instead, the system consumed her, transforming her in memory and perhaps even in fact into the "freak" and "crank" she was ultimately remembered to have been. Yet, in all her efforts and achievements throughout her life, Walker did nothing more significant than to expose the rigid core of the midcentury, middle-class gender system. By exposing this core and by sacrificing everything to undermine it, Walker demonstrated a unique sort of courage and persistence. And, while the Civil War saw thousands of women struggling to gain access to "territory" previously restricted to men, it witnessed only one Mary Walker, who, although defeated in the end, nonetheless, managed to achieve a brief but glorious victory against the very foundations of an entrenched gender system when she signed an army surgeon's contract in 1864. Despite all attempts to dismiss her achievements, Walker clung to that victory, pinning to her lapel for the next fifty-four years the proudest memento of it she possessed—the Medal of Honor.

CONCLUSION

I do not think we should quit the archives or abandon the
study of the past, but we do have to change some of the ways
we have gone about working, some of the questions we have
asked. We need to scrutinize our methods of analysis, clarify
our operative assumptions, and explain how we think change
occurs. Instead of a search for single origins, we have to
conceive of processes so interconnected that they cannot be
disentangled.

>   —JOAN W. SCOTT, "GENDER: A USEFUL CATEGORY
>   OF HISTORICAL ANALYSIS"

[T]he discipline of history, through its practices, produces
(rather than gathers or reflects) knowledge about the
past generally and, inevitably, about sexual difference as well.
In that way, history operates as a particular kind of
cultural institution endorsing and announcing constructions
of gender.

>   —JOAN W. SCOTT, *GENDER AND THE POLITICS OF HISTORY*

195

Joan Scott has described the discipline of history as operating "as a particular kind of cultural institution endorsing and announcing constructions of gender."[1] The involvement of northern, middle-class women in the Civil War, and the efforts of postwar historians to shape the women's stories to fit their mid-nineteenth-century model of middle-class womanhood, underscore the accuracy of Scott's insights. At any given time, historians play a key social role in the construction of gender, in the creation, maintenance, and occasional recasting of stereotypes of gender and patterns of gender interaction. Because wars are "gendering" events that also rend the social fabric and upset the status quo, postwar historians have an unusually significant opportunity to contribute to the establishment of new models by highlighting or by obscuring changes in the gender system that the war has wrought. The prominent post-Civil War historians chose the latter course.

Even historians, however, though they faithfully "endorse and announce constructions of gender," cannot unilaterally stem the tide of history, especially in the aftermath of events as unsettling as wars. Their efforts, in the wake of Appomattox, to limit the Civil War's social consequences for gender redefinition and the revision of gender relations were only partly successful. Middle-class women had participated in the war in numbers too large and in ways too unconventional and satisfying to permit conservative writers to achieve their goal uncontested. The prewar system, which depended on a definition of middle-class women as best-suited to fulfill the duties of the private household (versus men's fitness for public and professional life), had lost a good deal of its credibility under the pressure of northern women's wartime activities. Generations of women after the war would grow up in the context of a revised gender system that reflected the impact of the Civil War by assuming their capacity for and allowing them broader access to professional labor in nursing and institutional charity and, eventually, in clerical work and even in war itself.

Joan Scott has also suggested that in considering how change over time occurs, we need to "conceive of processes so interconnected that they cannot be disentangled."[2] The participation of northern, middle-class women in the Civil War exposed the complexity of the process of gender system change. To study these women reveals the enormous and varied pressures they exerted on the Victorian gender system during the Civil War, pressures that led to shifts and adjustments at particular points, and that met with rigid intractability at others.

The antebellum, middle-class gender system encompassed a variety of assumptions about women's and men's attributes and abilities. Like all systems, it had strengths and weaknesses, points of broad appeal and entrenchment, and points of potential dispute and change. The popular attribution of such qualities as fragility, emotionality, selflessness, and incapacity for public or professional life to middle-class women, and such qualities as sturdiness, rationality, competitiveness, and professional skill to middle-class men, reflected basic cultural values underlying Victorian Americans' rigid, complementary view of gender. These imputed characteristics helped shape and explain behavior and the relations of men and women within the household as well as without, and resulted in both the imagery and, to a great extent the functional reality, of "separate spheres" of life and labor, the private sphere or the "home" for women and the public sphere or the "world" for men.

The war damaged this imagery. Middle-class women threw themselves in large numbers into the war effort, quickly assessing and rejecting antebellum notions about their lack of endurance, courage, and clearheadedness. They scoffed at those who emphasized female limitations, pointing out that, in wartime, many of those so-called "limitations" had in fact become advantages. Who, after all, could better tend to the soldiers' needs than women, nature's chosen caretakers?

Above all, middle-class women challenged spatial boundaries in an unprecedented manner as thousands of them dramatically expanded the horizons of the middle-class female universe by travelling far from home to the front, or by linking in various ways their community undertakings on behalf of the soldiers to organizations national in scope. In vast numbers, women refused to accept the idea that war was "no place for women." Instead, they made the war their place, eagerly creating positions for themselves within the war context and adjusting their prewar patterns of behavior to fit public, wartime circumstances. Northern women declared themselves, like men, citizens and patriots who had a right to participate actively in the Union's defense. Perhaps, more importantly, they frequently demanded recognition in the form of pay and professional stature for their contributions, believing the paid and commissioned soldier's self-sacrifice the model to emulate.

In response to women's efforts, men necessarily, and in rare cases quite willingly, yielded ground, sharing and sometimes even surrendering territory, power, and status in the public realm. Men and women worked together for the preservation of the Union and for the protection of its uniformed defenders. The friction they experienced as they came into contact in military hospitals and sanitary organizations reflected the tension in the gender system that the war had produced, a tension that demanded relief. Relief came, for the most part, as women persisted and as men backed down, coming to appreciate and even depend upon women's contributions under the circumstances, learning to relinquish power.

There were many, of course, who failed to realize how quickly women had filled the area that the war had opened to them, and who expected the war's end to bring a similarly speedy end to such cooperative labor and a return to prewar arrangements. After 1865, however, attempts to restore the antebellum boundaries of gendered space met stiff resistance from women who had come greatly to enjoy their expanded domain. Under women's pressure and within the context of a national crisis, the middle-class gender system had shifted noticeably, its underlying values altered in consequence of women's wartime demonstration of the falsity of prewar images, and its prescriptions about proper behavior adjusted to incorporate functions for women for which they had proved themselves more than capable.

Still, the gender system, in the end, demonstrated remarkable rigidity and stability at its core. The very real adjustment of gender boundaries that resulted from middle-class women's wartime pressure did not, in turn, imply the possibility of the elimination of boundaries altogether; rather, it revealed the system's fundamental resilience and stubborn durability. Ironically, men's granting of new gender territory to women during and after the war itself highlighted the tragedy virtually inevitable when a singular figure such as Mary Walker altogether rejected the notion of delineated territory. That Walker alone managed to create such a stir and evoke such popular condemnation attests to her strength and courage, to the relentless vigor of her attacks upon gender conventions, and to the profound threat she posed to the system's basic complementary configuration. Mary Walker threatened the system as a whole, not just some of its individual components. As such, she did not resemble grit in the machinery, grinding but not endangering the gears but, rather, a misplaced wrench that if not removed would imperil the entire machine. Little wonder, then, that Walker suffered such abuse.

The swell of tens of thousands of middle-class women in Civil

War nursing and soldiers' aid, with their shrewd translations of prewar gender standards into the language appropriate for war, presented men with a problem they could not ignore. The appropriation by women of key aspects of prewar gender imagery—e.g., the "natural" selflessness and caretaking abilities of women and women's unique moral burden of maintaining the community—in the long run allowed them to subvert the system, to make claims in the public realm, and to expand the boundaries of women's proper place. They utilized a central aspect of the system, its definition of womanhood, to transform another aspect, its definition of women's ground of activity, and they thereby contributed significantly to a postwar redefinition of values about middle-class women's social role, and to the opening up of opportunities for the women who would follow.

Mary Walker, on the other hand, refused to settle for anything less than a complete dismissal of the notion that men and women were different, complementary, and permanently opposed, even though the ground of their opposition and the boundaries between them might shift. Walker's experience exposed the limits of the gender system's flexibility: Adjustments became necessary for the system's ultimate survival, but the dismantling of the system itself was absolutely unacceptable.

The stories of Sophronia Bucklin, Annie Wittenmyer, and Mary Walker, the postwar commemorators' efforts to domesticate the social repercussions of middle-class women's wartime experiences, and the unmistakable evidence of the expansive impact of northern women's wartime pressure on women's place in the Victorian gender system lead to conclusions at once encouraging and sad. Women in the Civil War, by virtue of their own determination and courage, brought forth positive changes in popular characterizations of middle-class womanhood that, in turn, opened new doors for women in the professions and in public life. At the same time, however, there was not enough determination or courage in the northern, middle-class female world, even in the singular person of Mary Edwards Walker, to bring about the demise of the gender system's fundamental structure—its organization around the basic concept of gender boundaries and limits—once and for all.

NOTES

NOTES TO INTRODUCTION

1 Mary Warden Bingham Diary, in the Mary Warden Bingham Papers, Kinsley Scott Bingham Collection. Michigan Historical Collections, Bentley Historical Library, University of Michigan, Ann Arbor (hereafter cited as the "Bingham Papers").

2 Mary Warden Bingham to James Bingham, 5 May 1862, in the Bingham Papers.

3 Mary Warden Bingham Diary, 14 May 1862, in the Bingham Papers.

4 Mary Warden Bingham to Lucina Warden, 2 February 1863, in the Bingham Papers.

5 Ethel Alice Hurn, *Wisconsin Women in the War Between the States* (Wisconsin History Commission, 1911), p. 2.

6 Needless to say, this is a paradigm that has been extended to reflect the intersection between women and war in general, as Nancy Huston discusses in her "Tales of War and Tears of Women," *Women's Studies International Forum* 5 (Summer 1982): 271–282.

7 James M. McPherson, *Battle Cry of Freedom: The Civil War Era* (New York: Ballantine Books, 1988), pp. 859–861.

8 See, for example, Dorothy and Carl J. Schneider, *Into the Breach: American Women Overseas in World War I* (New York: Viking, 1991); William H. Chafe, "World War II as a Pivotal Experience

for American Women," in *Women and War: The Changing Status of American Women from the 1930s to the 1950s*, ed. Maria Diedrich and Dorothea Fischer-Hornung (New York: Berg Publishers, Inc., 1990); D'Ann Campbell, *Women at War with America: Private Lives in a Patriotic Era* (Cambridge, MA: Harvard University Press, 1984); Doris Weatherford, *American Women and World War II* (New York: Facts on File, 1990); Mary Beth Norton, *Liberty's Daughters: The Revolutionary Experience of American Women, 1750–1800* (Boston: Little, Brown, 1980); and Linda K. Kerber, *Women of the Republic: Intellect and Ideology in Revolutionary America* (Chapel Hill: University of North Carolina Press, 1980). See also Ellen C. DuBois, *Feminism and Suffrage: The Emergence of an Independent Women's Movement in America, 1848–1869* (Ithaca, NY: Cornell University Press, 1978); Jean Fagan Yellin, *Women and Sisters: The Antislavery Feminists in American Culture* (New Haven, CT: Yale University Press, 1989); Ruth Bordin, *Woman and Temperance: The Quest for Power and Liberty, 1873–1900* (Philadelphia: Temple University Press, 1980); Barbara Epstein, *The Politics of Domesticity* (Middletown, CT: Wesleyan University Press, 1981); Jack S. Blocker, *"Give to the Winds thy Fears": The Women's Temperance Crusade, 1873–1874* (Westport, CT: Greenwood Press, 1985); Nancy Schrom Dye, *As Equals and as Sisters: Feminism, the Labor Movement, and the Women's Trade Union League of New York* (Columbia: University of Missouri Press, 1980); and Elizabeth Anne Payne, *Reform, Labor, and Feminism: Margaret Dreier Robins and the Women's Trade Union League* (Urbana: University of Illinois Press, 1988).

9 Schneider and Schneider, *Into the Breach*, p. 283; Chafe, "World War II as a Pivotal Experience," pp. 32–33; Norton, *Liberty's Daughters*, passim.

10 A few scholars in recent years have begun to focus on the topic of women and the Civil War. See, for example, George C. Rable, *Civil Wars: Women and the Crisis of Southern Nationalism* (Chicago: University of Illinois Press, 1989); Catherine Clinton and Nina Silber, eds., *Divided Houses: Gender and the Civil War* (New York:

Oxford University Press, 1992); Marilyn Mayer Culpepper, *Trials and Triumphs: The Women of the American Civil War* (East Lansing: Michigan State University Press, 1991); and Jane E. Schultz, *Women at the Front: Female Hospital Workers in Civil War America* (forthcoming). For shorter treatments, see Drew Gilpin Faust, "Altars of Sacrifice: Confederate Women and the Narratives of War," *Journal of American History* 76 (March 1990): 1200–1228; relevant chapters in Lori D. Ginzberg, *Women and the Work of Benevolence: Morality, Politics, and Class in the Nineteenth-Century United States* (New Haven, CT: Yale University Press, 1990); Anne Firor Scott, *Natural Allies: Women's Associations in American History* (Urbana: University of Illinois Press, 1991); and Catherine Clinton, *The Other Civil War: American Women in the Nineteenth Century* (New York: Hill & Wang, 1984). Few women's history textbooks go farther than to recognize the Civil War as the critical event dividing abolitionism from the woman suffrage movement. See Linda K. Kerber and Jane De Hart Mathews, *Women's America: Refocusing the Past* (New York: Oxford University Press, 1982); Mary Beth Norton, *Major Problems in American Women's History* (Lexington, MA: D. C. Heath & Co., 1989); and Sara M. Evans, *Born for Liberty: A History of Women in America* (New York: Free Press, 1989).

11 Daniel D. Addison, ed., *Lucy Larcom: Life, Letters and Diary* (Boston: Houghton, Mifflin, 1894; reprint ed., Detroit, MI: Gale Research Co., 1970), p. 89.

12 In fact, as the war progressed, Larcom yearned to contribute more than just "spirit" to the war effort. In late October, she wrote, "Little enough can one realize what war is, who sees it only in its picturesque aspect, who knows of it only by the newspapers, by knitting socks for soldiers, and sewing bed-quilts for the hospitals." Still, Larcom was reluctant to give of herself "in some more adequate way" (ibid., p. 109), troubled as she was by her awareness that the war continued to be a struggle for the Union, not for the slaves' emancipation.

George Rable and Drew Faust have both argued that, as the

war continued, in many ways it was the demise of this martial spirit among southern women that ultimately caused the Confederacy's defeat. See Rable, *Civil Wars*, and Faust, "Altars of Sacrifice."

13 R. Curtis Edgerton to Lydia Edgerton, 28 October 1861, in the R. Curtis Edgerton Letters, Special Collections, The Huntington Library, San Marino, CA.

14 Mary Elizabeth Massey, *Bonnet Brigades* (New York: Alfred A. Knopf, 1966). According to Linus Brockett and Mary Vaughan, there were ten thousand ladies' aid societies in the North. (Linus P. Brockett and Mary C. Vaughan, *Woman's Work in the Civil War: A Record of Heroism, Patriotism, and Patience* (Philadelphia: Zeigler, McCurdy & Co., 1867), p. 59.) Charles Stillé, in his *History of the United States Sanitary Commission: Being the General Report of its Work during the War of the Rebellion* (Philadelphia: J. B. Lippincott & Co., 1866), numbered the aid societies "tributary to the Sanitary Commission" at seven thousand (p. 172). Of course, Stillé's figure leaves open the possibility that numerous aid societies existed independently of the USSC (see below, Chapter Two).

15 Mary A. Livermore, *My Story of the War: A Woman's Narrative of Four Years Personal Experience as Nurse in the Union Army* (Hartford, CT: A. D. Worthington & Co., 1889), pp. 109–110. For early histories of the national relief organizations see, among others, Stillé, *History of the U.S. Sanitary Commission*; Jacob Gilbert Forman, *The Western Sanitary Commission* (St. Louis, MO: R. P. Studley & Co., 1864); and Lemuel Moss, *Annals of the United States Christian Commission* (Philadelphia: J. B. Lippincott & Co., 1868).

16 Annie Wittenmyer, *Under the Guns: A Woman's Reminiscences of the Civil War* (Boston: E. B. Stillings & Co., 1895), and below, Chapter Two.

17 Jane E. Schultz, "The Inhospitable Hospital: Gender and Professionalism in Civil War Medicine," *Signs* 17 (Winter 1992), p. 363. It should be noted that the women of the aid societies and the women who served as nurses and hospital attendants did not

constitute mutually exclusive groups. Many women served the Union in both capacities.

18 See below, Chapter One.

19 The United States Sanitary Commission, The Western Sanitary Commission, and the United States Christian Commission, all of which are discussed in greater detail in Chapter Two.

20 Schultz, "The Inhospitable Hospital," p. 367. See also Jane Ellen Schultz, "Women at the Front: Gender and Genre in Literature of the American Civil War" (Ph.D. dissertation, University of Michigan, Ann Arbor, 1988); Henrietta S. Jaquette, ed., *South After Gettysburg: Letters of Cornelia Hancock from the Army of the Potomac, 1863–1865* (Philadelphia: University of Pennsylvania Press, 1937); Margaret Davis, *Mother Bickerdyke: Her Life and Labors for the Relief of Our Soldiers* (San Francisco, CA: A. T. Dewey, 1886); Julia Chase, *Mary A. Bickerdyke, "Mother"* (Lawrence, KS: Journal Publishing House, 1896); Nina Brown Baker, *Cyclone in Calico: The Story of Mary Ann Bickerdyke* (Boston: Little, Brown, 1952); William F. Barton, *The Life of Clara Barton* (Boston: Houghton, Mifflin Co., 1922); Percy H. Epler, *The Life of Clara Barton* (New York: Macmillan Co., 1941); Ishbel Ross, *Angel of the Battlefield: The Life of Clara Barton* (New York: Harper, 1956); and Elizabeth Brown Pryor, *Clara Barton, Professional Angel* (Philadelphia: University of Pennsylvania Press, 1987). Needless to say, few women could achieve and maintain Bickerdyke's or Barton's independence of movement.

21 Some historians have argued that women nurses in the Civil War did not establish a new field but, rather, acted on their recognition that Civil War nursing offered an opportunity for women to force their way back into the general field of medicine, from which the increasing professionalization of training had excluded them. (See Ann Douglas Wood, "The War Within a War: Women Nurses in the Union Army," *Civil War History* 18 (September 1972), pp. 197–212.) For further discussion, see also below, Chapter One.

22 See below, Chapter Three. Women's roles in the Civil War

extended beyond those more common ones discussed here. For example, about four hundred northern women took male identities, dressed as soldiers, and joined the Union Army. (See Livermore, *My Story of the War*, p. 120; Frank Moore, *Women of the War: Their Heroism and Self-Sacrifice* (Hartford, CT: S. S. Scranton & Co., 1866), pp. 529–535; and Sarah Emma Edmonds, *Unsexed: Or, The Female Soldier* (Philadelphia: Philadelphia Publishing Co., 1864).) Other women travelled with individual regiments, dressed in modified uniforms, and even bore arms on occasion, but did not attempt to hide their sex. (Livermore, *My Story of the War*, p. 116; Brockett & Vaughan, *Woman's Work in the Civil War*, pp. 747–753, 770–774; and Moore, *Women of the War*, pp. 54–64, 109–112, 513–516.) These women's duties included at least a modicum of nursing when regimental conditions demanded it, but they primarily functioned in paramilitary capacities, typically bearing the title "daughter of the regiment." An unidentifiable number of women also served in various ways as secret transmitters of militarily significant information. "The ladies were terrific," wrote one historian. "In this war they made their American debut in espionage, and never since have the nation's women taken such an active part as spies." (Harnett T. Kane, *Spies for the Blue and Gray* (Garden City, NY: Doubleday & Co., Inc., 1954), pp. 12–13. See also F. L. Sarmiento, *The Life of Pauline Cushman, the Celebrated Union Spy and Scout* (Philadelphia: John E. Potter & Co., 1865), pp. 13–14.

23 Joan W. Scott and Linda Alcoff are among those who have demonstrated gender to be a critically important and powerfully influential social construct that develops and changes over time. Scott, invoking much of the new language of the history of gender, challenged scholars to refuse to accept "the fixed and permanent quality of binary opposition," and to strive for a genuine historicization . . . of the terms of sexual difference." It is necessary, Scott argued, for scholars to evaluate carefully and historically the manner in which gender mechanisms become "implicated in the conception and construction of power itself"; in other words, the ways in which gender relations are inter-

twined with shifting power relations. (Joan W. Scott, "Gender: A Useful Category of Historical Analysis," *American Historical Review* 91 (December 1986), pp. 1065, 1069.) Elsewhere, Scott leaned heavily on Jacques Derrida to indicate the ways in which "fixed oppositions . . . conceal the heterogeneity of either category" and the "extent to which the terms presented as oppositional are interdependent" and hierarchical. (Joan W. Scott, *Gender and the Politics of History* (New York: Columbia University Press, 1988), p. 7.) "Male," the "dominant term," exists necessarily in opposition to "female," the "subordinate term," the one requiring the other. Contextualized historically, the relationship between the two constitutes a relationship "signifying . . . power" (ibid.).

Linda Alcoff advanced the discussion of the historical unfolding of gender by calling for the interpretation of gender as a category "constructed through a continuous process, an ongoing constant renewal based on an interaction with the world," or experience (Linda Alcoff, "Cultural Feminism versus Post-Structuralism: The Identity Crisis in Feminist Theory," *Signs* 13 (1988), pp. 407, 415, 423). Alcoff argued that the subject "becomes engendered" (p. 423) through the "continuous engagement of a self or subject in social reality" (p. 424). Thus, for example, one can understand "feminine subjectivity" historically, as "construed here and now in such and such a way without this ever entailing a universalizable maxim about the 'feminine' " (p. 431). Any woman, then, or any man is both part of an "historicized, fluid movement" and also an active contributor to the "context within which her [or his] position can be delineated" (p. 434).

24 I use the term "gender system" with the following understanding: that at any given time in history, prevailing gender systems define, among other things, the appropriate use by men and women of space and time, furnishing answers to questions about how men and women customarily should fill their waking hours, in what activities, and in what physical contexts. The underlying assumption remains one in which a finite number of tasks must

be parcelled out appropriately and accomplished somehow in a given period of time in order for the individual and the society as a whole to function effectively. Gender systems interweave constraints and opportunities, and the opportunities commonly provided to one sex are typically matched by constraints on the other.

Gender systems also govern the basic nature and form of the relationships and interactions that occur between and among men and women. By placing conditions on interpersonal behavior, they lend themselves to the establishment of hierarchies of status and power. So, for example, mid-nineteenth-century, middle-class culture expected a man to support his wife and family financially—but not emotionally—by means of his labors; while it called for a woman to nurture her husband and family emotionally—but not financially—by applying her tender nature to the creation of a household that was a sanctuary from the stresses of the outside world. In this particular gender system, both men and women possessed power, but clearly the very context of a woman's power depended—at least in theory—on a man's fair exercise of his own.

25 Such fixed and binary explanatory concepts as "separate spheres" and "women's culture," which structured early explorations into the history of women, have recently begun to give way in the study of gender to mechanistic images ("gender systems"), which better highlight the interconnectedness of time, shifting gender roles, men's and women's respective struggles for power, social conflict, and the sustained human desire for social stability. Linda K. Kerber and others have increasingly and properly questioned the actuality of "separate spheres," as well as the overzealous adoption by women's historians of the public/private theme that permeated, with real purpose, the literature of the mid-nineteenth century. "To continue to use the language of separate spheres," wrote Kerber in 1988, "is to deny the reciprocity between gender and society and to impose a static model on dynamic relationships" (Linda K. Kerber, "Separate Spheres, Female Worlds, Woman's Place: The Rhetoric of Women's His-

tory," *Journal of American History* 75 (June 1988), p. 38). However, there is no doubt in my mind that the language of men's and women's separate spheres, which shaped Victorian discourse on gender in the mid-nineteenth-century United States, is still a valid starting point for understanding the ideological foundations of middle-class culture in that period. And despite real differences between ideology and reality (middle-class women, for example, were by 1848 at least sharply demanding—and claiming—public space and public voice), and despite women's ability to derive power from an ideology of private sphere disempowerment—as Nancy Cott noted, Victorian notions of middle-class womanhood "bound women together even as it bound them down" (Nancy F. Cott, *The Bonds of Womanhood: "Woman's Sphere" in New England, 1780–1835* (New Haven, CT: Yale University Press, 1977), p. 1)—even despite their participation in the perpetuation of separate spheres ideology (see Kathryn Kish Sklar, *Catharine Beecher: A Study in American Domesticity* (New York: W. W. Norton & Co., 1973)), it is wrong to ignore the fact that Victorian ideals of womanhood were at their core oppressive and aimed to keep middle-class women isolated and content in their domestic realm. It is from this premise that this study begins.

For significant early studies of "separate spheres" in the nineteenth century, see, among others: Barbara Welter, "The Cult of True Womanhood: 1820–1860," in *The American Family in Social-Historical Perspective*, ed. Michael Gordon (New York: St. Martin's Press, 1983), pp. 372–392; Carroll Smith-Rosenberg, "The Female World of Love and Ritual: Relations between Women in Nineteenth Century America," in *The American Family in Social-Historical Perspective*, ed. Michael Gordon, pp. 411–435; Sklar, *Catharine Beecher*, and Cott, *The Bonds of Womanhood*.

26 Cécile Dauphin and others have argued that the social construct denoted by the term "gender roles" (which can be defined as the designation in a given time and place of standards of appropriate behavior for men and women) has evolved in western culture

specifically "as a means to fight a system of undifferentiated roles which is considered fatal to societies." (Cécile Dauphin et al., "Theoretical and Methodological Dialogue on the Writing of Women's History," *Journal of Women's History* 1 (Spring 1989), p. 65.) Contrasting the ongoing historical modification of gender ideals with their unchanging purpose in the preservation of social order, Dauphin et al. joined Kerber, Scott, and Alcoff in chiding historians for clinging to notions of a transhistorical, binary, and hierarchically organized gender system, and along with it the idea that men's and women's "roles" always and in all places are discrete, complementary, and predominantly stable. Dauphin et al. encouraged the study of gender in the context of war, as an event that demonstrated conclusively the transitory nature of gender and gender systems.

27 Margaret Randolph Higonnet and others have described war itself as a "*gendering* activity, one that ritually marks the gender of all members of a society, whether or not they are combatants." In other words, war instantly demarcates, on the basis of sex, the theoretical position, role, and function of each individual in a society. In the simplest and most familiar pattern, this means that men become soldiers and warmakers, while women serve passively at home as the ones for whom the war is fought (see Huston, "Tales of War and Tears of Women"). Nevertheless, Higonnet pointed out, the physical, social, and economic demands of war simultaneously bring about temporary redefinitions of gender and gender and power relations for specific purposes (Margaret Randolph Higonnet et al., eds., *Behind the Lines: Gender and the Two World Wars* (New Haven, CT: Yale University Press, 1987), pp. 4–6, 17). The authors noted that wartime changes in gender definition and interaction rarely, if ever, challenge patterns of dominance and subordination. The simple fact that changes can and do occur, however, marks war as an event supremely capable of exposing the absolute arbitrariness of gender designations (ibid., p. 6).

Elsewhere, Barbara Freeman examined the dependence of "western representations of sexual difference" upon the structure of the "couple," itself a "precondition for war in the sense that a war cannot take place without at least two sides" (Barbara Freeman, "Epitaphs and Epigraphs," in *Arms and the Woman: War, Gender and Literary Representation*, ed., Helen M. Cooper, Adrienne Auslander Munich, and Susan Merrill Squier (Chapel Hill: University of North Carolina Press, 1989), p. 304). This perspective implies a necessary link between the very coupling of binary terms, which Freeman affirmed to be the "most basic [and fundamentally sexual] organizational pattern of Western thought" (ibid., p. 304) and war.

28 As noted above, recent studies have challenged the oversimplification of this typology, but they have done so more from the standpoint of the way that late-twentieth-century historians of women in particular have appropriated the typology for their own purposes, than from that of its accurate reflection of mid-nineteenth-century Victorian ideals of gender. See Kerber, "Separate Spheres"; and, among others, Mary Ryan, *Women in Public: Between Banners and Ballots, 1825–1880* (Baltimore, MD: Johns Hopkins University Press, 1990).

29 It should be noted, of course, that the Victorian gender system was already under stress as a result of the growing woman's rights movement (see, among others, DuBois, *Feminism and Suffrage*). However, I would contend that the Civil War, and women's participation in it, took such stresses to a dramatically new level.

30 A final note: I have chosen in the body of this study to resist making broad intersectional associations, especially in light of the far greater knowledge displayed by historians of the south who have gone before me. See, among others, Rable, *Civil Wars*, and Faust, "Altars of Sacrifice."

NOTES TO CHAPTER ONE

1 Jane E. Schultz estimates that "over twenty thousand [women] sought work in the military hospitals of the Confederacy and the Union" (Schultz, "The Inhospitable Hospital," p. 363).

2 Lincoln issued his proclamation three days after the attack, on April 15, calling for 75,000 ninety-day troops (James McPherson, *Battle Cry of Freedom*, p. 274). The ninety days was, not coincidentally, just coming to an end when plans were made to fight the Confederacy for the first time at Bull Run.

3 Sophronia E. Bucklin, *In Hospital and Camp: A Woman's Record of Thrilling Incidents among the Wounded in the Late War* (Philadelphia: John E. Potter & Co., 1869), pp. 33–34.

4 Mary A. Newcomb, *Four Years of Personal Reminiscences of the War* (Chicago, IL: H. S. Mills & Co., Publishers, 1893), p. 10.

5 Anna Holstein, *Three Years in Field Hospitals of the Army of the Potomac* (Philadelphia: J. B. Lippincott & Co., 1867), p. 10.

6 Sarah A. Palmer, *The Story of Aunt Becky's Army Life* (New York: John F. Trow & Co., 1867), p. 4.

7 Bucklin, *In Hospital and Camp*, p. 36.

8 A signed and notarized affidavit, dated 24 March 1893 and included with Bucklin's pension claim, states that she "has not married since her service as a nurse, and in fact was never married and of course has neither husband or sons." Sophronia E. Bucklin Pension File, National Archives, Washington, DC.

9 For examples of each of these types, both much lauded by the early historians of women in the war, see the chapters on Margaret Breckinridge in Brockett and Vaughan, *Woman's Work in the Civil War*, pp. 187–199; and Frank Moore, *Women of the War*, pp. 75–90; and on Bridget Divers ("Irish Biddy"), in Brockett and Vaughan, *Woman's Work in the Civil War*, pp. 771–773; and Moore, *Women of the War*, pp. 109–112.

10 Tompkins County City Directory, 1869–70. DeWitt Historical Society of Tompkins County, Ithaca, NY.

11 McPherson, *Battle Cry of Freedom*, p. 347.

12 Bucklin, *In Hospital and Camp*, p. 33. One could argue that Bucklin's emphasis on the immediate response of northern women to the battle cry reflected, at least in part, her desire to provide satisfying prose to a potential reading (and buying) audience in the late 1860s. And yet, the words of Mary New-

comb, Anna Holstein, Sarah Palmer, and others confirm the sentiments she expressed.

13 Bucklin, In Hospital and Camp, p. 35.

14 James Phinney Munroe, ed., Adventures of an Army Nurse in Two Wars (Boston: Little, Brown, & Co., 1904), p. 30.

15 Elvira J. Powers, Hospital Pencillings: Being a Diary while in Jefferson General Hospital, Jeffersonville, Indiana, and others at Nashville, Tennessee, as Matron and Visitor (Boston: Edward L. Mitchell, 1866), p. v. Jane Schultz's contention that "At the beginning of the war, the American press celebrated instances of spartan devotion and selfless sacrifice by women," and that "Newspapers from Boston to Montgomery recited a litany of supplies donated by prominent female citizens and ran the advertisements of aid societies in search of women to help care for the soldiers," is based on newspaper accounts from 1862 or later, and thus does not challenge the characterization presented here of the newspapers' basic reticence in the war's first twelve months on the topic of women's participation in military medical service (Schultz, "The Inhospitable Hospital," p. 364).

16 McPherson, Battle Cry of Freedom, p. 285.

17 See various biographies of Dix, including Francis Tiffany, Life of Dorothea Lynde Dix (Boston: Houghton, Mifflin & Co., 1891); Helen E. Marshall, Dorothea Dix: Forgotten Samaritan (New York: Russell & Russell, 1937; reprint ed., Chapel Hill: University of North Carolina Press, 1967); and Dorothy Clarke Wilson, Stranger and Traveler: The Story of Dorothea Dix, American Reformer (Boston: Little, Brown & Co., 1975).

18 Marshall, Dorothea Dix, p. 202: Wilson, Stranger and Traveler, pp. 283, 268.

19 Wilson, Stranger and Traveler, p. 269.

20 Marshall, Dorothea Dix, p. 218.

21 Marshall, Dorothea Dix, pp. 210–211.

22 McPherson, Battle Cry of Freedom, pp. 344–347.

23 Linda de Pauw, in an article dealing with the participation of women in the Revoluntionary War, noted that "no quota was

placed on women in the American army until 1802 when an act of Congress limited them to four per company, exclusive of nurses and hospital matrons" (Linda Grant de Pauw, "Women in Combat: The Revolutionary War Experience," *Armed Forces and Society* 7 (1981): p. 212). Although de Pauw's point is that the 1802 act *limited* formal positions for women in a given army company, conversely, one can interpret the act as continuing to *permit* a certain number of women to enlist or muster-in.

24 Junius Thomas Turner to "To Whom it May Concern," 22 August 1916, Catherine Oliphant Papers, Manuscript Division, Library of Congress, Washington, DC. Emphasis in the original.

25 Newcomb, *Four Years of Personal Reminiscences,* pp. 12–13, 37, 117.

26 Julia S. Wheelock, *The Boys in White: The Experience of a Hospital Agent in and around Washington* (New York: Lange & Hillman, 1870), pp. *v–vi.*

27 Rejean Attie, " 'A Swindling Concern': The United States Sanitary Commission and the Northern Female Public, 1861–1865" (Ph.D. dissertation, Columbia University, 1987), pp. 48–49.

28 Nina Bennett Smith, "The Women who Went to War: The Union Army Nurse in the Civil War" (Ph.D. dissertation, Columbia University, 1981), pp. 7–8. See also Ann Douglas Wood, "The War Within a War," p. 200.

29 Smith, "The Women who Went to War," p. 6.

30 Attie records a general "hostility" on the part of the medical community toward female physicians (Attie, " 'A Swindling Concern'," p. 52).

31 Attie, " 'A Swindling Concern'," pp. 97–98.

32 According to Wilson and others, Dix expended great energy contending with the influence of "non-regular" nurses, in large part because of her perceptions that they would threaten the integrity of her own nursing corps (Wilson, *Stranger and Traveler,* p. 271).

33 Bucklin, *In Hospital and Camp,* p. 36. Throughout the war, however, women continued to find their way into military nurs-

ing through the Commissions, through the regiments themselves, and through a variety of independent channels.

34 Bucklin, *In Hospital and Camp*, p. 44.

35 Bucklin, *In Hospital and Camp*, p. 52. Mary Livermore wrote similarly about her first experience in a military hospital. At first, she wrote, "The sickening odor of blood and healing wounds almost overpowered me. In the nearest bed lay a young man whose entire lower jaw had been shot away, and his tongue cut off. . . . [W]hen the bandages were removed by the surgeon for examination of the wound, its horrible nature became apparent. A deathly faintness came over me, and I was hurried from the ward to the outer air for recovery." She, too, soon learned to tolerate the intolerable, however, enduring scenes much worse than this "without a tremor of the nerves or a flutter of the pulse" (Mary Livermore, *My Story of the War*, p. 188).

36 Bucklin, *In Hospital and Camp*, p. 81. In the summer of 1863, Bucklin endured different but equally unpleasant conditions at the field hospital in Gettysburg, Pennsylvania. She wrote: "My tent contained an iron bedstead, on which for a while I slept with the bare slats beneath, and covered with sheets and blanket. . . . As time passed, and the heavy rains fell, sending muddy rivulets through our tents, we were often obliged in the morning to use our parasol handles to fish up our shoes from the water before we could dress ourselves. A tent cloth was afterwards put down for a carpet, and a Sibbly stove set up to dry our clothing. These were ofttimes so damp, that it was barely possible to draw on the sleeves of our dresses. By and by I had the additional comfort of two splint-bottomed rocking chairs, which were given me by convalescent patients. . . ." (Bucklin, *In Hospital and Camp*, pp. 144–145).

37 Palmer, *The Story of Aunt Becky's Army Life*, p. 1.

38 Sister Mary Denis Maher's work, *To Bind up the Wounds: Catholic Sister Nurses in the U.S. Civil War* (Westport, CT: Greenwood Press, 1989), testifies vividly to the persistence, even into the 1980s, of suspicions about the motivations of single, women

nurses. Maher's book draws comparisons between the lay and the Catholic women nurses in the war, clearly favoring the latter over the former. In a paragraph containing such comparisons, Maher addresses the resistance that many lay nurses encountered in a tone that suggests her own complicity with the women's opponents. She writes, "Most of the [lay] female nurses in the war were single, and many may have been looking for a soldier-husband" (p. 157).

39 According to Schultz, "an estimated half of the married nurses had at least one child who was left with a trusted neighbor or with next of kin—often a grandparent who lived with the family. Occasionally, a woman took a child with her to the front, especially if the hospital was not too far from home and if hospital quarters were spacious enough to permit private accommodations" (Jane Schultz, "Women at the Front," p. 91).

40 Bucklin, *In Hospital and Camp*, pp. 48–49.

41 Henrietta Jaquette, *South After Gettysburg*, p. 80. Had Hancock been married, no such reassurances would have been necessary.

42 Wheelock, *The Boys in White*, p. vi.

43 Dorothea Dix to Louisa Lee Schuyler, 29 April 1861, quoted in Wilson, *Stranger and Traveler*, pp. 270–271. In the same letter, Dix discouraged the WCRA from sending to Washington the nurses that had gathered under Dr. Blackwell's tutelage. She wrote, "They [the WCRA nurses] should by no means come on now. . . . If a conflict ensues let the leading surgeons of New York direct and decide the course which should be adopted . . ." (p. 270). Early on, Dix determined to adhere to a system of obtaining female nurses that tolerated no interference from the still independent WCRA, and that placed its reliance instead on the "leading surgeons of New York," who were exclusively male and, as Attie noted, bore a distinct hostility toward female physicians and their attempt to influence the field of Civil War nursing.

44 Surgeon General's Office Circular No. 8, 14 July 1862, Sophronia E. Bucklin Pension File, National Archives, Washington, DC. Also quoted in Bucklin, *In Hospital and Camp*, pp. 38–39.

Also in July 1862, simultaneous with its circular detailing the requirements for Dix's appointees, Surgeon General William Hammond's office issued a second circular "enjoining" medical officials to accept the appointment of one woman nurse to every two male nurses and to "organize their respective hospitals accordingly" (Surgeon General's Office Circular No. 7, 14 July 1862, Sophronia Bucklin Pension File, National Archives, Washington, DC. Also quoted in Bucklin, *In Hospital and Camp*, pp. 37–38.) Prior to this circular, the 3 August 1861 Congressional Act "For the Better Organization of the Military Establishment" had simply stated that women nurses could be substituted for men "when in the opinion of the surgeon general or medical officer in charge it is expedient to do so; the number of female nurses to be indicated by the surgeon general or surgeon in charge of the hospital" (Julia Catherine Stimson, "Women Nurses with the Union Forces During the Civil War," *Military Surgeon* (January-February, 1928); Ann Arbor, MI, University Microforms International, 1982, pp. 2–3). Although it had seemed to be making a place for women nurses in military hospitals, the Congressional Act had actually made it possible, if they so desired, for the male medical authorities of individual hospitals to keep Dix's nurses off the premises. Surgeon General Hammond's circular of 1862 was less compromising, demanding that women nurses be accepted and, paradoxically, demonstrating that the resistance of surgeons to female nurses in their hospitals remained strong. Unfortunately, Hammond's circular could not legislate anything more than superficial compliance, and it certainly could not ensure the women nurses a pleasant and welcoming environment in which to work.

45 Dix appointed just over three thousand women to nursing positions (Schultz, "The Inhospitable Hospital," p. 367).

46 John R. Brumgardt, *Civil War Nurse: The Diary and Letters of Hannah Ropes* (Knoxville: University of Tennessee Press, 1980), p. 123.

47 Bucklin, *In Hospital and Camp*, pp. 40, 60–61.

48 Jaquette, *South After Gettysburg*, p. 4.

49 Ibid., p. *vii*.

50 Bucklin, *In Hospital and Camp*, p. 58.

51 Bucklin, *In Hospital and Camp*, p. 90. Schultz summed up the duties of Civil War nurses in the following manner: "A hospital worker's daily activities varied with her experience and the rigor of the assignment. The larger the hospital, the greater the specialization of tasks; the longer a worker had served, the more likely she was to have more responsibility. The great majority of workers, however, had limited responsibilities: they were expected to keep their charges clean and clothes and bedding in order, to prepare and serve food in accordance with surgeons' instructions, to administer medicines, and to write letters for patients and otherwise help them pass the time. Depending on surgeons' confidence in them, women workers . . . were allowed to change wound dressings and to assist in operations, particularly when huge numbers of casualties overwhelmed medical personnel after battles" (Schultz, "The Inhospitable Hospital," p. 370). "The Civil War nurse," Nina Bennett Smith wrote in 1981, "was generally the workhorse of the military hospital. . . . She did everything that no one else could or would do" (Smith, "The Women who Went to War," p. 57).

52 In general, Bucklin wrote, it was Dix's desire that her nurses be allowed to perform this task, but surgeons frequently refused to permit them to do so. At Judiciary Square, for example, "we were peremptorily ordered from the ward, when that process was in operation" (Bucklin, *In Hospital and Camp*, p. 60).

53 Bucklin, *In Hospital and Camp*, p. 88.

54 George Worthington Adams, *Doctors in Blue: The Medical History of the Union Army in the Civil War* (New York: Henry Schuman, Inc., 1952), pp. 159–160. Bucklin briefly described the staff makeup at the Hammond General Hospital: "Our corps of women nurses numbered seventeen. Miss Heald . . . was at the dignified post of matron. The number of patients reached nearly three thousand. Six surgeons were in our medical corps, who each had a round of patients, such as would have astonished the country

practitioners. . . . Of men nurses we had the usual liberal supply. A general ward master had supervision over all the wards, and each ward had its master" (Bucklin, *In Hospital and Camp*, p. 79). Typically, the only other women employed by the hospital were laundresses and sometimes cooks and, after mid-1863, special diet-kitchen managers. Of course, soldiers' female relatives visited when they could and often helped around the wards however they were able.

55 Jaquette, *South After Gettysburg*, p. 33 (emphasis in the original). Later, Hancock provided her own evaluation of Dix's nurses. They were, she wrote diplomatically, like all female nurses, "Some excellent, some good, some positively bad" (p. 122).

56 Marshall, *Dorothea Dix*, p. 207.

57 "Address of Amanda Shelton Stewart on her Experiences as a Civil War Nurse," Shelton Family Papers, Special Collections, University of Iowa, Iowa City, IA.

58 Surgeon General William A. Hammond's Circular No. 8, 14 July 1862, Sophronia E. Bucklin Pension File, National Archives, Washington, DC. White volunteer soldiers in the Union Army at this time earned $13 per month, which included a $3 per month clothing allowance, plus rations (Dudley Taylor Cornish, *The Sable Arm: Black Troops in the Union Army, 1861–1865* (Lawrence, KS: University Press of Kansas, 1987), pp. 184–185). This means that the army nurses' wages were only $1 per month less than the wages of the common soldier. Significantly, black soldier recruits received only $10 per month (when they received anything at all), out of which $3 were set aside for clothing, plus rations (Cornish, *The Sable Arm*, p. 185), and women who served in hospitals as cooks and laundresses, who were also frequently black and who typically did nursing duty as well but without the title, earned only between $6 and $10 per month (Schultz, "The Inhospitable Hospital," p. 367).

59 Bucklin, *In Hospital and Camp*, p. 70.

60 Stimson, "Women Nurses with the Union Forces," pp. 2–3.

61 Almira Chase to Sophronia Bucklin, 7 February 1863, Sophronia

G. Bucklin Papers, DeWitt Historical Society of Tompkins County, Ithaca, NY (hereafter cited as "Bucklin Papers").

62 Almira Chase to Sophronia Bucklin, 26 September 1864, Bucklin Papers.

63 Lewis Hawkins to Sophronia Bucklin, 27 November 1861, Bucklin Papers. It is unclear why Bucklin did not go directly to the hospital from which Hawkins wrote. Perhaps she was unable to establish the sort of direct contact with someone capable of employing her that seemed to be necessary in order to legitimize her service and also protect her from the accusations of impropriety that certainly would have followed any attempt to travel alone and unsolicited to the front.

64 Schultz has argued that patriotism, in fact, took a back seat to wages for many women who served in hospitals during the war. Patriotism, she writes, "was not the prime mover for thousands of black and white working- and middle-class women, who drew sustenance from (and, if fortunate, pay for) their labor" (Schultz, "The Inhospitable Hospital," p. 365).

65 Newcomb, *Four Years of Personal Reminiscences*, p. 18.

66 Ibid., pp. 57–58.

67 Mary A. Newcomb Pension File, National Archives, Washington, DC. The National Archives's Collection of Carded Service Records of Hospital Attendants, Matrons and Nurses, 1861–1865, consists of the pay records of thousands of women who served in the Union's military hospitals. In a sub-sample of 40 women for whom pay began to be recorded in 1862, thirty (or 75%) began to receive pay after July, when the Surgeon General's Office issued its circular stipulating the allocation of wages for nursing service. If nothing else, this implies that once the Medical Department established bureaucratic channels to permit payment, women on duty unhesitatingly accepted it.

68 Bucklin, *In Hospital and Camp*, p. 22. I have found it impossible to determine with certainty the identity or even the gender of "S. L. C.," whose use of initials may have been nothing more than a typical Victorian gesture of modesty. However, two letters to Bucklin from her nephew, Charlie Chase, refer to an "S. C.

Chase," who seems to have been a relative in Cincinnati connected somehow with the publishing business. On March 22,
1863, Charlie wrote, "I received a letter from . . . S. C. C. a
few days ago[.] His powerful book [perhaps on the war?] is published and he has sent [F]rank a copy . . ." (Charlie Chase to
Sophronia Bucklin, 22 March 1863, Bucklin Papers). On April
28 of the same year, he wrote, "S. C. Chase sent me his powerful
work[.] I took it down to the camp and sold it for 120 cents to a
[D]utchman name[d] Nickolas . . ." (Charlie Chase to Sophronia
Bucklin, 28 April 1863, Bucklin Papers). If Charlie was mistaken
about Mr. Chase's middle initial, this relative of both Bucklin's
and Charlie's may well have been the unknown author of the
introduction to *In Hospital and Camp*. Recalling that Bucklin
published her memoir privately, one finds even more convincing
the suggestion that S. L. C. was a relative in the publishing
business, as was Charlie's "S. C. Chase."

69 Bucklin, *In Hospital and Camp*, p. 23.

70 Ibid., p. 23. S. L. C. seems to have felt a strong need to emphasize
the harsh conditions Bucklin withstood and the sheer devotion
with which she bore them. He wrote, "For nearly three long
years she led the life of an actual soldier. She partook of their
rude fare, lived under unsubstantial tents, shared their weary
marches to new hospital grounds, from the transports on which
they had been borne over river and bay, starving through long
days and nights of waiting, sick from exposure to the sun and
dews: in all things, save the wild, deadly charges of battle, A
TRUE SOLDIER OF THE UNION" (pp. 21–22). And he went
on: "The well ordered hospital, in which every sight which might
shock a sensitive nature was carefully hidden—where lemonades,
and jellies, and fruits, and flowers could, at fixed hours be distributed . . .—*was not* the field hospital, into which men were
brought direct from the awful place of carnage, with the dirt of
rifle pits mingling with their own gore, unable to meet nature's
demands, with worms rioting over the putrifying flesh. Yet, it
was in the field hospitals that Miss Bucklin did her greatest work"
(pp. 23–24).

71 On this note, see, among others, Barbara Welter, "The Cult of True Womanhood: 1820–1860," pp. 372–392; and Kathryn Kish Sklar, *Catharine Beecher.*

72 Brockett and Vaughan, *Woman's Work in the Civil War,* p. 60.

73 The August 1861 Congressional Act "For the Better Organization of the Military Establishment" anticipated this, when it provided for women nurses to be "substituted for soldiers, when in the opinion of the surgeon general or medical officer in charge it is expedient to do so . . ." (Stimson, "Women Nurses with the Union Forces," pp. 2–3).

74 McPherson, *Battle Cry of Freedom,* pp. 541, 540. According to McPherson, "The casualties at Antietam numbered four times the total suffered by American soldiers at the Normandy beaches on June 6, 1944" (p. 544).

75 Holstein, *Three Years in Field Hospitals,* p. 10.

76 Palmer, *The Story of Aunt Becky's Army Life,* p. 58.

77 Brumgardt, *Civil War Nurse,* p. 69.

78 Amanda Akin Stearns, *The Lady Nurse of Ward E* (New York: Baker & Taylor Com., 1909), pp. 14–15, 35.

79 Powers, *Hospital Pencillings,* p. 209.

80 Bucklin, *In Hospital and Camp,* p. 71.

81 Adams, *Doctors in Blue,* p. 159.

82 Theophilus Parsons, *Memoir of Emily Elizabeth Parsons* (Boston: Little, Brown & Co., 1880), p. 83.

83 T. B. Hood to "To Whom it May Concern," 29 March 1894, Harriet A. Sharpless Pension File, National Archives, Washington, DC.

84 Bucklin, *In Hospital and Camp,* p. 121.

85 Ibid., p. 125.

86 Ibid., p. 125.

87 Ibid., pp. 24–25.

88 Ibid., pp. 59, 94.

89 Ibid., pp. 61, 119. Mary von Olnhausen told a similar story. On the way to the Mansion House Hospital in Alexandria, she was informed by Dorothea Dix that "the surgeon in charge was deter-

mined to give her [Dix] no foothold in any hospital where he reigned, and that I was to take no notice of anything that might occur, and was to make no complaint whatever might happen" (Munroe, *Adventures of an Army Nurse*, p. 32).

90 Bucklin, *In Hospital and Camp*, pp. 91–92.

91 Ibid., pp. 96–100.

92 Ibid., p. 128.

93 McPherson, *Battle Cry of Freedom*, p. 664.

94 Bucklin, *In Hospital and Camp*, pp. 137, 139–140.

95 Ibid., p. 142.

96 Ibid., p. 143.

97 Ibid., p. 172.

98 Ibid., p. 173.

99 Ibid., p. 186.

100 Ibid., pp. 108–109.

101 Newcomb, *Four Years of Personal Reminiscences*, pp. 34–35.

102 Wood, "The War Within a War," pp. 206–207. Wood overstated her case when she argued that women nurses sought to "replace the captain with the mother, the doctor with the nurse, and even to out-soldier the soldiers" (p. 207). Some years later, Schultz rightly criticized Wood's position for being too comfortably couched in the terms of a power struggle between malicious men determined to exclude women from the medical profession, and aggressive nurses equally determined to retaliate and, eventually, take over the profession. As Schultz pointed out in regard to her own work, "not a single nurse in my study suggests that she could be a replacement for a doctor" (Schultz, "Women at the Front," p. 74).

103 See Smith, "The Women who Went to War," p. 8.

104 Schultz has recently argued that "Military surgeons' reception of women at the front was beclouded by internecine struggle within the medical profession over the standardization of medical training and practice" (Schultz, "The Inhospitable Hospital," p. 371). According to Schultz, the numerous factors contributing to the doctors' resistance to and frequent thwarting of women nurses

(including the doctors' insecurities about their own poor training and the frustrations they experienced due to overwork and meager facilities) created a "divisive arena" in which the women then struggled to maintain their position and their sanity (p. 373).

105 Palmer, *The Story of Aunt Becky's Army Life*, p. 2.

106 Bucklin, *In Hospital and Camp*, pp. 112–113. Bucklin could not explain the power that Mrs. Gibbons wielded in the hospital. "It was a mystery to many . . . why she was not responsible to Miss Dix like other nurses and matrons and why . . . she still retained her position, and removed surgeons and nurses alike" (p. 113).

107 Bucklin, *In Hospital and Camp*, pp. 303–304.

108 Charlotte E. McKay, *Stories of Hospital and Camp* (Philadelphia: Claxton, Remsen & Haffelfinger, 1876; reprint ed., Freeport, NY: Books for Libraries Press, 1971), p. 28.

109 Stearns, *The Lady Nurse of Ward E*, pp. 277–278.

110 Katharine Prescott Wormeley, *The Other Side of War with the Army of the Potomac* (Boston: Ticknor & Co., 1889), p. 118.

111 Munroe, *Adventures of an Army Nurse*, p. 82.

112 Palmer, *The Story of Aunt Becky's Army Life*, p. 187.

113 Bucklin, *In Hospital and Camp*, p. 379.

114 Ibid., p. 52.

115 Ibid., p. 53.

116 Parsons, *Memoir of Emily Elizabeth Parsons*, pp. 67–68.

117 Mary H. Porter, *Eliza Chappell Porter, A Memoir* (Chicago, IL: Fleming Revell, Co., 1892), p. 193.

118 Bucklin, *In Hospital and Camp*, p. 52.

119 Wheelock, *The Boys in White*, p. 265.

120 Bucklin, *In Hospital and Camp*, p. 106.

121 Parsons, *Memoir of Emily Elizabeth Parsons*, p. 45.

122 Stearns, *The Lady Nurse of Ward E*, p. 31.

123 Brumgardt, *Civil War Nurse*, p. 66.

124 Jaquette, *South After Gettysburg*, p. 170.

125 Parsons, *Memoir of Emily Elizabeth Parsons*, p. 40.

126 Jaquette, *South After Gettysburg*, p. 12.

127 Stearns, *The Lady Nurse of Ward E*, p. 31.

128 Wormeley, *The Other Side of War*, pp. 19, 43–44.

129 Brockett and Vaughan, *Woman's Work in the Civil War*, p. 62.

130 Ibid., p. 62.

131 See Schultz, "The Inhospitable Hospital," and below, Chapter Four.

NOTES TO CHAPTER TWO

1 Ruth A. Gallaher, "Annie Turner Wittenmyer," *Iowa Journal of History and Politics* 29 (October 1931), p. 520.

2 "Annie Wittenmyer," *Standard Encyclopedia of the Alcohol Problem* (Westerville, OH: American Issues Pub. Co., 1925–30), VI, p. 2888. Wittenmyer had grown up in Ohio, the descendant of forebears who served in the Seven Years' War, the Revolutionary War, and the War of 1812 ("Mrs. Annie Wittenmyer," *Annals of Iowa* (January 1900), p. 277). Both her parents hailed from the south. Her father, John G. Turner, came from a long line of southern gentlemen planters and slaveholders in Kentucky, and her mother, Elizabeth Smith Turner, claimed descent from John Smith, the Virginia soldier of fortune (Gallaher, "Annie Turner Wittenmyer," p. 519). But the Turners had moved to Ohio by the time of Wittenmyer's birth, in 1827, and so her own roots lay in northern soil. As one biographer wrote, Wittenmyer's character displayed the "warm, fervid temperament of the south, united with the cool, calculating reason of the North" (Frances E. Willard, *Woman and Temperance; or, the Work and Workers of the Woman's Christian Temperance Union* (Hartford, CT: Park Publishing Co., 1883), p. 160).

3 See, for example, Willard, *Woman and Temperance*, p. 160.

4 Tom Sillanpa, *Annie Wittenmyer: God's Angel* (Evanston, IL: Signal Press, 1972), p. 11.

5 "Mrs. Annie Wittenmyer," *Annals of Iowa*, p. 279. For a full study of middle-class women and benevolent work before, during, and after the war, see Lori Ginzberg, *Women and the Work of Benevolence*.

6 "Mrs. Annie Wittenmyer," *Annals of Iowa*, p. 279.

7 Annie Wittenmyer, *Under the Guns*, pp. *i–ii*.

8 Wittenmyer had three brothers in the military service, William (a surgeon in the Second Iowa Infantry), James (First Iowa Cavalry), and sixteen-year-old Davis, who followed James into the First Iowa Cavalry and mustered in by claiming to be nineteen. A fourth brother was unable to enter the service "because of a physical disability" (See Gallaher, "Annie Turner Wittenmyer," pp. 519–520).

9 Sillanpa, *Annie Wittenmyer*, p. 12.

10 *The Gate City*, 31 May 1861.

11 "Report of the Ladies' Soldiers' Aid Society," *The Gate City*, 15 April 1862.

12 Ibid.

13 Ibid.

14 Gallaher, "Annie Turner Wittenmyer," p. 521; Sillanpa, *Annie Wittenmyer*, p. 14.

15 *The Gate City*, 16 September 1861.

16 In June, Mrs. C. D. Allen of Iowa City wrote to Mrs. Chittenden of the Keokuk Society requesting "further information, about the sending of boxes, to the care of Mrs. Whittenmyer [sic] . . ." (Mrs. C. D. Allen to Mrs. Chittenden, 20 June 1861, in the War Correspondence of Annie Wittenmyer, 1861–1865, Iowa State Historical Library, Des Moines, IA, hereafter cited as the "War Correspondence").

17 "Report of the Ladies' Soldiers' Aid Society," *The Gate City*, 15 April 1862.

18 Rejean Attie, " 'A Swindling Concern'," pp. 126, 131.

19 The 1862 "Report" indicated that, by the end of September, some forty local relief associations in Iowa had come under the Keokuk Society's authority ("Report of the Ladies' Soldiers' Aid Society," *The Gate City*, 15 April 1862).

20 *The Gate City*, 5 August 1861.

21 "Report of the Ladies' Soldiers' Aid Society," *The Gate City*, 15 April 1862.

22 Ibid.

23 *The Gate City*, 21 October 1861.

24 For one example of such a request, see Mrs. Mattie Senard to Annie Wittenmyer, 9 August 1861, in the War Correspondence. There are many other similar letters throughout the Correspondence, and an article in *The Gate City* of 22 April 1862 indicates that the Keokuk Society, at least by that date, had begun "making efforts to secure experienced female nurses" to serve in military hospitals.

25 Mrs. O. Amigh to Annie Wittenmyer, 1 November 1861, in the War Correspondence.

26 J. B. Sample to Annie Wittenmyer, 27 October 1861, in the War Correspondence.

27 Earl S. Fulbrook, "Relief Work in Iowa during the Civil War," *Iowa Journal of History and Politics* (April 1918), p. 198.

28 Fulbrook, "Relief Work in Iowa during the Civil War," pp. 198–199. As the secretary of the Keokuk Society would later describe them, the other key members of the State Sanitary Commission consisted of "two Bishops, two or three Reverends, three or four Honorables and three or four Bankers" ("Report of the Ladies' Soldiers' Aid Society," *The Gate City*, 15 April 1862).

29 *The Gate City*, 28 October 1861.

30 *The Gate City*, 18 November 1861.

31 Ibid.

32 Ibid.

33 Samuel Kirkwood to Annie Wittenmyer, 6 November 1861, in the War Correspondence.

34 A. S. Marsh to Annie Wittenmyer, 21 November 1861, in the War Correspondence.

35 Mrs. J. B. Howell to Annie Wittenmyer, 9 December 1861, in the War Correspondence.

36 Mary Strong to Annie Wittenmyer, 18 March 1862, in the War Correspondence.

37 Lucretia Knowles to Annie Wittenmyer, 4 February 1862, in the War Correspondence.

38 Mary Strong to Annie Wittenmyer, 18 March 1862, in the War Correspondence.

39 "Report of the Ladies' Soldiers' Aid Society," *The Gate City*, 15 April 1862.

40 Lucretia Knowles to Annie Wittenmyer, 4 March 1862, in the War Correspondence.

41 Annie Wittenmyer to Mrs. Chittenden, 2 December 1861, in the War Correspondence.

42 Annie Wittenmyer to Mrs. J. B. Howell, 3 December 1861, in the War Correspondence.

43 Annie Wittenmyer to Captain Parsons, 28 February 1862, in the War Correspondence.

44 "Report of the Ladies' Soldiers' Aid Society," *The Gate City*, 15 April 1862. In *Under the Guns*, Wittenmyer quite proudly displayed her intimacy with General and Mrs. Ulysses S. Grant, providing numerous anecdotes in which the three figured together. Indeed, Julia Dent Grant composed the book's introduction.

45 Annie Wittenmyer to Samuel J. Kirkwood, 20 March 1862, in the Correspondence of the Adjutant General, Civil War Years, Iowa State Historical Library, Des Moines, IA (hereafter cited as the "Adjutant General's Correspondence").

46 Chaplain Ingalls to Annie Wittenmyer, 11 January 1862, in the War Correspondence.

47 "Report of the Ladies' Soldiers' Aid Society," *The Gate City*, 15 April 1862.

48 "*Be it enacted by the General Assembly of the State of Iowa*," read the bill, "That the Governor be and he is hereby authorized and required to appoint two or more agents (one of whom shall be Mrs. Annie Wittenmyer) as Sanitary Agents for the State of Iowa" ("Mrs. Annie Wittenmyer," *Annals of Iowa*, p. 280).

49 Annie Wittenmyer to Samuel J. Kirkwood, 10 January 1862, in the Adjutant General's Correspondence. Wittenmyer may well have lacked sincerity when she asserted that she was "exceedingly anxious for a union of the two organizations," but she certainly knew that open conflict was counterproductive for the Society.

Her attempt, sincere or not, to assuage the concerns of the Governor could only reflect well upon herself and the Society.

50 Mary Strong to Annie Wittenmyer, 18 March 1862, in the War Correspondence.

51 "Report of the Ladies' Soldiers' Aid Society," *The Gate City*, 15 April 1862.

52 Annie Wittenmyer to Samuel J. Kirkwood, 30 March 1862, in the Adjutant General's Correspondence.

53 Mrs. C. D. Allen to Mary Strong, 29 February 1862, in the War Correspondence.

54 Lucretia Knowles to Annie Wittenmyer, 21 March 1862, in the War Correspondence.

55 "Report of the Ladies' Soldiers' Aid Society," *The Gate City*, 15 April 1862.

56 Amelia Bloomer to Annie Wittenmyer, 2 March 1862, in the War Correspondence.

57 Copy of a statement sent to the *Iowa City State Press* by Annie Wittenmyer, 3 March 1863, in the War Correspondence.

58 Note by Wittenmyer attached to a letter in the War Correspondence, C. D. Allen to Annie Wittenmyer, 13 April 1863. Wittenmyer noted also that the arrangement had proved impracticable, "as the men had not been payed [sic]," and that she had ended up giving away the supplies she had purchased. She requested in the future "to be excused from any further duty on that line."

59 N. H. Brainerd to Annie Wittenmyer, 30 March 1863, in the War Correspondence.

60 "S. H. H." to Annie Wittenmyer, 31 July 1863, in the War Correspondence.

61 N. H. Brainerd to Annie Wittenmyer, 30 March 1863, in the War Correspondence.

62 N. H. Brainerd to Annie Wittenmyer, 19 May 1863, in the War Correspondence.

63 Fulbrook, "Relief Work in Iowa during the Civil War," pp. 212–235.

64 A. J. Kynett to Samuel J. Kirkwood, 1 December 1863, in the

General Correspondence of Governor Samuel J. Kirkwood, Iowa State Historical Library, Des Moines, IA.

65 Fulbrook, "Relief Work in Iowa during the Civil War," p. 225.

66 Ibid., pp. 230–231. Mrs. N. H. Brainerd's March 1864 letter to Annie Wittenmyer included a list of resolutions passed by the Iowa City Ladies' Aid Society in her favor, and forwarded to the Iowa Senate and House of Representatives. Among other things, the Iowa City organization threatened to reject all connection with the "official State Agencies for the relief of our suffering heroes and seek those who *do not discard* merit but who honor patriotic devotion to the work in which we are engaged" (Mrs. N. H. Brainerd to Annie Wittenmyer, 11 March 1864, in the War Correspondence).

67 Nettie Sanford to Annie Wittenmyer, 12 November 1863, in the War Correspondence.

68 In February 1864, before resigning her official position, Wittenmyer filed a formal account of her fifteen months as a State Sanitary Agent, and a summary of her suggestions for improving the relief work already underway and for developing new avenues of labor for the duration of the war. The state subsequently published her report. See Annie Wittenmyer, *Reports of Mrs. Annie Wittenmyer, State Sanitary Agent* (Des Moines, IA: F. W. Palmer, State Printer, 1864).

69 Wittenmyer, *Under the Guns*, p. 251.

70 Mary E. Shelton to "My Dear Friend," 7 February 1864, in the War Correspondence.

71 Wittenmyer, *Under the Guns*, p. 251.

72 "Mrs. Annie Wittenmyer," *Annals of Iowa*, p. 281.

73 For more detailed accounts of Wittenmyer's establishment of various orphans' homes, see Wittenmyer, *Under the Guns*, pp. 251–258; "Mrs. Annie Wittenmyer," *Annals of Iowa*, p. 281; Sillanpa, *Annie Wittenmyer*, pp. 28–30; and the Diaries of Mary E. Shelton, 1 January 1864 through 30 December 1864, in the Shelton Family Papers, Special Collections, University of Iowa, Iowa City, IA. According to Sillanpa, the Davenport home

became a tax-supported public institution in June 1866 (Sillanpa, *Annie Wittenmyer*, p. 30). Sara Dunlap Jackson reported that the Davenport home continued to function until 1975, having been renamed the "Annie Wittenmyer Home" in 1949 (Annie Wittenmyer, *A Collection of Recipes for the Use of Special Diet Kitchens in Military Hospitals* (N.P., 1864; reprint ed., Sara D. Jackson and John M. Carroll & Co., 1983), Sara Dunlap Jackson's introduction).

74 Wittenmyer, *Under the Guns*, p. 252.

75 In *Women and the Work of Benevolence*, Lori Ginzberg argued that benevolent women during the war learned that a class-based alliance with men in benevolent work resulted in greater efficiency, and that middle-class women readily abandoned their notions of gender superiority for a new class strategy. Wittenmyer's experience suggests that the transition from gender alliance to class alliance in benevolent work by no means occurred universally. In Wittenmyer's case, gender continued to be crucial, for she continued to believe that she was doing "women's work," but she recognized that men held the reins of power in her society and determined, in a calculated political fashion, to associate herself with precisely those men whose influence could help her to achieve her goals. Her growing political acumen exerted significant pressure on the gender system because it defied prevailing notions about women's incapacity for public and specifically political work. Her successes reflected a yielding in the system, as men in power found themselves compelled to endorse Wittenmyer's irreproachable activities.

76 Sillanpa, *Annie Wittenmyer*, p. 30.

77 Ibid.

78 Wittenmyer, *Under the Guns*, pp. 23ff, 62ff, 230ff.

79 Ibid., p. 72–73.

80 Annie Wittenmyer to William Stone, 23 January 1864, in the War Correspondence.

81 Fulbrook, "Relief Work in Iowa during the Civil War," p. 176ff.

82 Apparently, the popularity of the USCC had begun generally to

surge among middle-class women in 1863, in part on account of the religious image it aggressively displayed. See Attie, " 'A Swindling Concern'," p. 164ff.

83 Wittenmyer, *A Collection of Recipes*, Sara Dunlap Jackson's introduction.

84 "Mrs. Annie Wittenmyer," *Annals of Iowa*, pp. 282, 283.

85 Wittenmyer, *A Collection of Recipes*, Sara Dunlap Jackson's introduction.

86 Wittenmyer, *Under the Guns*, p. 260.

87 Ibid., pp. 209–210.

88 Ibid., pp. 210–212. In her earlier *Collection of Recipes*, Wittenmyer included a recipe for "beef tea," commonly served from all of her kitchens: "Mince four pounds of beef very fine, and pour over it one pint of cold water. Boil it hard for five minutes, skim it well and pour it through a colander. When perfectly cold, strain it through a cloth, and season with salt" (p. 10).

89 Letter from "E. W. J." to Annie Wittenmyer, 10 January 1865, quoted in Lemuel Moss, *Annals of the United States Christian Commission*, p. 677.

90 See Moss, *Annals of the United States Christian Commission*, p. 664.

91 Gallaher, "Annie Turner Wittenmyer," pp. 546, 552.

92 Wittenmyer, *Under the Guns*, pp. 260–261. See also "Mrs. Annie Wittenmyer," *Annals of Iowa*, p. 282. Her *Collection of Recipes* emphasized Wittenmyer's concern that kitchen workers prepare foods that were nutritious, but also appetizing. "Many soldiers," she wrote for example, "have lived on rice so long, prepared so badly that the taste of rice is disgusting to them; and although a healthy article of food for the sick, and best suited to many patients, it is rejected by them with loathing unless the taste is disguised in some way. . . . It is useless to cook rice for sick men, unless it can be served in such a way as to be eaten and relished by them" (p. 30). From a modern perspective, however, Wittenmyer's recipe for coffee seems to defy these instructions about rice. "Have the water boiling, and just before the coffee is to be

served, add one pint of ground coffee to every gallon of water; stir well, and boil briskly for fifteen minutes; set the kettle off the stove, pour into it a pint of cold water, and allow to settle. Sugar and milk to suit the taste. When eggs can be obtained, one egg to each pint of ground coffee, beaten and stirred in, will make the coffee very clear" (p. 9).

93 Wittenmyer, *Under the Guns*, p. 261.

94 M. S. Underwood to S. E. Cox, 6 May 1864, in the War Correspondence.

95 Just as some nurses insisted that women's caretaking of the soldiers should be strictly a voluntary (unpaid) expression of their "nature," and others believed in their right to be paid, so too among the kitchen managers the dispute over money for what was perceived to be women's work arose. Julia Clark and her daughter Catharine, who participated in the diet-kitchen project and whose story is detailed below, apparently disagreed over the matter of a kitchen manager's receipt of a salary. Wrote Catharine in a February 1865 letter to her mother,

> You speak of my not receiving Mrs. W's compensation. Don['] t feel badly about it dear mother. I think it is perfectly right that I should, I feel no hesitation about it at all. All the other ladies do . . . and I think I ought to too. (Catharine Clark to Julia A. (Smith) Clark, Sr., 13 February 1865, in the Lincoln Clark Papers, Special Collections, The Huntington Library, San Marino, CA (hereafter cited as the "Clark Papers"))

To Catharine, "compensation," even for works of mercy, had a genuine appeal. Financial remuneration gave this young single woman an unfamiliar degree of independence. In addition, by virtue of her employment, Catharine achieved a measure of public status for which her mother, the wife of a judge and congressional representative, had no concern.

96 Wittenmyer, *Under the Guns*, pp. 217–218.

97 Wittenmyer, *A Collection of Recipes*, pp. 38–39.

98 Ibid., p. 37.

99 As noted in Chapter One, Amanda Shelton, who worked for Wittenmyer, years later noted that Wittenmyer's employment requirements were actually *less* stringent than those of Dix. As Shelton wrote, Dix generally "selected elderly, homely, women on the theory that female nurses should not be too attractive" (Amanda Shelton Stewart, "An Address of Amanda Shelton Stewart on her Experiences as a Civil War Nurse," in the Shelton Family Papers, Special Collections, University of Iowa, Iowa City, IA). A letter Wittenmyer received from a colleague in the field, filled with harsh criticism of a new but "fossilized" employee, suggested strongly that Wittenmyer believed good looks (if matched by chastity) heightened the positive influence a woman could have in hospital service. "I asked you," wrote the frustrated "D,"

> if Mrs Allen was competent to select one suitable for this work. You tho[ugh]t she was. What could she be thinking of! Such a selection! I've no doubt there may be a good deal of benevolence & kindness [in her]. But you don[']t want the sick men [made] sicker by the appearance of—plain looks & plainer dress! ("D" to Annie Wittenmyer, 28 August 1864, in the War Correspondence)

100 Wittenmyer, *A Collection of Recipes*, introduction.

101 Brockett and Vaughan, *Woman's Work in the Civil War*, p. 378.

102 Julia A. (Smith) Clark to Julia Clark [her daughter], 1 June 1864, in the Clark Papers. Also at home were the older Julia's husband of twenty-seven years, Lincoln, Sr., and their son, also named Lincoln.

103 Julia A. (Smith) Clark to Julia Clark, 1 June 1864, in the Clark Papers.

104 Julia A. (Smith) Clark to Mrs. Edward P. Smith, 3 June 1864, in the Clark Papers.

105 Catharine Clark to Lincoln Clark, Sr., 5 June 1864, in the Clark Papers.

106 Julia A. (Smith) Clark to Lincoln Clark, Sr., 25 June 1864, in the Clark Papers.

107 Ibid.

108 Julia A. (Smith) Clark to B. E. Fryer, 1 July 1864, in the Clark Papers.

109 Julia A. (Smith) Clark to Lincoln Clark, Sr., 1 July 1864, in the Clark Papers.

110 Julia A. (Smith) Clark to Lincoln Clark, Sr., 2 July 1864, in the Clark Papers.

111 Catharine Clark to Lincoln Clark, Sr., 12 January 1865, in the Clark Papers.

112 Catharine Clark to Julia Clark, 28 January 1865, in the Clark Papers.

113 Catharine Clark to Julia A. (Smith) Clark, 23 January 1865, in the Clark Papers.

114 Dr. Kienon to Annie Wittenmyer, 23 July 1864, in the War Correspondence.

115 Ibid.

116 A letter from one of the women Wittenmyer assigned to the Adams Hospital provided further information about the resistance of Dr. Kienon to their taking up the diet-kitchen work that they had come to do. "I wish you were here to make it all right," wrote Helen Beckett, displaying confidence in Wittenmyer's ability to work the problem out. "[I]t is no more [of a problem] than I expected, but it makes me feel unhappy and rather discouraged" (Helen Beckett to Annie Wittenmyer, 12 July 1864, in the War Correspondence).

117 W. A. Banks to Annie Wittenmyer, 7 November 1864, in the War Correspondence.

118 Catharine Clark to Lincoln Clark, Sr., 19 February 1865, in the Clark Papers.

119 Wittenmyer, *Under the Guns*, pp. 193–210. Webster's Dictionary describes logwood as the "hard, brownish-red wood of a tropical tree native to Central America and the West Indies, used in dyeing." Apparently, unscrupulous military cooks combined log-

wood with the old coffee grounds to provide color and give the visual illusion of freshness.

120 S. E. Vance to Annie Wittenmyer, 6 May 1865, in the War Correspondence.

121 S. E. Vance to Annie Wittenmyer, 2 June 1865, in the War Correspondence.

122 There is substantial evidence to the effect that Wittenmyer took her own position very seriously, first in Iowa state sanitary affairs, and then in the national context. She occasionally provoked formal accusations about her imperious attitude, as shown by a long and conciliatory letter from R. G. Orwig, Governor Stone's private secretary, to Mrs. J. E. Horner, who in 1864 succeeded Wittenmyer to her position as Iowa Sanitary Agent. Orwig wrote,

> I regret exceedingly that you should meet with annoyance, and be embarrassed in your duties, and by one [Wittenmyer] too whose experience and interest in the suffering soldier should enable her to assist, and be a guide to you, and her heart be cheered by the increased number of laborers in the field of humanity. Her conduct, as narrated by you, must be condemned, and I feel grieved that one in whom I have felt so deep an interest as being an earnest, self-denying, and Christian woman, should from any motive whatever, refuse a hearty welcome to any one as honestly devoted to the soldiers' welfare as she herself can be. . . . (R. G. Orwig to Mrs. J. E. Horner, 9 June 1864, in the Governor's Letter Books Collection, 1864–1865, Iowa State Historical Library, Des Moines, Iowa, hereafter cited as the "Governor's Letter Books")

Orwig also wrote a letter to Wittenmyer herself, gently scolding her for her tendency to impress other sanitary agents with her personal lack of "kindly feeling toward them." "I know that you entered the field early," he conceded, and

> that no honors or payment that can be offered to you will be to a Christian woman worth what the remembrance of bless-

ings from the lips of dieing [sic] soldiers must be, and that cannot be taken away from you, but while I remember this I cannot be blind to the opposition you have and must believe that some inadvertence on your part, some imprudent words or acts, not with evil design, but no less effective, repel rather than induce confidence and cooperation of those engaged with you in the holy mission of ministering to those giving their lives for the country's cause. (R. G. Orwig to Annie Wittenmyer, 9 June 1864, in the Governor's Letter Books)

Apparently, what Wittenmyer had learned by 1864 in the area of political skills she had not yet entirely translated into interpersonal skills.

123 Brockett and Vaughan, *Woman's Work in the Civil War*, p. 379.

124 The wartime story of Mary Livermore provides a similar example of individual transformation and gender-system shift as the story of Annie Wittenmyer. See Mary Livermore, *My Story of the War*.

125 Brockett and Vaughan, *Woman's Work in the Civil War*, p. 56.

126 Ibid., pp. 56, 58.

NOTES TO CHAPTER THREE

1 Charles McCool Snyder, *Dr. Mary Walker: The Little Lady in Pants* (New York: Vantage Press, 1962; reprint ed., New York: Arno Press, 1974), pp. 12, 16–20.

2 Snyder, *Dr. Mary Walker*, pp. 9–14.

3 Richard Harrison Shryock distinguished Blackwell as the nation's first woman recipient of a "regular" medical degree, in contrast with those few women who might already have received M.D. degrees from "irregular" colleges around the country (Richard Harrison Shryock, *Medicine in America: Historical Essays* (Baltimore, MD: Johns Hopkins Press, 1966), p. 188). See below for more discussion of "regular" versus "non-regular" medicine in the mid-nineteenth century.

4 Nancy Ann Sahli, "Elizabeth Blackwell, M.D. (1821–1910): A Biography" (Ph.D. dissertation, University of Pennsylvania, 1974), pp. 118–119.

5 John B. Blake, "Women and Medicine in Ante-bellum America," *Bulletin of the History of Medicine* 39 (March–April, 1965), pp. 100–108. According to James Cassedy, there were only five medical schools in existence in the United States in 1800. By 1860, there were over sixty, if "regular" and "non-regular" schools are counted together (James Cassedy, *Medicine and American Growth, 1800–1860* (Madison: University of Wisconsin Press, 1986), pp. 67–69).

6 Cassedy, *Medicine and American Growth*, pp. 172, 68. See also Mary A. E. Wager, "Women as Physicians," *The Galaxy* 6 (December 1868), p. 788. Wager noted that some of these women physicians had made quite a success of their careers, earning "professional incomes of ten thousand dollars per annum, which certainly must be quite as pleasant to a woman as to eke out a pittance over a washtub or cambric needle" (p. 788). Among these women, noted the author, most were "gentle, modest, and womanly" (p. 788). Some, however, were "bold, bad women . . . who try to be as much like men as possible," a trait she characterized as "obnoxious" (p. 789). The author did not mention Mary Walker by name anywhere in the article.

7 Cassedy, *Medicine and American Growth*, p. 171.

8 Lester S. King, *Transformations in American Medicine: From Benjamin Rush to William Osler* (Baltimore, MD: Johns Hopkins University Press, 1991), p. 210. King asserts that economic pressure from increasingly popular non-regulars was a major factor in the AMA's establishment (p. 195).

9 John Duffy, *The Healers: A History of Medicine in America* (Chicago: University of Illinois Press, 1979), pp. 110–115. See also William G. Rothstein, *American Physicians in the Nineteenth Century: From Sects to Science* (Baltimore, MD: Johns Hopkins University Press, 1972); and James Bordley and A. McGehee Harvey, *Two Centuries of American Medicine, 1776–1976* (Philadelphia: W. B. Saunders Co., 1976).

10 Duffy, *The Healers*, p. 273. According to Cassedy, the "conspicuous welcome" that some non-regular schools offered women had at least as much to do with their need to draw tuition in a highly competitive situation, as it did with any philosophical commitment to women's equality (Cassedy, *Medicine and American Growth*, p. 171). In 1855, a spokesperson for Syracuse Medical College revealed that the decision to admit women was made with some difficulty: "The admission of females to our privileges, formed no part of the original design [of the college], but Mrs. L. N. Fowler, Mrs. S. O. Gleason, Mrs. Montgomery, Miss Taylor and Miss Warren; ladies of superior literary attainments and accomplishments, made personal application and were admitted at the first session. Since that time, each session, has enjoyed the harmonizing and refining influence of woman in these halls, and between 40 and 50 others have here been qualified to go forth . . ." (Report on the 1855 commencement at Syracuse Medical College, in the *American Medical and Surgical Journal* 7 (April 1855), p. 152).

11 Cassedy, *Medicine and American Growth*, p. 171.

12 Mary Edwards Walker's medical school commencement speech, quoted in the *American Medical and Surgical Journal* 7 (April 1855), p. 150.

13 A strong association between the woman's rights movement that was getting underway at midcentury, and middle-class women's growing determination to establish a place for themselves in the medical profession (particularly in obstetrics and gynecology), may have exacerbated popular resistance to both. Shryock has argued that "the potency of the feminist crusade in this country explains both the pioneer character of the woman's medical movement here and the intense opposition which it encountered"; whereas it seems that in Europe, where feminism was weaker, small numbers of women seem to have gained relatively easy access to schools in France, Switzerland, and Russia (Shryock, *Medicine in America*, p. 198). Thomas N. Bonner has recently argued that the "opposition to women doctors was overwhelming in Europe and only slightly less hostile in

America" (Thomas N. Bonner, *To the Ends of the Earth: Women's Search for Education in Medicine* (Cambridge: Harvard University Press, 1992), p. 11). Although he seems to contradict Shryock's conclusion and present Europe as the more antagonistic environment for women seeking medical degrees, Bonner's observation that non-regular schools did not exist in Europe (p. 15) suggests that those women who made it into medical school at all attended regular schools, where they no doubt experienced the "overwhelming hostility" that Bonner described. In contrast, in the U.S., the non-regular schools themselves absorbed a good portion of the antipathy that regulars might otherwise have aimed directly at women seeking medical educations.

14 Needless to say, one component of the dispute raging in American medicine at midcentury was the issue of precisely what material a formal education in medicine should entail, and how long a student should be required to attend a school. It was common for opponents to challenge the quality of each other's degrees as a means of asserting the superiority of the type of medicine each was practicing. Certainly in her own time, but also long after her death, critics questioned the validity of the education Walker had received at Syracuse. One particularly unkind biographer, who betrayed her dislike of Walker by asking rhetorically, "By what chemical process . . . does a proud, ambitious girl of more than average intelligence coagulate into a freak?" (Helen Beal Woodward, *The Bold Women* (Freeport, NY: Books for Libraries Press, 1971), p. 290), insisted that the "M.D." behind Walker's name did not "bear anything like the luster of Miss Blackwell's Geneva Medical College degree" (Woodward, *The Bold Women*, p. 282). In fact, setting aside the non-regular philosophy of Syracuse Medical College, Walker's medical degree had a par value not only with that of the celebrated Elizabeth Blackwell, but also generally with the degrees granted in her era. Syracuse, not unlike the "regular" Geneva Medical College, required students to master, in two sixteen-week terms over a span of two years, basic courses in Anatomy, Principles and Practices of Sur-

gery, Theory and Practice of Medicine and Pathology, Obstetrics
and Diseases of Women and Children, Physiology and Medical
Jurisprudence, Materia Medica, Therapeutics and Pharmacy, and
Chemistry and Botany (Doris Lawson, "Dr. Mary E. Walker: A
Biographical Sketch" (M.A. thesis, Syracuse University, 1954),
p. 10).

James Bordley and A. McGehee Harvey have written that
Yale Medical School attempted, in 1827, to set a new standard
for medical education not only by tightening its requirements for
admission and graduation, but also by lengthening the course of
study to three of four years (Bordley and Harvey, *Two Centuries
of American Medicine*, p. 19). Yale rapidly abandoned this exper-
iement when other schools that had failed to follow suit began
to draw away potential candidates for admission to the ambitious
Ivy League institution. Some years later, the University of Pennsylvania also tried to increase the time students remained in
school, only to encounter the same problem. The University of
Pennsylvania, like Yale, reverted to the common schedule of two
sixteen-week courses of lectures in order to protect its enrollments
(p. 20).

It is worth noting that both Syracuse Medical College and
Geneva Medical College were absorbed into the Syracuse Uni-
versity Medical School in 1872 (Sahli, "Elizabeth Blackwell,
M.D.," p. 65).

15 On June 14, 1866, *The New York Times* published an article
regarding Walker's appearance in court following her arrest for
being dressed in men's clothing. The article read, in part,

It having been bruited about that . . . Dr. Mary E. Walker,
Brevet Major of the United States Volunteers, would appear
against Patrolman Patrick H. Pickett, of Capt. Mills' Precinct,
an uncommonly large number of spectators attended Police
Trials on Wednesday, expecting a treat. Mrs. Walker, who is
an attractive woman and may have seen thirty summers, was
habited in black broadcloth, her coat, from the shoulders to

the waist, closely resembling a woman's ordinary attire; but from the waist downward the cut of both coat and pantaloons is masculine. Her hat is the merest chip of straw, trimmed as the milliners usually trim that indescribable article of dress. Her dainty parasol, her bijoutry, indeed everything but the ample pantaloons and coat terminating at the knees betokened the moderately fashionable woman. . . .

The substance of Mrs. Dr. Walker's charge against Policeman Pickett is, that he arrested her for wearing male attire. Her testimony was as follows: "I . . . am a practicing physician and surgeon . . . I have worn this style of dress for many years, as many female medical students and practitioners have done. . . . Between 5 and 6 o'clock P. M. on the 5th inst., I entered a millinery in Canal-street, and a gaping crowd gathered at the door; the lady of the shop invited me to stay until the unmannerly multitude had gone; presently a policeman approached me in the store and took me to the Wooster-street Police Station. . . ." (*The New York Times*, 14 June 1866)

Ultimately, Walker's charges were dismissed. The Police Department argued successfully that Officer Pickett had not arrested Walker because of her clothing, but because of the crowd that she had drawn by wearing such clothing, and the hazards that posed to her safety and the safety of others. There is some indication that Walker took a sarcastic tone in her initial response to the officer's questions while she was at the millinery on Canal Street, which may well have prompted him to arrest her.

The Times ran subsequent articles about Walker being arrested for her manner of dress on 6 December 1878, 12 March 1886, and 2 February 1913.

16 Snyder, *Dr. Mary Walker*, p. 13.
17 Elizabeth Cady Stanton, *Eighty Years and More: Reminiscences, 1815–1897* (New York: T. Fisher Unwin, 1898; reprint ed., New York: Schocken Books, 1971), p. 200. Amelia Bloomer (the same Amelia Bloomer who wrote to Annie Wittenmyer—see

above, Chapter Two—regarding the takeover of the Council Bluffs, Iowa, Ladies' Aid Society by the Iowa State Army Commission) promoted the cause of women's dress reform in her journal *The Lily*, but, according to Stanton, the originator of the outfit that came to bear her name was Stanton's own cousin, Elizabeth Smith Miller. After seeing Miller in the outfit for the first time in 1852, Stanton herself "promptly donned a similar attire," at least for a period of time (p. 201). According to Stanton,

> A few sensible women, in different parts of the country, adopted the costume, and farmers' wives especially proved its convenience. It was also worn by skaters, gymnasts, tourists, and in sanitariums. But, while the few realized its advantages, the many laughed it to scorn, and heaped such ridicule on its wearers that they soon found that the physical freedom enjoyed did not compensate for the persistent persecution and petty annoyances suffered at every turn. (pp. 201–202)

Prominent reform women such as Stanton, Lucy Stone, Susan B. Anthony, and others, soon gave up wearing the "bloomer" costume because they felt that it drew attention away from more pressing issues such as woman's suffrage, and elicited a mocking critique of woman's rights activists that the movement did best to avoid. Not surprisingly, Mary Walker herself eventually came to be perceived by many as a liability to the woman's rights movement, in part because her convictions about the connection between women's health and women's dress forbid her to back down on the issue of reform dress, and thus she continued to be a source of unwanted publicity (Snyder, *Dr. Mary Walker*, p. 98ff).

18 Lida Poynter, "Dr. Mary Walker, M.D.: Pioneer Woman Physician," *Medical Woman's Journal* (October 1946), p. 45.

19 Mary E. Walker, *Hit* (New York: American News Co., 1871), p. 66.

20 According to Charles Neilson Gattey, midcentury women's skirts

typically "trailed on the ground" to such an extent that sweeping and floor cleaning were rarely necessary (Charles Neilson Gattey, *The Bloomer Girls* (London: Femina Books Ltd., 1967), p. 48). Some gowns, wrote Gattey, "took between twenty and thirty yards of material to make" (ibid.).

21 Walker, *Hit*, p. 84 (see photo at the beginning of this chapter). Walker attributed the design of her wartime version of the reform dress to a "Mrs. Littlejohn" of Delhi, Iowa (Letter from Mary Edwards Walker to *The Sibyl: A Review of the Tastes, Errors, and Fashions of Society*, January 1862).

According to Gattey, the one-piece undergarment replaced many. On the average middle-class woman's fully-dressed body, he wrote, "First one would probably find a white cambric petticoat with a border of *broderie anglaise*. Under this might be a plain white longcloth petticoat—then a flannel petticoat, followed by another flannel petticoat, both with scalloped hems. Next would come a petticoat, lined and corded with horsehair, which had a straw plait six feet long in its hem to make it stand out. Last of all, the lace-trimmed drawers" (Gattey, *The Bloomer Girls*, p. 48).

Later in her life, Walker increasingly turned to clothes tailored for her according to the dictates of styles worn by men, which she nonetheless insisted were not "men's clothes." An 1880 article in the *Oswego Palladium* recounted a brief conversation that had occurred some days before between Walker and a "pert young fellow" who confronted her at a polling place to which she had come to cast her (technically illegal) vote in a local election. Noting her appearance and her determination to vote, the young man commented to her that "if she was going to vote, they might as well dress up all their women folks in men's clothes and bring them down and vote them," to which Walker responded, "I don't wear men's clothes, I wear my own clothes" (*Oswego Palladium*, 4 November 1880).

Recently, scholars have begun to deal extensively with the issue of cross-dressing as an historical and sociological phenomenon. Majorie Garber has studied a vast number of examples of cross-dressing, both past and present, and argues strongly against the tendency to deny the uniqueness of the cross-dresser and to "appropriate the cross-dresser 'as' one of the two sexes." Such a tendency, she contends, is "emblematic of a fairly consistent critical desire to look away from the transvestite as transvestite, not to see cross-dressing except as male or female manqué, whether motivated by social, cultural, or aesthetic designs. And this tendency might be called an *underestimation* of the object" (Marjorie Garber, *Vested Interests: Cross-Dressing and Cultural Anxiety* (New York: Routledge, 1992), p. 10). For Garber, the cross-dresser is an indicator of " 'category crisis,' disrupting and calling attention to cultural, social, or aesthetic dissonances" (p. 16).

It may not be precisely accurate to use the term "cross-dresser" for Walker, who repeatedly claimed to be choosing her clothing for practical reasons, and who never tried to hide her sex. However, Garber's analysis of the "dissonances" that the cross-dresser occasioned certainly apply to Walker's experience.

22 Walker, *Hit*, pp. 58–59.

23 Ibid. Gattey agreed, observing that, "it was the trousers that caused all the excitement. For mid-Victorians in England and their American contemporaries certainly had a complex about trousers. . . . Trousers were the symbol of the male and of male domination and the proposal that women should adopt them (almost entirely concealed by the skirt as they were) was seen as a threat to the whole structure of society" (Gattey, *The Bloomer Girls*, p. 13).

24 Letter from Mary Edwards Walker to *The Sibyl* (January 1862).

25 The divorce proceedings seem to have been complicated, lengthy, and unpleasant. A September 1861 document from the Supreme Court of the State of New York decreed dissolution of the marriage on the basis of Miller's adultery (Mary Edwards Walker Papers, Syracuse University Library Special Collections Department, Syracuse, NY, hereafter cited as the "Walker Papers, Syracuse"), but some time in the mid-1860s one of the parties reopened the case, which finally settled in 1866.

Towards the end of her life, many no longer remembered that Walker had ever married, and newspaper accounts frequently described her as having been a "spinster" all her life.

26 Walker's papers contain more than one letter whose writer displays romantic inclinations towards her. See "J. H. W." to Mary Walker, 31 January 1865; M. Harry Johnson to Mary E. Walker, 12 March 1866; Gus Richmond to Mary E. Walker, 18 June 1866; Oscar Ruben to Mary E. Walker, 3 June 1869; all in the Walker Papers, Syracuse.

27 Walker, *Hit*, pp. 19, 30.

28 Over the course of her life, Walker, who never retreated on any of the culturally troubling causes dear to her heart, experienced increasing notoriety. In 1893, a reporter, who had gone to interview the now 61-year-old Walker, expressed surprise at finding her to be nothing like the person others had commonly portrayed her to be. Instead of the angry fanatic he expected to meet, the reporter wrote, Walker turned out to be

> one of the most pleasant and courteous persons to interview that can be imagined and answered all of the reporter's questions in a most kindly manner. Dr. Walker is one of the most widely advertised persons in America. She is called a crank, insane, and has been abused by the press and in private more times than any other woman in the country and yet to sit down and talk with her on any subject relating to the welfare or uplifting of her fellowmen and women she at once appears as a liberal minded, earnest and self sacrificing advocate of all methods that tend to the enobling [sic] or elevating of her fellow creatures. Many of her ideas in this respect are advanced and doubtless far ahead of the majority of people and yet they are for the betterment of society rather than for its debasement. . . . Her methods and acts may be questionable, but the principle that prompts them seems to be sincere. (*Nashua Telegraph*, 11 November 1893)

29 Without a desire to serve her country in the emergency, of course,

Walker might just as well have remained in Rome. And, if it was pure adventure she sought, she might instead have headed west to the frontier, where doctors were in short supply. But Walker travelled to Washington, urged on by patriotic fervor. A poem Walker wrote after the war read, in part,

> I love it! I love it! Oh, who shall dare
> To chide me for loving that flag so fair?
> I treasured it long for the patriot's pride
> And wept for the heroes who for it died.
>
> . . .
>
> When I am buried 'neath the ground,
> Wrap that flag my corpse around,
> Plant that flag above my grave,
> There let it wave! Let it wave!

(Quoted in Lida Poynter, "Dr. Mary Walker, The Forgotten Woman," unpublished manuscript, pp. 66–67; in the Lida Poynter Papers, Archives and Special Collections on Women in Medicine, Medical College of Pennsylvania, Philadelphia, PA (hereafter cited as the "Poynter Papers").)

Undoubtedly, the lure of celebrity had its own distinct influence on Walker, who had already experienced considerable public notice for her dress, her medical degree, and her outspoken advocacy of woman's rights in such radical reform journals as *The Sibyl: A Review of the Tastes, Errors, and Fashions of Society*. The journal, which appeared monthly between the mid-1850s and mid-1860s, published articles by men as well as women, on all aspects of reform, but particularly those relating to women and the woman's rights movement. Even before the war, Walker was an occasional contributor. In a May 15, 1859, issue, for example, Walker published an article in which she commented on a scandal involving a wife's adultery, and argued that the woman should be held no more culpable than the man who seduced her or even her own husband, whose "wanderings" from home and hearth were well known. "Never," she wrote, "until women as a mass are better educated physiologically—until they are considered something besides a drudge or a doll—until they have all the social education and political advantages that men enjoy; in a word, *equality* with them, shall we consider vice in our own sex any more culpable than in men!" (*The Sibyl*, 15 May 1859, p. 554).

There is much in Walker's life that indicates a passion for public notice, and yet, although Walker never shied away from the public eye, she was also deeply hurt by it over the course of her life. She earned a reputation as a freak and a crank, and in her later years was reduced to recounting her wartime exploits in travelling shows called "dime museums." An 1893 notice in a Buffalo, New York, newspaper announced that "Dr. Mary Walker will be at Wonderland all next week. There was a time when this remarkable woman stood upon the same platform with Presidents and the world's greatest women. There is something grotesque in her appearance on a stage built for freaks" (clipping from an unnamed newspaper, 25 March 1893, in the Walker Papers, Syracuse). Nevertheless, to the end of her life, Walker consciously employed her maverick qualities in the work of achieving advances for women. In the case of the Civil War, she undoubtedly recognized the potential significance for future women physicians of her own success at the front. Her persistence in Washington after her initial rejection by the Medical Department revealed her depth of principle, combined with elements of both arrogance and naïveté. An interpretation of Walker's motivation for going to the front and remaining there to pursue a surgeon's commission requires an acknowledgement of the issue's complexity. Mary Walker was neither a megalomaniac nor a saint.

30 Walker carried with her a letter signed by Dr. J. M. Mackenzie, "formerly engaged in the practice of medicine in Sacramento City, Cal.," which read, in part, "I am happy to bear testimony to the moral worth of Miss Walker who is a graduate of Syracuse

Medical College and is well versed in the science of medicine and whose unbounded patriotism and love of humanity prompts her to seek a position where she can be useful to our soldiary [sic] . . ." (J. M. Mackenzie to "To Whom it May Concern," 28 October 1861, in the Walker Papers, Syracuse).

It is interesting to note Mackenzie's concern with establishing not only Walker's medical competence but also her "moral worth." Although there is little doubt that hospital and military administrators tried to gauge the "moral worth" of male physicians seeking commissions, one suspects that the official scrutiny of a woman seeking a formal position was significantly more intense. Women who pursued employment as military nurses typically endured others' misgivings about their "virtue" (see above, Chapter One). No doubt because of the controversial nature of Walker's ambition, Mackenzie, and Walker herself, hoped to avert from the start all possible suspicion about her moral character.

The War Department's records relating to Mary Walker contain an additional letter, dated 1855, expressing confidence in Walker's medical abilities. It is most likely she presented this letter as well in connection with her repeated requests for an official appointment. The letter, signed by Professor E. H. Stockwell, M.D. of Cincinnati, Ohio, read:

It gives the undersigned much pleasure to certify that Mary E. Walker, M.D. is a lady of many virtues, of a good education, of talent, of tact, of energy, and of independence; that she has been studying medicine for three years; that she has attended three [sic] regular courses of Medical Lectures in a regularly incorporated Medical College; that she pursued her professional studies with enthusiasm, eagerness and pleasure; that she was a faithful and diligent student; that she made rapid and meritorious progress; that she graduated with honor; and that she received the honorable Degree of Doctor of Medicine.

251

The undersigned cordially recommends Mary E. Walker, M.D. to the confidence, friendship, and patronage of those who may demand the aid of a skillful, faithful and competent physician. (E. H. Stockwell to "To Whomsoever it May Concern," 3 June 1855, in the Records of the War Department, Office of the Adjutant General, Records Group #94, Re: Dr. Mary Walker, National Archives, Washington, DC, hereafter cited as the "War Department Records")

31 George Washington Adams, *Doctors in Blue*, p. 9.
32 Ibid., p. 10. See also pp. 42–58, for details on the complicated hierarchy of surgeons and physicians in the Union military.
33 Ibid., p. 4. By April 1865, over 12,000 physicians and surgeons had served the Union military (p. 47).
34 Adams, *Doctors in Blue*, pp. 24–41.
35 According to Adams, American medical schools, regular and non-regular, were "never worse than in the middle years of the nineteenth century." Lester S. King concurred, writing that, by the 1840s, the "proprietary medical schools [those run by practitioners who devoted part of their time to teaching] had debased medical education and were turning out vast numbers of practicing physicians, many of whom were thoroughly ignorant of science" (Adams, *Doctors in Blue*, p. 49; King, *Transformations in American Medicine*, p. 195). Adams added, however, that although most Civil War surgeons and physicians were "deplorably ignorant and badly trained," in comparison with their predecessors they nonetheless "appear in a better light. Nearly all had diplomas from medical schools, while as recently as the second quarter of the century most American practitioners had been office-trained" (p. 49). For modern as well as contemporary critics, the "retrogression" of American medicine affected the standards and requirements of many schools to such a degree as to make the exclusion of women superfluous.
36 Mary Edwards Walker to "Brother and Sister" [Lyman and Aurora Coats], 13 November 1861, in the Mary Edwards Walker Papers,

Oswego County Historical Society, Oswego, NY (hereafter cited as the "Walker Papers, Oswego").

37 Mary Edwards Walker, "Incidents Connected with the Army," n.d., in the Walker Papers, Syracuse. The "Incidents" is a collection of typed accounts of key events in Walker's Civil War career, probably written by her shortly after the war in connection with a speaking tour she took, and possibly with an eye toward eventual publication. The pages are not numbered, and the accounts are not ordered in the file in any way.

38 J. N. Green to [Assistant Surgeon General] R. C. Wood, 5 November 1861, in the War Department Records.

39 Walker must have shown Dr. Green her credentials. It seems quite likely to me that Dr. Green's use of the phrase "regular Medical College," rather than to mislead his letter's readers, was meant to identify Syracuse Medical College as a fully accredited medical school—if not an "orthodox" school—whose graduate, Walker, was worthy of confidence by regular doctors.

One notes also that Dr. Green addressed Walker as "Miss Dr. Walker," which suggests that he was unaware of her previous marriage, most likely because Walker chose not to inform him. Throughout her life, as will be seen, people used a variety of forms by which to address Walker, among them "Miss Dr. Walker," "Mrs. Dr. Walker," and "Miss Maj. Mary E. Walker," the last reflecting postwar confusion about the precise nature of her wartime status.

40 Adams, *Doctors in Blue*, pp. 6, 8.

41 Walker, "Incidents Connected with the Army," in the Walker Papers, Syracuse.

42 J. N. Green to "To Whom it May Concern," 11 December 1861, in the War Department Records. (A copy of this letter also exists in the Walker Papers, Syracuse.) A century later, one observer characterized Walker's role for the "first three years of the Civil War" as that of a "nurse in the Union Army," a description Walker would have found demeaning (William E. Shea, "Mary Edwards Walker," in Dumas Malone, ed., *Dictionary of American*

Biography, X (New York: Charles Scribner's Sons, 1964), p. 352.) Another further reduced the importance of her medical role, specifically at the Indiana Hospital, by describing her not even as a nurse, but as Dr. Green's "administrative assistant" (Snyder, *Dr. Mary Walker*, p. 29). Such comments diminish Walker's accomplishments and fail to reflect her actual experience.

43 Walker, "Incidents Connected with the Army," in the Walker Papers, Syracuse.

44 Ibid.

45 Stewart Brooks, *Civil War Medicine* (Springfield, IL: Charles C. Thomas, 1966), p. 25; Adams, *Doctors in Blue*, p. 175.

46 Adams, *Doctors in Blue*, p. 47.

47 Walker, "Incidents Connected with the Army," in the Walker Papers, Syracuse.

48 Ibid.

49 Synder, *Dr. Mary Walker*, pp. 33–34. Walker may have hoped to improve her standing in the medical profession by attending the Hygeia Therapeutic College, but a certificate from yet another non-regular institution can only have added to the ammunition regular doctors turned against her.

50 See James McPherson, *Battle Cry of Freedom*, pp. 369–590.

51 Ibid., pp. 532, 555.

52 Ibid., p. 572.

53 Walker, "Incidents Connected with the Army," in the Walker Papers, Syracuse. Walker claimed that at Warrenton, "medical supplies were inadequate and the medical staff was undermanned and exhausted" (Snyder, *Dr. Mary Walker*, p. 35).

54 General Ambrose Burnside to "To Whom it May Concern," 15 November 1862, in the War Department Records.

55 Walker, "Incidents Connected with the Army," in the Walker Papers, Syracuse.

56 McPherson, *Battle Cry of Freedom*, p. 572.

57 Ibid., p. 573.

58 Walker, "Incidents Connected with the Army," in the Walker Papers, Syracuse.

59 Preston King to Mary Edwards Walker, 10 January 1863, in the War Department Records.

60 It is true that Walker did not, in her own accounts, explicitly discuss performing surgery with her own hands, although she did mention providing assistance. Even under the emergency conditions she encountered at Warrenton and Fredericksburg, the willingness of military authorities to allow a woman to tend medically to soldiers may well not have extended to the performance of surgery, and certainly there were enough otherwise ill and postsurgical soldiers to occupy her full medical attention.

61 *Oswego Times*, 19 June 1863.

62 Adams called the dispute over the merits of amputation "the great surgical controversy of the war," exacerbated by the great numbers of casualties particularly at Antietam (Adams, *Doctors in Blue*, pp. 131–132). In 1864, he noted, the medical director of the Army of the Ohio declared that experience shaped each of the two sides of the debate: "[t]hose who had done much reading but had seen little were ardent 'conservatives,' . . . while those who had done little reading but had seen much were the pro-amputation extremists." Certainly, careful and lengthy deliberation over proper surgical procedures was a luxury battlefield surgeons could not enjoy. And yet, there is much evidence to suggest that amputations—particularly those performed under unsanitary conditions—resulted in higher mortality rates (p. 131).

63 Walker, "Incidents Connected with the Army," in the Walker Papers, Syracuse.

64 In December 1863, a Mr. Sherburne wrote to the Mayor of Washington concerning this project. "Miss Dr. Walker of N.Y.," he wrote, "is in search of a house confiscated or otherwise—for the purpose of establishing a house for unprotected females and children who are frequently found about the streets of Wash. . . . Thinking perhaps you might be of some assistance in this praiseworthy matter I have taken the liberty to refer her to you—she has been connected with the service in many capacities since the breaking out of the rebellion" (Mr. Sherburne to R. Wallach,

14 December 1863, in the Walker Papers, Syracuse). Walker retained Sherburne's letter among her papers and later pasted to the back of it a newspaper announcement that read "Women's Free Lodging Rooms—Dr. Mary E. Walker has accepted a room in the east end of the City Hall building, where she will transact all business pertaining to receiving and classifying friendless females, between eleven and twelve o'clock A. M."

65 Walker, "Incidents Connected with the Army," in the Walker Papers, Syracuse.

66 Edwin F. DeFoe to Mary Edwards Walker, 10 February 1864, in the Walker Papers, Syracuse.

67 Ibid.

68 "Women in the Army," The Sibyl 7 (September 1863), p. 1171.

69 Fitzhough McChesney to Mary Edwards Walker, 27 September 1863, in the Walker Papers, Syracuse.

70 Mary Edwards Walker to "Medical Director," 9 November 1863, in the Walker Papers, Syracuse.

71 Alex S. Springsteen to Mary Edwards Walker, 19 November 1863, in the Walker Papers, Syracuse.

72 Undated, unidentified newspaper clipping in the Walker Papers, Syracuse.

73 Mary Edwards Walker to Edwin Stanton, 2 November 1863, in the War Department Records.

74 Ibid.

75 McPherson, Battle Cry of Freedom, p. 672; Adams, Doctors in Blue, p. 95. Adams called Chickamauga "one of the worst medical failures of the war," due to the "improper location of the hospitals and the lack of a well equipped supply base" (p. 94).

76 Copy of a telegram from George H. Thomas to E. D. Townsend, undated, in the War Department Records.

77 Mary Edwards Walker to Abraham Lincoln, 11 January 1864, in the Walker Papers, Syracuse.

78 Ibid.

79 Abraham Lincoln to Mary Walker, 16 January 1864, in the Walker Papers, Syracuse.

80 As Lida Poynter observed years later, a contract surgeon was "low in the scale compared to a commissioned officer," but it nevertheless represented official recognition as well as a salary of at least $80 per month (Poynter, "Dr. Mary Walker, M.D.," p. 47).

81 Snyder, *Dr. Mary Walker*, p. 41.

82 According to Adams, contract surgeons "were expected to be medical school graduates," but many had in fact "never seen the inside of a professional school." The examination system was established to root out incompetents (Adams, *Doctors in Blue*, p. 174).

83 Mary Edwards Walker to Andrew Johnson, 30 September 1865, in the War Department Records.

84 Copy of a letter, Roberts Bartholow to the Editor of the *New York Medical Journal*, 20 January 1867, in the Charles McCool Snyder Papers, Special Collections, Penfield Library, State University of New York, Oswego, NY (hereafter cited as the "Synder Papers").

85 Ibid.

86 Adams, *Doctors in Blue*, p. 175.

87 Adams notes that, despite federal regulations, some states either issued commissions (and presumably contracts) without any examinations at all, and others chose laxity over strictness in their exams simply in order to be able to secure sufficient numbers of physicians—regular or non-regular (Adams, *Doctors in Blue*, p. 48). In contrast, Walker's gender seems to have propelled her particular examiners to a new level of severity.

88 Mary Edwards Walker to Andrew Johnson, 30 September 1865, in the War Department Records.

89 After the war, Cooper voiced his own disdain for Walker in a letter to the Surgeon General's office. He wrote, "She is useless, ignorant, trifling and a consummat [sic] bore & I cannot immagine [sic] how she ever had a contract made with her as Actg. Asst. Surgeon" (George E. Cooper to the Surgeon General, 10 September 1865, in the War Department Records).

90 Walker, "Incidents Connected with the Army," in the Walker Papers, Syracuse.

91 Rev. Nixon B. Stewart, *Dan McCook's Regiment, 52nd O.V.I.: A History of the Regiment, Its Campaigns and Battles* (privately printed, 1900), pp. 84–85, 91.

92 Stewart, *Dan McCook's Regiment*, pp. 90–91, 93.

93 Snyder, *Dr. Mary Walker*, p. 42. According to Adams, soldiers were most susceptible to diseases of camp life—dysentery, diarrhea, typhoid—during the period from July through September (Adams, *Doctors in Blue*, pp. 199–200).

94 Walker, "Incidents Connected with the Army," in the Walker Papers, Syracuse.

95 McPherson, *Battle Cry of Freedom*, p. 620.

96 Walker, "Incidents Connected with the Army," in the Walker Papers, Syracuse.

97 Stewart, *Dan McCook's Regiment*, p. 91.

98 George H. Thomas to E. D. Townsend, copy of an undated telegram, in the War Department Records.

99 "Women in the Army," *The Sibyl* 8 (September 1863), p. 1171.

100 Ibid.

101 Moreover, although many women did function as formal or informal spies during the war—their sex serving them in good stead as a cover—Walker's name does not appear in any of the accounts of their exploits. See, among others, Sarah Emma Edmonds, *Unsexed: Or, the Female Soldier*; Ferdinand Sarmiento, *Life of Pauline Cushman*; and Harnett T. Kane, *Spies for the Blue and Gray*.

102 Walker, "Incidents Connected with the Army," in the Walker Papers, Syracuse.

103 Quote from *The Richmond Enquirer* (14 April 1864) in Poynter, "Dr. Mary Walker, The Forgotten Woman," p. 85, in the Poynter Papers. According to another Confederate source, also cited by Poynter, Walker, "presuming on her connection with the medical fraternity and her sex, rode boldly up to our picket and asked if he would take some letters which she wished deliv-

ered within our lines." The picket, wrote Poynter, "very gallantly replied that he would take her and them too" (p. 85).

A Senate report from 1880 asserted that Walker's capture itself had been contrived "in accordance with a preconcerted arrangement entered into between her and the Federal officers, the petitioner thinking that she might obtain information while in the hands of the enemy which would be of value to the Federal officers" (Senate Report No. 637 (1888) from the Committee on Pensions, in the Walker Papers, Syracuse).

104 B. J. Semmes, quote in Jane E. Schultz, "Women at the Front," pp. 3–4.

105 William M. Gardner, quoted in Schultz, "Women at the Front," p. 4.

106 McPherson, *Battle Cry of Freedom*, p. 792.

107 Poynter, "Dr. Mary Walker, The Forgotten Woman," p. 87, in the Poynter Papers.

108 Snyder, *Dr. Mary Walker*, p. 45.

109 McPherson, *Battle Cry of Freedom*, pp. 796–797. See also William B. Hesseltine, ed., *Civil War Prisons* (Kent, OH: Kent State University Press, 1972) and Warren Lee Goss, *The Soldier's Story of his Captivity at Andersonville, Belle Isle, and Other Rebel Prisons* (Boston: Lee & Shepard, 1868).

110 Poynter, "Dr. Mary Walker, M.D.," p. 48; see also clipping from an unidentified newspaper, dated 25 March 1893, in the Walker Papers, Syracuse.

111 Poynter, "Dr. Mary Walker, The Forgotten Woman," pp. 86–89, in the Poynter Papers.

112 Various documents in the Walker Papers, Syracuse, testify to Walker's postwar health problems and her attempts to bring the federal government to see the justice of her pension requests if only in light of her physical suffering as a prisoner of war. See, for example, Senate Report No. 237 (1880) from the Committee on Pensions.

113 Snyder, *Dr. Mary Walker*, pp. 46–47.

114 Stewart, *Dan McCook's Regiment*, p. 91.

115 Mary Edwards Walker to William T. Sherman, 14 September 1864, in the War Department Records.

116 George H. Thomas to "To Whom it May Concern," 15 September 1864, in the War Department Records.

117 Snyder, *Dr. Mary Walker*, p. 49. A letter from Assistant Adjutant General E. D. Townsend to General Thomas shortly after Walker's release from Castle Thunder revealed continuing bureaucratic confusion over her association with the 52nd Ohio. Townsend wrote,

> The female doctor Mary E. Walker has been released and is here. There is no evidence of her being connected with the service so as to entitle her to pay and allowances. She claims to have been appointed by you for special service assistant surgeon of fifty second Ohio. She is in need of funds. Please inform me how she was employed, at what rate of pay, and how payment should be made. (E. D. Townsend to George H. Thomas, 19 August 1864, in the War Department Records)

In return, Thomas sent to Townsend a copy of Walker's orders, a copy of Colonel McCook's acknowledgment of her arrival, and a recommendation that she be "paid as contract surgeon from the 11th of March [1864] to the present time at a rate of $80.00 per month" (George H. Thomas to E. D. Townsend, undated, in the War Department Records). Apparently, Thomas and Walker had not signed a formal contract at the time of her appointment to the 52nd Ohio, a mistake they did not repeat on the occasion of her next assignment.

118 Contract drawn up between R. C. Wood and Mary Edwards Walker for her service at the Female Military Prison in Louisville, Kentucky, in the War Department Records.

119 Susan E. Hall to Mary Edwards Walker, 10 October 1864, in the Walker Papers, Syracuse.

120 E. O. Brown to R. C. Wood, 4 October 1864, in the War Department Records.

121 Mary Edwards Walker to J. H. Hammond, 4 October 1864, in the War Department Records.

122 J. H. Hammond to R. C. Wood, 4 October 1864, in the War Department Records.

123 For a good discussion of the perception (and self-perception) of middle-class women as the bearers and conservators of morality in the nineteenth century, see Lori Ginzberg, *Women and the Work of Benevolence.*

124 Note appended to the letter from J. H. Hammond to R. C. Wood, 4 October 1864, in the War Department Records.

125 Affidavit of Charles W. Griswald, June 1873, in the War Department Records.

126 Affidavit of Cary C. Conklin, 8 July 1873, in the Walker Papers, Syracuse.

127 Snyder, *Dr. Mary Walker,* p. 49.

128 Inmates of the Female Military Prison at Louisville, Kentucky, to Colonel Fairleigh, 24 October 1864, in the War Department Records.

129 Mary Edwards Walker to J. H. Hammond, 7 October 1864, in the War Department Records.

130 R. C. Wood to Colonel Fairleigh, 13 November 1864, in the War Department Records.

131 Mary Edwards Walker to Lieutenant Colonel Coyle, 15 January 1865, in the Walker Papers, Syracuse.

132 C. C. Gray to Mary Edwards Walker, 21 January 1865, in the War Department Records.

133 Daniel J. Dill to "E. B. [sic] P. Mil Comdr" (E. E. Phelps), 21 March 1865, in the War Department Records.

134 For the stories of these widely acclaimed and very independent Civil War women, see, among others, Margaret Davis, *Mother Bickerdyke*; Nina Brown Baker, *Cyclone in Calico*; William E. Barton, *The Life of Clara Barton*; Ishbel Ross, *Angel of the Battlefield: The Life of Clara Barton*; and Elizabeth Brown Pryor, *Clara Barton: Professional Angel.*

135 Mary Edwards Walker to E. E. Phelps, 22 March 1865, in the War Department Records.

136 E. E. Phelps to Daniel J. Dill, 21 March 1865, in the War Department Records.

137 E. E. Phelps to "To Whom it May Concern," 10 August 1865, in the War Department Records.

138 Snyder, *Dr. Mary Walker*, p. 50.

139 George E. Cooper to Mary Edwards Walker, 5 May 1865, in the Walker Papers, Syracuse.

140 See Gerald Schwartz, ed., *A Woman Doctor's Civil War: Esther Hill Hawks' Diary* (Columbia: University of South Carolina Press, 1984). Dr. Hawks served not as an army physician but as a missionary to the black refugees in the south during the war. Nevertheless, her diary includes passages describing her dispensation of medical services to the blacks who were under her care, with little evidence that she was considered by observers to be acting inappropriately.

141 W. H. De Motte to Andrew Johnson, 12 June 1865, in the War Department Records. Many misunderstood Walker's position as surgeon-in-charge of the Female Military Hospital to imply a commission, which in the case of a full surgeon would have entitled her to the rank of Major. In fact, she served under a contract, and as a contract surgeon received no commission or rank, although her salary was the same as that of a first lieutenant (Adams, *Doctors in Blue*, pp. 174–175, 47).

142 D. E. Millard to Andrew Johnson, 16 June 1865, in the War Department Records.

143 W. A. Benedict to Andrew Johnson, 15 June 1865, in the War Department Records.

144 Andrew Johnson to Edwin Stanton, 24 August 1865, in the War Department Records.

145 M. B. Ames to Andrew Johnson, undated, in the War Department Records.

146 J. Collamer to Edwin Stanton, 28 August 1865, in the War Department Records.

147 F. E. Spinner to "To Whom it May Concern," 9 September 1865, in the War Department Records.

148 Mary Edwards Walker to Andrew Johnson, 30 September 1865, in the War Department Records.

149 J. Holt to Edwin Stanton, 30 October 1865, in the War Department Records.

150 Ibid.

151 Ibid.

152 Ibid.

153 E. D. Townsend to Mary Edwards Walker, 2 November 1865, in the War Department Records.

154 The Congressional Medal of Honor, "the highest military award for bravery that can be given to any individual in the United States of America," was conceived during the Civil War as a means of "recognizing the deeds of American soldiers, sailors, and marines who were distinguishing themselves in the fighting" (U.S., Congress, Senate, *Committee Report on Medal of Honor Recipients, 1863–1978*, Print No. 3, 96th Cong., 1st sess., 1979: pp. 1,2). In 1862, Congress adopted the Medal of Honor resolution, which provided for the medal's presentation to enlisted men and officers distinguished (retroactive to the beginning of the war) by their "gallantry in action, and other soldierlike qualities" (p. 4).

155 Snyder, *Dr. Mary Walker*, pp. 53–54.

156 Ibid., p. 54. According to the Senate Committee Report, the original legislation regarding the presentation of the medal allowed for a number of abuses, including frequent delayed claims of ex-soldiers whose documentation of their "gallantry" at war was negligible. In 1916, after years of consideration and investigation, a board of retired military officers determined that the regulations governing the medal's presentation should be made more strict: i.e., the medal could only be earned by "action involving actual conflict with an enemy, distinguished by conspicuous gallantry or intrepidity, at the risk of life, above and beyond the call of duty," and any application for a medal must be accompanied by "official documents describing the deed involved." Furthermore, the board agreed that any prior recipients who no longer met the revised guidelines would have their medals revoked, theoretically in order to "protect" the honor of the

medal as a whole. Walker fell into this category, along with 909 others (864 of whom were members of a single Civil War regiment to whom President Lincoln had granted the medal in June 1863 as a means of convincing the regiment to reenlist) (*Medal of Honor Recipients*, pp. 4–10). Walker's medal was reinstated posthumously in 1977, in large part as a result of feminist activists' lobbying activities.

157 See Henry Bellows's introduction to Brockett and Vaughan, *Woman's Work in the Civil War*.

158 Alma Lutz to Lida Poynter, 21 May 1931, in the Poynter Papers. These words might just as well have been written today, for late into the twentieth century, it is Mary Walker's lifelong advocacy of dress reform for women—and the "peculiarity," at least in Victorian terms, of her own personal decision to shun traditional women's dress in favor of clothing considered fundamentally masculine in style—that keeps her alive in the popular memory.

NOTES TO CHAPTER FOUR

1 The National Archives in Washington, DC, has a multitude of records related to women nurses' requests for and receipt of postwar pensions.

2 Almira Chase to Sophronia Bucklin, 2 January 1865, in the Bucklin Papers. Another letter in the collection suggests that, the year before her death, Bucklin received a marriage proposal, which she rejected. "Dear Aunty Phrone," wrote Bucklin's niece Grace from Webster, Iowa,

> So you had a proposal of marriage did you Auntie? Well it seems funny but I am glad you had the grit to answer him as you did. Surely you do not need anyone else to take care of, and there are few men who want to take care of the women. . . . (Grace N. Thorburn to Sophronia Bucklin, 6 January 1901, in the Bucklin Papers)

3 Affidavit signed by Sophronia Bucklin, 24 March 1893, in the Sophronia E. Bucklin Pension File, National Archives, Washington, DC.

4 Woman's Relief Corps Representative to Sophronia Bucklin, 20 November 1871; Julia Albright to Sophronia Bucklin, 9 June 1878; S. C. Millard to Sophronia Bucklin, 17 April 1884, in the Bucklin Papers.

5 City Directories for Ithaca locate "S. E. Bucklin, Tailoress" on East State Street, in the years 1869–70; and "Sophronia Bucklin" on West Seneca (1892–93), North Tioga (1894–95), and Falls (1896–1901) Streets (Tompkins County City Directories, 1869–1902, DeWitt Historical Society of Tompkins County, Ithaca, NY).

6 Sophronia E. Bucklin, *In Hospital and Camp.*

7 In 1868, Calvin Lawrence, a former soldier and friend of Bucklin's, wrote to her regarding the process of getting the book published: "I should think if you could see a publisher yourself you might arrange business more satisfactory to your mind & his too than any one else. Everyone in this world is looking out for himself & it is so with a publisher if he thinks your book would have a good run he would publish without hesitancy but if he thought it doubtful you would have to make an advance to him & run the risk yourself . . . (Calvin Lawrence to Sophronia Bucklin, 14 February 1868, Bucklin Papers). Apparently, Bucklin found it necessary to "run the risk" of providing an advance to the publisher. In 1885, G. C. Caldwell, a former agent of the United States Sanitary Commission, addressed a letter to Bucklin to accompany her application for a government pension, in which he confirmed her "very straitened circumstances" following the publication of the book. Caldwell also recalled his original doubts concerning the book's salability. "Your book," he wrote, "though a faithful account of certain phases of army and hospital life, I never supposed would meet with a ready sale: such is too often the case with privately printed books" (G. C. Caldwell to Sophronia Bucklin, 1 August 1885,

Sophronia E. Bucklin Pension File, National Archives, Washington, DC).

One cannot avoid the possibility the book's sales were further dampened by the gap between Bucklin's sharply critical observations about the military medical establishment and her blunt address of issues of wartime gender discord, and the dominant images of self-sacrificial Yankee womanhood that filled the pages of the popular commemoratives of northern women in the Civil War—Frank Moore's *Women of the War* and Brockett and Vaughan's *Woman's Work in the Civil War*—which had appeared, respectively, two and three years before the release of *In Hospital and Camp* (see discussion below). Jane Schultz has written that "Bucklin came as close as any Civil War nurse to recognizing that her problems with hospital authorities were located in gendered relationships" (Jane E. Schultz, "The Inhospitable Hospital," p. 389). A memoir with this sort of consciousness, in the afterglow of a Union victory and the return of peace, may have turned some popular audiences away.

Interestingly, recognition denied to Bucklin's work in the years immediately following the war has been granted steadily in the late twentieth century. Beginning with Agatha Young's *The Women and the Crisis: Women of the North in the Civil War* (New York: McDowell, Obolensky) published in 1959, *In Hospital and Camp* has received consistent citations throughout the literature dealing with Union nurses in the Civil War.

8 The Bucklin Papers contain numerous documents related to Bucklin's membership in the WRC in the 1890s, among them letters from various officials in the organization discussing the details of Bucklin's application for a pension in 1892. See in particular a letter from an unidentified WRC representative to Sophronia Bucklin, 20 November 1871, in the Bucklin Papers.

9 It is true, of course, that one key aspect of the WRC's work after 1892 lay in ensuring that former nurses could gain access to the pensions that the federal government had agreed to provide. Had she joined after 1892, one could argue that Bucklin's motive for

membership was her financial need, and her expectation that the WRC could help with her pension application. On the contrary, Bucklin joined twenty years before nurses' pensions became available, and, in any case, she ultimately petitioned the government, with success, on her own (see Sophronia E. Bucklin Pension File, National Archives, Washington, DC). Thus, her WRC membership must have fulfilled other needs, specifically the need to associate with women likewise distinguished by their active participation in the Civil War.

10 Bucklin, *In Hospital and Camp*, pp 379–80.

11 Annie Wittenmyer, *History of the Woman's Temperance Crusade* (Boston: J. H. Earle, 1882).

12 Annie Wittenmyer, *Woman's Work for Jesus* (New York: Nelson & Phillips, 1873), pp. 49–50.

13 Ruth A. Gallaher, "Annie Turner Wittenmyer," p. 563.

14 Annie Wittenmyer, *The Women of the Reformation* (New York: Phillips & Hunt, 1885); Annie Wittenmyer, *Under the Guns*; "Annie (Turner) Wittenmyer," *National Cyclopedia of American Biography* (New York: James T. White & Co., 1904), XII, p. 363; Gallaher, "Annie Turner Wittenmyer," p. 564.

15 Wittenmyer also wrote the organization's handbook: see Annie Wittenmyer, *The Woman's Relief Corps Red Book* (E. B. Stillings & Co., 1897).

16 Frank L. Byrne, "Annie Turner Wittenmyer," in *Notable American Women, 1607–1950: A Biographical Dictionary*, ed. Edward T. James et al. (Cambridge, MA: Belknap Press, 1971), pp. 636–637; Gallaher, "Annie Turner Wittenmyer," p. 562.

17 Frances E. Willard, *Woman and Temperance*; p. 164.

18 Byrne, "Annie Turner Wittenmyer," p. 637.

19 Wittenmyer, *Woman's Work for Jesus*, pp. 5–6.

20 Charles McCool Snyder, *Dr. Mary Walker*, pp. 55–77. See also various letters from Walker's friends and acquaintances in Great Britain dealing with arrangements for speaking engagements and responding to speeches already presented, in the Walker Papers, Syracuse; and the Mary Edwards Walker Papers, Archives and

Special Collections on Women in Medicine, Medical College of Pennsylvania, Philadelphia, PA. The *New York Medical Journal* published a vicious article in January 1867 about Walker's British tour: see *New York Medical Journal* 4 (January 1867), pp. 314–316. A handwritten introduction to one such speech is preserved in the Walker Papers, Syracuse.

21 The Walker Papers, Syracuse, contain a large number of documents related to Walker's struggle first to convince the United States Government to pension her at all for her military service, and then to convince them to increase the amount of her pension from $8.50 per month to $20 per month. See, for example, a letter from the Commissioner of the Law Division, Department of the Interior Bureau of Pensions, to Mary E. Walker, 13 April 1898; and a copy of the *Congressional Record* from 4 July 1898 (pp. 7443–7445) containing a discussion of the bill (HR 9732) written regarding the increase. Beginning in 1892, military nurses received pensions of $12 per month (ibid.). Wittenmyer, it bears repeating, received almost three times the amount allotted to Mary Walker, twice that allotted to the nurses (Gallaher, "Annie Turner Wittenmyer," pp. 562–563).

22 Snyder, *Dr. Mary Walker*, pp. 78–152. See Mary E. Walker, M.D., *Hit*; Mary E. Walker, M.D., *Unmasked, or the Science of Immorality* (Philadelphia: William H. Boyd, 1878); and Mary E. Walker, M.D., "Crowning Constitutional Argument" (Oswego, NY: privately printed, 1907).

23 Walker, "Crowning Constitutional Argument," pp. 3–9; Louis Filler, "Mary Edwards Walker," in *Notable American Women*, p. 532. Jane Bliss Taylor, whose mother and sisters were founders of a suffrage group in Walker's hometown of Oswego, New York, recalled that members of the group feared the negative effects of "any link or association with Dr. Mary Walker in the *public mind* . . . for they felt she would *hurt the cause*" (Jane Bliss Taylor's "Reminiscence of Mary Edwards Walker" in the Jane Bliss Taylor Papers, Archives and Special Collections on Women in Medicine, Medical College of Pennsylvania, Philadelphia, PA, hereafter cited as the "Taylor Papers.")

At least one account exists of Walker herself attempting to vote. A newspaper article dated 4 November 1880 noted that,

> At the polls of the first election district in Oswego Town, last Tuesday, Dr. Mary Walker stepped up and offered her vote.
>
> The inspectors said that she was not a legally qualified voter and they could not receive the ballot.
>
> She insisted on her right to vote, and the oath respecting the qualification of the voter being read to her, she said: "I'll take that oath; I am a fe-male citizen and therefore a male citizen." Some say that she said, "I am a free male citizen," but that could hardly be.
>
> The inspectors refused to receive her vote and she warned them that she should commence proceedings against them. (Unidentified clipping, 4 November 1880, in the Mary Edwards Walker Papers, Oswego County Historical Society, Oswego, NY)

24 Transcript of an interview with DeWitt Groat of Oswego, New York. Transcript #OH 096, in the Mary Edwards Walker Papers, Special Collections, State University of New York at Oswego, Oswego, NY. Various people applied the term "queer" to Walker. Jane Bliss Taylor similarly noted of Walker that "people said she was 'plain queer' " (Jane Bliss Taylor, "Reminiscence of Mary Edwards Walker," in the Taylor Papers). Carrie Chapman Catt, the famous suffragist, wrote to Lida Poynter of meeting Walker for the first time at a national suffrage convention: "She was very queer and everybody laughed at her. . . . She led a queer life and did queer things. . . . Dr. Walker was the queerest person I ever saw" (Carrie Chapman Catt to Lida Poynter, 1 April 1931, in the Lida Poynter Papers, Archives and Special Collections on Women in Medicine, Medical College of Pennsylvania, Philadelphia, PA).

25 Snyder, *Dr. Mary Walker*, pp. 150–151.

26 Prior to her publication of "Jenny Wade of Gettysburg" (Philadelphia: J. B. Lippincott & Co., 1864), Eastman—born in Virginia

but married to a Maine native who served in the Union Army—
was probably best known for her novel, *Aunt Phillis' Cabin*
(1852), a basically *proslavery* work she wrote in reply to Harriet
Beecher Stowe's *Uncle Tom's Cabin*. For an introduction to Eastman's life and writings, see Lina Maniero, ed., *American Women
Writers* (New York: Frederick Ungar Publishing Co., 1979), pp.
568–569.

27 Eastman, "Jenny Wade of Gettysburg," pp. 23–24.

28 Ibid., pp. 32–33.

29 This is a reference to Bell Irvin Wiley's *The Life of Billy Yank, The
Common Soldier of the Union* (Indianapolis, IN: Bobbs-Merrill,
1952). See also Bell Irvin Wiley, *The Life of Johnny Reb, The
Common Soldier of the Confederacy* (Indianapolis, IN: Bobbs-
Merrill, 1943).

30 Jenny Wade's story appears in other places as well, among them
Brockett and Vaughan, *Woman's Work in the Civil War*, pp. 88,
775–776. Brockett and Vaughan listed Jenny Wade among a
group of women martyrs whose names "should be inscribed upon
the ever during granite, for they were indeed the most heroic
spirits of the war, and to them, belong its unfading laurels and
its golden crowns" (p. 88), and they identified the location of
her house in Gettysburg as "between Oak Ridge and Seminary
Hill" (p. 775).

31 John Greenleaf Whittier, "Barbara Frietchie," in Brockett and
Vaughan, *Woman's Work in the Civil War*, pp. 761–763. See also
Dorothy Quynn, *Barbara Frietschie* (Baltimore, MD: Historical
Quarterly, 1942).

32 Moore's other historical works include *American Eloquence: A
Collection of Speeches and Addresses by the Most Eminent Orators
of America* (New York: D. Appleton & Co., 1857); *The Civil
War in Song and Story, 1860–1865* (New York: P. F. Collier,
1889); *Diary of the American Revolution from Newspapers and Original Documents* (New York: Charles Scribner, 1860); and *Rebellion
Record: A Diary of American Events, with Documents, Narratives,
Illustrative Incidents, Poetry, etc.* (New York: G. P. Putnam,
1861–1863; D. Van Nostrand, 1864–1868).

33 Brockett and Vaughan collaborated only on this one book. See also Brockett's *The Camp, the Battlefield and the Hospital* (Philadelphia: National Publishing Co., 1866); *The Great War of 1870 between France and Germany* (New York: Gaylord Watson, 1871); *The History and Progress of Education* (New York: A. S. Barnes & Burr, 1866); and *The Life and Times of Abraham Lincoln* (Rochester, NY: R. H. Curran, 1865).

34 Because of what we know about the supreme value of female selflessness in mid-nineteenth-century, northern, middle-class culture, it comes as no surprise that Moore and Brockett and Vaughan should emphasize these qualities above all others in their treatment of women in the war. See, among others, Barbara Welter, "The Cult of True Womanhood: 1820–1860," in *The American Family in Social-Historical Perspective*, ed., Michael Gordon (New York: St. Martin's Press, 1983), pp. 372–392.

35 Moore, *Women of the War*, p. *iv*.

36 Ibid., pp. *iv*, 22, 77, 177, 170–171.

37 Ibid., p. *v*.

38 Ibid.

39 Brockett and Vaughan, *Woman's Work in the Civil War*, dedication.

40 Ibid., pp. 149, 187.

41 Ibid., p. 60.

42 Brockett and Vaughan's title, which employed the phrase "Woman's Work" rather than "Women's Work," even seemed to attribute an essential nature to women, and to women's response to the crisis presented by the Civil War. See Nancy F. Cott, *The Grounding of Modern Feminism* (New York: Yale University Press, 1987), introduction.

43 Brockett and Vaughan, *Woman's Work in the Civil War*, p. 58.

44 Mary Livermore, *My Story of the War*, p. 120.

45 See Moore, *Women of the War*, pp. 54–64, 109–112, 513–516, 529–535. See also Brockett and Vaughan, *Woman's Work in the Civil War*, pp. 747–753, 770–774.

46 Moore, *Women of the War*, p. 529.

47 Ibid., p. 109.

48 Ibid., pp. 110, 514.
49 Brockett and Vaughan, *Woman's Work in the Civil War*, p. 747.
50 Ibid., p. 770.
51 Ibid.
52 Ibid.
53 According to Schultz, Frank Moore solicited Mary Walker's story for inclusion in *Women of the War*, but Walker refused his request with the explanation that she was saving her material for her own book and had no interest in giving him the information for free (Jane E. Schultz to Elizabeth D. Leonard, 9 January 1992). Given the general tone of his book and his obvious determination to domesticate the wartime experiences of women who had severely threatened gender stereotypes during the war, it is unclear to me that Moore would have included a chapter on Walker, even had she been more forthcoming with her material. Certainly, he would have substantially reshaped Walker's story somehow to fit the model of Civil War womanhood he was trying to create.

Mary Livermore recognized Walker's contributions to the Union effort in a book she coedited with Frances Willard in 1893 (See Frances Willard and Mary Livermore, eds., *A Woman of the Century: Fourteen Hundred-Seventy Biographical Sketches Accompanied by Portraits of Leading American Women in All Walks of Life* (Buffalo, NY: Moulton, 1893), p. 740). In her memoir of the war, however, Livermore gave no space to Walker, although one of the first chapters in *My Story of the War* dealt with the issue of armed women in uniform who served the Union. Like Moore and Brockett and Vaughan, Livermore looked individually at some of the "half-soldier heroines" (p. 119), like Bridget Divers and Annie Etheridge, and reached no more favorable opinion of them. In general, she commented, "Such service was not the noblest that women rendered the country during its four years' struggle for life, and no one can regret that these soldier women were exceptional and rare" (p. 120). After all, she added, "It is better to heal a wound than to make one" (p. 120). This remark, along with Walker's absence from the volume, highlights the discomfort that an individual woman who failed to fit acceptable middle-class models could evoke, even among her female observers.

54 See *The New York Times*, 16 August 1864, 14 June 1866, 21 September 1869, 27 May 1871, 7 September 1876, 16 January 1877, 24 March 1877, 26 March 1877, 27 March 1877, 8 December 1877, 26 January 1878, 4 March 1878, 20 March 1878, 6 December 1878, 18 February 1880, 11 February 1881, 10 January 1881, 26 June 1881, 30 April 1882, 12 March 1886, 8 March 1887, 3 December 1890, 30 September 1891, 5 October 1893, 18 November 1893, 6 April 1896, 9 November 1901, 17 August 1911, 28 January 1912, 18 March 1912, 19 March 1912, 20 March 1912, 21 March 1912, 23 March 1912, 24 March 1912, 25 March 1912, 26 March 1912, 2 February 1913, 26 October 1913, 4 March 1914, 14 April 1915, 16 December 1915, 23 February 1919.

55 See Snyder, *Dr. Mary Walker*. Lida Poynter's biography of Walker, which was never published, is entitled "Dr. Mary Walker, the Forgotten Woman," and offers a perspective on Walker rather more favorable than the more common one shared by Snyder. A copy of the Poynter manuscript is in the Poynter Papers.

56 Moore, *Women of the War*, pp. 213–237; Brockett and Vaughan, *Woman's Work in the Civil War*, pp. 374–379.

57 Moore, *Women of the War*, pp. 213–237. Like Brockett and Vaughan, Moore compiled his accounts of the women in his book in large part by soliciting from these women information about their wartime activities, and it is possible that his relegation of Wittenmyer's story to a section of the Mary Shelton chapter is a consequence of his having been unable to solicit enough information from Wittenmyer directly. Still, Wittenmyer's war work was so well-known by the time Moore set about putting his book together that he should have been able to provide a more complete account had he so desired.

58 Brockett and Vaughan, *Woman's Work in the Civil War*, p. 374.

59 Ibid., p. 379.

60 Ibid., p. 791. Mary A. Gardner Holland did include Bucklin (under a misspelled name: "Sophronia E. Brecklin") in her *Our Army Nurses: Interesting Sketches, Addresses, and Photographs of nearly One Hundred of the Noble Women who served in Hospitals and on Battlefields during our Civil War* (Boston: B. Wilkins & Co., 1895) (pp. 443–444), but Holland's book differed from works like those of Moore and Brockett and Vaughan in that it consisted of a collection of apparently unedited anecdotal statements supplied by the women themselves concerning their military service. Apparently, Holland solicited such statements from as many of the nurses as she could identify, and published as many as she received.

61 Moore, *Women of the War*, p. 177.

62 In a letter dated 29 July 1885, Charles Eddy of Auburn, New York, wrote to Bucklin, probably in connection with her quest for a government pension, ". . . in answer to your letter of the 27th inst to Father and me Would say that I have been acquainted with you for Thirty years at least and know that you have been a hard working woman and have known about your cicumstance [*sic*] at different times and can say that as to riches you never had . . ." (Charles Eddy to Sophronia Bucklin, 29 July 1885, the Bucklin Papers).

63 Bits and pieces of the story of northern women's wartime activities appeared in other nineteenth-century works, including Mary Livermore's *My Story of the War*, a combined memoir and tribute to northern women's Civil War involvement. "Who," Livermore asked,

> has fully narrated the consecrated and organized work of women, who strengthened the sinews of the nation with their unflagging enthusiasm, and bridged over the chasm between civil and military life . . . ? (p. 9)

Although her introductory question seemed to promise a fuller telling of the tale of northern women's Civil War efforts and accomplishments, in the end, Livermore, despite being herself an active supporter of woman's rights and suffrage throughout the late nineteenth century, essentially only added her own mild gloss to what had quickly become the standard postwar view of women's participation in the Civil War. For Livermore, writing in the late 1880s, middle-class women's most significant wartime role lay in serving as mediators, ameliorating the most unpleasant consequences of war, "bridging over the chasm" and holding American society together by "infusing homogeneousness of feeling into the army and the people," and by "keeping the men in the field civilians, and making the people at home, of both sexes, half soldiers" (ibid., p. 9). Women's key patriotic purpose was, ultimately, the maintenance of the social balance, even if this required temporary adjustments in their own prescribed antebellum role. By leaving their homes for the front, involving themselves in the public business of sanitary work, and actively supporting and promoting the war at home, middle-class women in the war, Livermore recognized, stretched peacetime gender limits, but they did so only for the sake of safeguarding the world that the war might otherwise have shattered. For Livermore, as for Moore and Brockett and Vaughan, women's altered wartime position was not transformative, but defensive, a function of woman's role as the protector and transmitter of culture even, or perhaps especially, in periods of crisis.

The few books on women in the war that appeared from the end of the nineteenth until the middle of the twentieth century shed little additional light on the nature and impact of women's participation in the war for women and for American culture, tending instead to confirm, in one form or another, the image projected in the early writings of women's perfect self-sacrifice for the cause, their splendid cooperation with men in the Union effort, and their uncontested postwar return to their place in the prewar gender system. Among them were Mary Holland's *Our Army Nurses*; George Barton's *Angels of the Battlefield* (Philadelphia: Catholic Art Publishing Co., 1897) and Ellen Jolly's *Nuns of the Battlefield* (Providence, RI: Providence Visitor Press, 1927), both of which studied the activities of various Catholic sisterhoods during the war; such works as Julia Chase's *Mary A. Bickerdyke* and William E. Barton's *Life of Clara Barton* (both cited above), which examined specific female Civil War figures on a larger scale; and books like Phebe A. Hanaford's *Daughters of America* (Augusta, ME: True & Co., 1883); Willard and Livermore's *A Woman of the Century*, which included either general discussions of "women in the Civil War" or biographical entries devoted to particular female Civil War figures, such as Clara Barton or Mary Walker. Occasional books, like Ethel Hurn's *Wisconsin Women in the War Between the States*, detailed the contributions made by women of one particular state to the war effort.

Only with the passage of a century and more since Appomattox have scholars actively begun to reach behind the images presented in the early postwar works for more information about women's wartime activities and experiences. In 1959, Agatha Young argued, for the first time, that the Civil War had left a permanent legacy of greater freedom to women. "It came about," she wrote, "because during the Civil War the old restrictions and conventions relating to women's activities were lifted, as a matter of expediency, to meet the unusual demands of the war." For Young, involvement in the Civil War provided middle-class women with precisely the opportunity they had been waiting for to advance their social status and to take their first clear steps along the path to "liberation" (Young, *The Women and the Crisis*, pp. 3, 5, 12). Young resisted calling the women of her study overtly "political," however, characterizing them instead as "working from the premise of their *ideals*" (p. 3). Sylvia G. L. Dannett argued similarly, in 1959, that the Civil War "swept aside" previous restrictions on women, finally giving them an opportunity "not only to prove their ability but to demonstrate that women could be as courageous as men" (Sylvia G. L. Dannett, *Noble Women of the North* (New York: Thomas Yoseloff,

1959)). Young's and Dannett's works emerged from an intellectual environment in which scholars had begun to exchange the *Godey's Ladies' Book* image of nineteenth-century, middle-class womanhood, the "angel of the house," for an image of women as actors in the transformation of their own lives and history (see, for example, Simone de Beauvoir, *The Second Sex*, trans. H. M. Parshley (New York: Knopf, 1953); and Mary R. Beard, *Woman as Force in History: A Study of Traditions and Realities* (New York: Macmillan Co., 1946).) Yet, their work, which notably lacked any evidence of gender conflict or stress, also reflected the influence of Brockett and Vaughan and other earlier writers. Young's and Dannett's women slid gracefully, and without contest from men, into new wartime roles, which constituted nothing more than the logical extensions of their roles in antebellum society. In a section dealing with female "sanitary agents," for example, Young explained that "The women knew nothing about army sanitation, but they knew bad housekeeping when they saw it, and the conditions in the camps seemed to them bad housekeeping on a colossal scale." And, of Civil War nurses, she wrote, "The women did all that was possible to preserve the ties with home in the camps and hospitals and . . . whether young or old, considered motherliness their first duty" (Young, *The Women and the Crisis*, pp. 90, 9). For Young, as for the earlier writers, the middle-class Union women who participated actively in the Civil War did so literally as an extension of their work in the home, in their "sphere." The difference was that Young believed these activities to be permanently transformative and good, resulting in a "new freedom," which permitted women to operate, for the first time, as homemakers in the public sphere as well as the private.

A few years later, Mary Elizabeth Massey's *Bonnet Brigades* (1966) (cited above) dealt with women in both the north and the south and shared many of the same convictions about the war's impact on women. "The Civil War," wrote Massey, "compelled women to become more active, self-reliant, and resourceful, and this ultimately contributed to their economic, social and intellectual advancement" (p. x). She concluded, "When sheltered timid women came out of their homes to join with others in patriotic endeavors, when bold resourceful ones stepped into the 'man's sphere' and did his work, when determined, courageous, or foolhardy ones ignored masculine criticism and Victorian decorum, the individual was inevitably affected, but more important, she was helping to change the position and image of all. Experience acquired during the four years of conflict equipped women for their 'war of independence' and enabled them to prove their capabilities as they could never have done, according to Clara Barton, during 'continued peace' " (p. 366).

Since the 1970s, scholars have begun to refine, even more substantially, past interpretations of women's participation in the Civil War. In 1972, Ann Douglas Wood argued that the Civil War gave women an opportunity to return to the ranks of the medical profession, from which they had gradually been excluded over the course of the late eighteenth and early nineteenth centuries. "Basic to these women's complicated urge to make the front truly a home-front," she wrote, "was their sense that they were being kept out, of medicine, of war, of *life itself*, by a complicated professional code that simply boiled down to men's unwillingness to let anyone—including themselves—know what a mess they had made. And the first thing the volunteers wanted to reveal was the mess in all its enormity (Ann Douglas Wood, "The War Within a War," pp. 206–207). The angry, ambitious female nurses in Wood's account contrast sharply with the selfless, all-sacrificing women described by Brockett and Vaughan and others, just as Wood's image of a "war within a war" defies early descriptions of the vast realm of wartime activity in which men and women worked harmoniously toward a common cause.

In the 1980s, Nina Bennett Smith and Jane Ellen Schultz both discussed female Civil War nurses extensively in their dissertations (Nina Bennett Smith, "The Women who Went to War"; and Schultz, "Women at the Fror

Douglas Wood, Smith argued that, although the female nurses believed in their own unique healing skills, and although they often scorned male doctors as inadequately trained "creatures endowed with arbitrary bureaucratic power" (p. 8), nonetheless, they brought to the front no professional ambitions. Instead, they brought the determination to exert their special moral and restorative powers, "to provide men with those things that only women could provide" (p. 10). Smith rejected, in theory, the early writers' image of a universally harmonious northern response to the war, as well as Wood's theory of middle-class women's conscious appropriation of the opportunities afforded by the war to mount a calculated assault on the medical profession. Smith's nurses did more than just fit into spaces already made for them—they made their *own* spaces. But, they acted subtly, unlike the strident nurses of Wood's depiction, carefully and shrewdly paying attention to the political surroundings, and their actions were guided above all by the mid-nineteenth-century values of patriotism, personal duty, and female moral force.

Schultz, on the other hand, focused on the ways in which female nurses at the front shaped military life and concerns, compelling military leaders for the first time to "consider the well-being of the individual soldier" (Schultz, "Women at the Front," p. 348). She also noted the internal transformations for women at the front, their achievement of "self-reliance" and "tough-mindedness," qualities, wrote Schultz, "that many Americans believed were characteristics reserved for men" (p. 348). According to Schultz, the war front represented common ground on which old definitions of gender could no longer stand, and as a result, both men and women found it necessary to adjust not only their expectations but also their behavior. Schultz's view projected a postwar, middle-class gender balance painfully birthed in war, different from that of the antebellum period, but, nevertheless, essentially harmonious.

From a different perspective, Lori Ginzberg has argued, in her broad study of nineteenth-century women and benevolence, that the war years played a crucial role in reshaping the whole field of middle-class women's charity work toward a model of men's and women's cooperation. Wartime experiences with the United States Sanitary Commission, in particular, Ginzberg contended, led middle-class women to abandon their antebellum model of benevolence, with its notions concerning women's ability to harness their superior virtue to the task of society's moral transformation. In the context of all-out war, superior virtue seemed a poor substitute for the simple efficiency of institutionally based action. The Civil War gave to women still clinging to the "moral suasion" model an opportunity to witness and participate in the "new virtues of efficiency and order" via organizations like the USSC (Lori Ginzberg, *Women and the Work of Benevolence*, p. 133). Rejean Attie, in contrast with Ginzberg, examined the struggle of the USSC to achieve and maintain control over northern women's Civil War relief activities (Rejean Attie, " 'A Swindling Concern' "). Attie argued that the leadership of the USSC comprised a group of "reformers and intellectuals" who firmly believed that participation in the Commission's activities offered to all northerners "an occasion to rehearse relinquishing local power over voluntary—predominantly female—labor in favor of a centrally-directed institution that assessed charitable needs in national terms" (pp. 10–11). Many of the local societies, however, found the USSC's system far too rigid and oppressively controlling, and chose either to resist its influence and continue working independently, or to channel and systematize their efforts instead through the more compatible United States Christian Commission. In the end, local women's defiance of the USSC contributed substantially to the Commission's demise and, ultimately, to a partial postbellum retreat, by the "reformers and intellectuals," from the wartime goals of the centralization of benevolence and the cultural control it implied.

64 Brockett and Vaughan, *Woman's Work in the Civil War*, p. 92.
65 Ibid., p. 93.
66 See Mary P. Ryan, *Cradle of the Middle Class: The Family in*

Oneida County, New York, 1790–1865 (New York: Cambridge University Press, 1981). See also Ginzberg, *Women and the Work of Benevolence.*

67 Linus P. Brockett, *Woman: Her Rights, Wrongs, Privileges and Responsibilities* (Hartford, CT: L. Stebbins, 1869; reprint ed., Plainview, NY: Books for Libraries Press, 1976), pp. 301, 357.

68 Ibid., p. 359.

69 See, for example, Charles Stillé, *History of the United States Sanitary Commission.*

70 Ginzberg, *Women and the Work of Benevolence,* p. 175.

71 Ginzberg has described late-nineteenth-century developments in institutional benevolence in terms of a shift by middle-class women from "gender alliance" to "class alliance," characterized by the acceptance by mid-nineteenth-century, middle-class women of the superiority of men's "scientific," institutional efficiency over antebellum women's "moral suasion" as a model for social uplift (Ginzberg, *Women and the Work of Benevolence,* pp. 174–213). Annie Wittenmyer's story indicates that it is important for current historians of benevolence not to unduly hasten and oversimplify the process by which gender-alliance yielded to class-alliance in postwar public charity, nor to downplay the endurance of middle-class women's certainty about their unique, gender-based capacity for the social uplift of the less fortunate. "Women are the governors of the race for the first and best half of human life," wrote Annie Wittenmyer in 1882. "They are the character builders for the future generations" (Wittenmyer, *History of the Woman's Temperance Crusade,* p. 803). It is clearly correct to note middle-class women's conscious and intentional development of connections with male-dominated organizations in the postwar period. Still, by aligning themselves with such organizations and by constructing similar organizations of their own (such as the WCTU), many women were actually exercising skills in political strategy that had grown out of the practical wartime experience of trying to protect their perceived territory of patriotic expression, soldiers' aid.

Women across the Union had carved out this territory months before the national, male-administered commissions came into being, and they were determined to defend their claim. By the time the war ended, Annie Wittenmyer had indeed learned to seek male allies for her charitable endeavors, and she had also learned to adjust her ideas and methods to fit a "male" institutional model. But, Wittenmyer had learned these things in order to retain control over those enterprises that she considered representative of women's proper work in the larger world, in order to guarantee that the business of charity—at the national level as at the level of the local community—might ultimately remain within the wise and gentle grasp of women like herself. Even Wittenmyer, although she herself expressed a rather conservative postwar vision for middle-class women, in practice clearly tested the limits of propriety that the postwar historians established, as she rose more than once to administrative supremacy in organizations of benevolence whose boundaries encompassed the whole United States.

72 Erva M. Smith to Sophronia Bucklin, 3 December 1899, in the Bucklin Papers.

73 Ibid.

74 Schultz, "The Inhospitable Hospital," pp. 389–90. As Schultz noted, the idea that nurse training programs should recruit *young* women excluded from professional training most of the former Civil War nurses who, by 1873, were typically in their forties or older.

According to James Cassedy, the construction of hospitals and the development of hospital services constituted one of the "most sweeping of the post-Civil War changes in formal health care arrangements. . . . Following the Civil War the numbers of such institutions proliferated from hardly more than 100 hospitals in all parts of the nation in 1870, not including mental asylums, to over 6,000 in the next fifty years, largely in cities" (James Cassedy, *Medicine in America: A Short History*, p. 73).

75 According to Schultz, the transformation of nursing into a paid

profession stood in sharp contrast to Civil War nurses' frequent postwar "insistence that they had nursed because their help was needed and not because they wished to be paid" (Schultz, "The Inhospitable Hospital," p. 390). The nurses who made this claim revealed more about the postwar tenacity of antebellum imagery concerning the impropriety of middle-class women earning money for their "natural" caretaking abilities, than they did about the reality of Civil War nurses' common receipt of regular pay. Certainly, self-sacrifice and patriotism factored into women's decisions to take up nursing during the war. Even Bucklin, whose memoir sharply addressed the question of nurses' wages, presented her primary motivation for travelling to the front as love of country. But, as I have argued above, the "foot soldiers" of Civil War nursing, such as Bucklin, could not have gotten along, and did not really try to make do, without wages. Even Superintendent of Army Nurses Dorothea Dix, who had initially hoped to draw into her nursing corps only women who could partially or fully support themselves, soon abandoned that notion in favor of a plan in which her nurses would receive pay and rations. Dix realized, early on, that only the few could meet her early standard of self-support, and that the development of a steady and consistent supply of female nurses for the Union Army required reaching out to those women who yearned to serve but could only do so if they could be assured that their financial needs would be met.

76 Other women doctors may have entered the military service as nurses. Dr. Esther Hill Hawks, for example, found her way to the Sea Islands of South Carolina and into the work of aiding contraband and freed slaves there. Hawks exercised her skills as a physician among the former slaves, but she was not recognized in any official way for doing so. See Gerald Schwartz, A Woman Doctor's Civil War.

77 Cassedy, Medicine in America, p. 94. Over the same period of time, Cassedy noted, "well-trained women were increasingly employed as technical assistants in hospital laboratories and other

departments where they offered little challenge to the authority or economic position of the male doctors" (Ibid.).

78 Richard Harrison Shryock, *Medicine in America*, p. 185.

79 Cassedy, *Medicine in America*, p. 94; Shryock, *Medicine in America*, p. 185.

Notes to Conclusion

1 Joan W. Scott, *Gender and the Politics of History*, p. 9.

2 Joan W. Scott, "Gender: A Useful Category of Historical Analysis," pp. 1066–1067.

SELECT BIBLIOGRAPHY

ARCHIVAL MATERIALS

Correspondence of the Adjutant General, Civil War Years. Iowa State Historical Library, Des Moines, IA.

Mary Ann Ball Bickerdyke Papers. Manuscripts Division, Library of Congress, Washington, DC.

Sophronia E. Bucklin Papers. DeWitt Historical Society of Tompkins County, Ithaca, NY.

Sophronia E. Bucklin Pension File. National Archives, Washington, DC.

Leonard Caplinger Correspondence. Special Collections, The Huntington Library, San Marino, CA.

Carded Service Records of Female Hospital Attendants, Matrons and Nurses During the Civil War. National Archives, Washington, DC.

Julia A. (Smith) Clark Correspondence. Lincoln Clark Papers. Special Collections, The Huntington Library, San Marino, CA.

R. Curtis Edgerton Letters. Special Collections, The Huntington Library, San Marino, CA.

General Correspondence of Governor Samuel J. Kirkwood. Iowa State Historical Library, Des Moines, IA.

George Mellish Correspondence. Special Collections, The Huntington Library, San Marino, CA.

Governor's Letter Books Collection. Iowa State Historical Library, Des Moines, IA.

Mary A. Newcomb Pension File. National Archives, Washington, DC.

Catherine Oliphant Papers. Manuscripts Division, Library of Congress, Washington, DC.

Lida Poynter Papers. Archives and Special Collections on Women in Medicine, Medical College of Pennsylvania, Philadelphia, PA.

Harriet A. Sharpless Pension File. National Archives, Washington, DC.

Amanda Rhoda Shelton Diary, 15 April 1864 to 11 September 1866. Shelton Family Papers, Special Collections, University of Iowa, Iowa City, IA.

Mary E. Shelton Diary, 1 January 1864 to 30 December 1864. Shelton Family Papers, Special Collections, University of Iowa, Iowa City, IA.

Charles McCool Snyder Papers. Special Collections Department, Penfield Library, State University of New York, Oswego, NY.

Amanda Shelton Stewart. "Address of Amanda Shelton Stewart on her Experiences as a Civil War Nurse." Shelton Family Papers, Special Collections, University of Iowa, Iowa City, IA.

Jane Bliss Taylor Papers. Archives and Special Collections on Women in Medicine, Medical College of Pennsylvania, Philadelphia, PA.

Tompkins County City Directories. DeWitt Historical Society of Tompkins County, Ithaca, NY.

Mary E. Walker Papers. Syracuse University Library Special Collections Department, Syracuse, NY.

Mary E. Walker Papers. Oswego County Historical Society, Oswego, NY.

Mary E. Walker Papers. Records of the War Department, Office of the Adjutant General, Record Group #94, National Archives, Washington, DC.

War Correspondence of Annie Wittenmyer, 1861–1865. Iowa State Historical Library, Des Moines, IA.

Published Materials and Dissertations

Adams, Elmer C., and Warren Dunham Foster. *Heroines of Modern Progress*. New York: Sturgis & Walton Co., 1913.

Adams, George Worthington. *Doctors in Blue: The Medical History of the Union Army in the Civil War*. New York: Henry Schuman, Inc., 1952.

Addison, Daniel D., ed. *Lucy Larcom: Life, Letters and Diary*. Boston: Houghton, Mifflin, 1894; reprint ed., Detroit, MI: Gale Research Co., 1970.

Alcoff, Linda. "Cultural Feminism versus Post-Structuralism: The Identity Crisis in Feminist Theory." *Signs* 13 (Spring 1988): 405–436.

Alcott, Louisa May. *Hospital Sketches*. Boston: J. Redpath, 1863.

"Mrs. Annie Wittenmyer." *Annals of Iowa* (January 1900): 276–288.

Attie, Rejean. " 'A Swindling Concern': The United States Sanitary Commission and the Northern Female Public, 1861–1865." Ph.D. dissertation, Columbia University, 1987.

Austin, Anne. *The Woolsey Sisters of New York: A Family's Involvement in the Civil War and a New Profession*. Philadelphia: American Philosophical Society Memoirs, 1971.

Bacon, Georgeanna. *Three Weeks at Gettysburg*. New York: Anson Randolph, 1863.

Bacon, Georgeanna, and Eliza W. Howland. *Letters of a Family During the War for the Union*. New Haven, CT: Tuttle, Morehouse & Taylor, 1899.

Baker, Nina Brown. *Cyclone in Calico: The Story of Mary Ann Bickerdyke*. Boston: Little, Brown, 1952.

Barton, George. *Angels of the Battlefield: A History of the Labors of the Catholic Sisterhoods in the Late Civil War*. Philadelphia: Catholic Art Publishing Co., 1897.

Barton, William E. *The Life of Clara Barton*. Boston: Houghton, Mifflin Co., 1922.

Beers, Fannie. *Memories: A Record of Personal Experience and Adventures during Four Years of War*. Philadelphia: J. B. Lippincott, 1891.

Blake, John B. "Women and Medicine in Ante-Bellum America." *Bulletin of the History of Medicine* 39 (March-April 1965): 99–123.

Bonner, Thomas N. *To the Ends of the Earth: Women's Search for Education in Medicine.* Cambridge, MA: Harvard University Press, 1992.

Bordley, James, and A. McGehee Harvey. *Two Centuries of American Medicine, 1776–1976.* Philadelphia: W. B. Saunders Co., 1976.

Brockett, Linus P. *Woman: Her Rights, Wrongs, Privileges, and Responsibilities.* Hartford, CT: L. Stebbins, 1869; reprint ed., Plainview, NY: Books for Libraries Press, 1976.

Brockett, Linus P., and Mary C. Vaughan. *Woman's Work in the Civil War: A Record of Heroism, Patriotism, and Patience.* Philadelphia: Zeigler, McCurdy & Co., 1867.

Brooks, Stewart. *Civil War Medicine.* Springfield, IL: Charles C. Thomas, 1966.

Brumgardt, John R., ed. *Civil War Nurse: The Diary and Letters of Hannah Ropes.* Knoxville: University of Tennessee Press, 1980.

Bucklin, Sophronia E. *In Hospital and Camp: A Woman's Record of Thrilling Incidents among the Wounded in the Late War.* Philadelphia: John E. Potter & Co., 1869.

Byers, S. H. M. *Iowa in War Times.* Des Moines, IA: W. D. Condit & Co., 1888.

Cassedy, James. *Medicine and American Growth, 1800–1860.* Madison: University of Wisconsin Press, 1986.

Chase, Julia. *Mary A. Bickerdyke, "Mother".* Lawrence, KS: Journal Publishing House, 1896.

Clinton, Catherine. *The Other Civil War: American Women in the Nineteenth Century.* New York: Hill & Wang, 1984.

Collis, Septima. *A Woman's War Record, 1861–1865.* New York: G. P. Putnam's Sons, 1889.

Cooper, Helen, Adrienne Auslander Munich, and Susan Merrill Squier, eds. *Arms and the Woman: War, Gender, and Literary Representation.* Chapel Hill: University of North Carolina Press, 1989.

Cornish, Dudley Taylor. *The Sable Arm: Black Troops in the Union Army, 1861–1865.* Lawrence: University of Kansas Press, 1987.

Coryell, Janet L. *Neither Heroine Nor Fool: Anna Ella Carroll of Maryland*. Kent, OH: Kent State University Press, 1990.

Dannett, Sylvia G. L. *Noble Women of the North*. New York: Thomas Yoseloff, 1959.

Dannett, Sylvia G. L. *She Rode with the Generals: The True and Incredible Story of Sarah Emma Seelye, alias Franklin Thompson*. New York: Thomas Nelson & Sons, 1960.

Dauphin, Cécile, et al. "Theoretical and Methodological Dialogue on the Writing of Women's History." *Journal of Women's History* 1 (Spring 1989): 63–107.

Davis, Margaret. *Mother Bickerdyke: Her Life and Labors for the Relief of Our Soldiers*. San Francisco, CA: A. T. Dewey, 1886.

DuBois, Ellen, et al. "Politics and Culture in Women's History: A Symposium." *Feminist Studies* 6 (Spring 1980): 28–63.

Eastman, Mary. "Jenny Wade of Gettysburg." J. B. Lippincott & Co., 1864.

Edmonds, Sarah Emma. *Unsexed: Or, The Female Soldier, The Thrilling Adventures, Experiences and Escapes of a Woman, as Nurse, Spy and Scout, in Hospitals, Camps and Battlefields*. Philadelphia: Philadelphia Publishing Co., 1864.

Edwards, Linden F. "Dr. Mary Edwards Walker (1832–1919); Charlatan or Martyr?" (Parts I and II). *Ohio State Medical Journal* 54 (September 1958): 1160–1162; and 54 (October 1958): 1296, 1298.

Elshtain, Jean Bethke. "On Beautiful Souls, Just Warriors, and Feminist Consciousness." *Women's Studies International Forum* 5 (Summer 1982): 341–348.

Elshtain, Jean Bethke. *Women and War*. New York: Basic Books, 1987.

Epler, Percy H. *The Life of Clara Barton*. New York: Macmillan Co., 1941.

Faust, Drew Gilpin. "Altars of Sacrifice: Confederate Women and the Narratives of War." *Journal of American History* 76 (March 1990): 1200–1228.

Forman, Jacob Gilbert. *The Western Sanitary Commission: A Sketch of its Origin, History, Labors for the Sick and Wounded of the Western Armies and Aid Given to Freedmen and Union Refugees: With Incidents of Hospital Life*. St. Louis, MO: R. P. Studley & Co., 1864.

Freidel, Frank, ed. *Union Pamphlets of the Civil War, 1861–1865*, 2 vols. Cambridge, MA.: Belknap Press, 1967.

Fulbrook, Earl S. "Relief Work in Iowa during the Civil War." *Iowa Journal of History and Politics* (April 1918): 115–274.

Gallaher, Ruth A. "Annie Turner Wittenmyer." *Iowa Journal of History and Politics* 29 (October 1931): 518–569.

Garber, Marjorie. *Vested Interests: Cross-Dressing and Cultural Anxiety*. New York: Routledge, 1992.

Gattey, Charles Neilson. *The Bloomer Girls*. London: Femina Books, 1967.

Ginzberg, Lori D. *Women and the Work of Benevolence: Morality, Politics, and Class in the Nineteenth-Century United States*. New Haven, CT: Yale University Press, 1990.

Greenbie, Marjorie. *Lincoln's Daughters of Mercy*. New York: G. P. Putnam, 1944.

Greenbie, Marjorie. *My Dear Lady: The Story of Anna Ella Carroll, the "Great Unrecognized Member of Lincoln's Cabinet"*. New York: Whittlesey House, 1940; reprint ed., New York: Arno Press, 1974.

Hammond, Harold Earl. *Diary of a Union Lady, 1861–1865*. New York: Funk & Wagnalls Co., 1962.

Hanaford, Phebe A. *Daughters of America: or, Women of the Century*. Augusta, ME: True & Co., 1883.

Hass, Paul, ed. "A Volunteer Nurse in the Civil War: The Letters of Harriet Douglas Whetten." *Wisconsin Magazine of History* 48 (1964): 131–151 and 48 (1965): 205–221.

Haviland, Laura. *A Woman's Life-Work: Labors and Experiences of Laura S. Haviland*. Cincinnati, OH: Walden & Stowe, 1882; reprint ed., Salem, NH: Ayer Co., 1984.

Higonnet, Margaret Randolph, et al., eds. *Behind the Lines: Gender and the Two World Wars*. New Haven, CT: Yale University Press, 1987.

Holland, Mary. *Our Army Nurses: Interesting Sketches, Addresses, and Photographs of nearly One Hundred of the Noble Women who served in Hospitals and on Battlefields during our Civil War.* Boston: B. Wilkins & Co., 1895.

Holland, Rupert Sargent, ed. *Letters and Diary of Laura M. Towne: Written from the Sea Islands of South Carolina, 1862–1864.* Cambridge, MA.: Riverside Press, 1912; reprint ed., New York: Negro University Press, 1969.

Holstein, Anna. *Three Years in Field Hospitals of the Army of the Potomac.* Philadelphia: J. B. Lippincott & Co., 1867.

Howe, Julia Ward. *Reminiscences.* Boston & New York: Houghton, Mifflin & Co., 1899.

Hurn, Ethel A. *Wisconsin Women in the War Between the States.* Wisconsin History Commission, 1911.

Huston, Nancy. "Tales of War and Tears of Women." *Women's Studies International Forum* 5 (Summer 1982): 272–282.

Jaquette, Henrietta Stratton, ed. *South After Gettysburg: Letters of Cornelia Hancock from the Army of the Potomac, 1863–1865.* Philadelphia: University of Pennsylvania Press, 1937.

James, Edward T., and Janet W. James, eds. *Notable American Women, 1607–1950: A Biographical Dictionary.* Cambridge, MA: Belknap Press, 1971.

Jolly, Ellen. *Nuns of the Battlefield.* Providence, RI: Providence Visitor Press, 1927.

Kalisch, Philip, and Margaret Scobey. "Female Nurses in American Wars: Helplessness Suspended for the Duration." *Armed Forces and Society* 9 (1983): 215–244.

Kane, Harnett T. *Spies for the Blue and Gray.* Garden City, NY: Doubleday & Co., 1954.

Kelly, Joan. *Women, History and Theory.* Chicago, IL: University of Chicago Press, 1984.

Kerber, Linda K. "Separate Spheres, Female Worlds, Woman's Place: The Rhetoric of Women's History." *Journal of American History* 75 (June 1988): 9–39.

King, Lester S. *Transformations in American Medicine: From Benjamin*

Rush to William Osler. Baltimore, MD: Johns Hopkins University Press, 1991.

Lawson, Doris. "Dr. Mary E. Walker: A Biographical Sketch." M.A. thesis, Syracuse University, 1954.

Livermore, Mary A. *My Story of the War: A Woman's Narrative of Four Years Personal Experience As Nurse in the Union Army, and in Relief Work at Home, in Hospitals, Camps, and at the Front, During the War of the Rebellion*. Hartford, CT: A. D. Worthington & Co., 1889.

Livermore, Mary A. *The Story of My Life; or, the Sunshine and Shadow of Seventy Years*. Hartford, CT: A. D. Worthington & Co., 1899.

Logan, Mrs. John A. (Mary S.). *The Part Taken by Women in American History*. Wilmington, DE: Perry-Nalle Publishing Co., 1912; reprint ed., New York: Arno Press, 1972.

Logan, Mrs. John A. (Mary S.). *Reminiscences of the Civil War and Reconstruction*. Carbondale: Southern Illinois University Press, 1970.

Macdonald, Sharon, Pat Holden, and Shirley Ardener, eds. *Images of Woman in Peace and War: Cross-Cultural and Historical Perspectives*. London: Macmillan Education Ltd., 1987.

McKay, Charlotte E. *Stories of Hospital and Camp*. Philadelphia: Claxton, Remsen & Haffelfinger, 1876; reprint ed., Freeport, NY: Books for Libraries Press, 1971.

McPherson, James M. *Battle Cry of Freedom: The Civil War Era*. New York: Ballantine Books, 1988.

Maher, Sister Mary Denis. *To Bind up the Wounds: Catholic Sister Nurses in the U.S. Civil War*. Westport, CT: Greenwood Press, 1989.

Marshall, Helen E. *Dorothea Dix: Forgotten Samaritan*. New York: Russell & Russell, 1937; reprint ed., Chapel Hill: University of North Carolina Press, 1967.

Massey, Mary Elizabeth. *Bonnet Brigades*. New York: Alfred A. Knopf, 1966.

Maxwell, William. *Lincoln's Fifth Wheel: The Political History of the United States Sanitary Commission*. New York: Longman's Green, 1956.

Michigan Women in the Civil War. Lansing, MI: Civil War Centennial Observance Commission, 1963.

Moore, Frank. *Women of the War: Their Heroism and Self-Sacrifice.* Hartford, CT: S. S. Scranton & Co., 1866.

Moss, Lemuel. *Annals of the United States Christian Commission.* Philadelphia: J. B. Lippincott & Co., 1868.

Munroe, James Phinney, ed. *Adventures of an Army Nurse in Two Wars.* Boston: Little, Brown & Co., 1904.

Newcomb, Mary A. *Four Years of Personal Reminiscences of the War.* Chicago, IL: H. S. Mills & Co., Publishers, 1893.

Palmer, Sarah. *The Story of Aunt Becky's Army Life.* New York: John F. Trow & Co., 1867.

Parsons, Theophilus. *Memoir of Emily Elizabeth Parsons.* Boston: Little, Brown & Co., 1880.

de Pauw, Linda Grant. "Women in Combat: The Revolutionary War Experience." *Armed Forces and Society* 7 (1981): 209–226.

Pearson, Elizabeth Ware, ed. *Letters from Port Royal, Written at the Time of the Civil War.* Boston: W. B. Clarke, 1906; reprint ed., New York: Arno Press, 1969.

Phelps, Mary Mervin. *Kate Chase, Dominant Daughter.* New York: Thomas Y. Crowell Co., 1903.

Pierson, Ruth, et al., eds. *Women and Peace: Theoretical, Historical and Practical Perspectives.* London: Croom Helm, 1987.

Pinkerton, Allan. *The Spy of the Rebellion.* New York: G. W. Carleton & Co., 1885.

Poovey, Mary. *Uneven Developments: The Ideological Work of Gender in Mid-Victorian England.* Chicago, IL: University of Chicago Press, 1988.

Porter, Mary H. *Eliza Chappell Porter, A Memoir.* Chicago, IL: Fleming Revell, 1892.

Powers, Elvira J. *Hospital Pencillings, Being a Diary while in Jefferson General Hospital, Jeffersonville, Indiana, and others at Nashville, Tennessee, as Matron and Visitor.* Boston: Edward L. Mitchell, 1866.

Poynter, Lida. "Dr. Mary Walker, M.D.: Pioneer Woman Physician." *Medical Woman's Journal* (October 1946): 43–51.

Pryor, Elizabeth Brown. *Clara Barton, Professional Angel.* Philadelphia: University of Pennsylvania Press, 1987.

Quynn, Dorothy. "Barbara Frietschie." Baltimore, MD: Historical Quarterly, 1942.

Rable, George. *Civil Wars: Women and the Crisis of Southern Nationalism.* Chicago: University of Illinois Press, 1989.

Ross, Ishbel. *Angel of the Battlefield: The Life of Clara Barton.* New York: Harper, 1956.

Ross, Ishbel. *Proud Kate: Portrait of an Ambitious Woman.* New York: Harper, 1953.

Rothstein, William G. *American Physicians in the Nineteenth Century: From Sects to Science.* Baltimore, MD: Johns Hopkins University Press, 1972.

Ryan, Mary P. *Women in Public: Between Banners and Ballots, 1825–1880.* Baltimore, MD: Johns Hopkins University Press, 1990.

Sahli, Nancy Ann. "Elizabeth Blackwell, MD. (1821–1910): A Biography." Ph.D. dissertation, University of Pennsylvania, 1974.

Sarmiento, Ferdinand. *The Life of Pauline Cushman, the Celebrated Union Spy and Scout.* Philadelphia: John E. Potter & Co., 1865.

Schultz, Jane E. "The Inhospitable Hospital: Gender and Professionalism in Civil War Medicine." *Signs* 17 (Winter 1992): 363–392.

Schultz, Jane Ellen. "Women at the Front: Gender and Genre in Literature of the American Civil War." Ph.D. dissertation, University of Michigan, Ann Arbor, 1988.

Schwartz, Gerald, ed. *A Woman Doctor's Civil War: Esther Hill Hawks' Diary.* Columbia: University of South Carolina Press, 1984.

Scott, Joan W. *Gender and the Politics of History.* New York: Columbia University Press, 1988.

Scott, Joan W. "Gender: A Useful Category of Historical Analysis." *American Historical Review* 91 (December 1986): 1053–1075.

Shryock, Richard Harrison. *Medicine in America: Historical Essays.* Baltimore, MD: Johns Hopkins University Press, 1966.

Sillanpa, Tom. *Annie Wittenmyer: God's Angel.* Evanston, IL: Signal Press, 1972.

Smith, Nina Bennett. "The Women who Went to War: The Union Army Nurse in the Civil War." Ph.D. dissertation, Northwestern University, 1981.

Snyder, Charles McCool. *Dr. Mary Walker: The Little Lady in Pants.* New York: Vantage Press, 1962; reprint ed., New York: Arno Press, 1974.

Souder, Mrs. Edmund A. *Leaves from the Battle-field of Gettysburg.* Caxton Press of C. Sherman, Son & Co., 1864.

Stanton, Elizabeth Cady. *Eighty Years and More: Reminiscences, 1815–1897.* New York: T. Fisher Unwin, 1898; reprint ed., New York: Schocken Books, 1971.

Stearns, Amanda Akin. *The Lady Nurse of Ward E.* New York: Baker & Taylor Co., 1909.

Stewart, Nixon B. *Dan McCook's Regiment, 52nd O.V.I.: A History of the Regiment, Its Campaigns and Battles.* Privately printed, 1900.

Stillé, Charles. *History of the United States Sanitary Commission: Being the General Report of its Work during the War of the Rebellion.* Philadelphia: J. B. Lippincott & Co., 1866.

Stimson, Julia Catherine. "Women Nurses with the Union Forces During the Civil War." *Military Surgeon* (January-February 1928); Ann Arbor, MI, University Microforms International, 1982.

Summers, Anne. *Angels and Citizens: British Women as Military Nurses, 1854–1914.* London: Routledge & Kegan Paul, 1988.

Tiffany, Francis. *Life of Dorothea Lynde Dix.* Boston: Houghton, Mifflin & Co., 1891.

Venet, Wendy Hammand. *Neither Ballots Nor Bullets: Women Abolitionists and the Civil War.* Charlottesville: University Press of Virginia, 1991.

Wager, Mary A. E. "Women as Physicians." *The Galaxy* 6 (December 1868): 774–778.

Walker, Mary E. *Hit.* New York: American News Co., 1871.

Walker, Mary E. *Unmasked, or the Science of Immorality.* Philadelphia: William H. Boyd, 1878.

Walker, Mary E. "What Can Woman Do?" *The Sibyl: A Review of Tastes, Errors and Fashions of Society* (15 May 1859): 1011.

Werlich, Robert. "Mary Walker: From Union Army Surgeon to Side Show Freak." *Civil War Times Illustrated* 6 (1967): 46–49.

Wheelock, Julia S. *The Boys in White: The Experience of a Hospital Agent in and around Washington.* New York: Lange & Hillman, 1870.

Wiley, Bell Irvin. *The Life of Billy Yank, The Common Soldier of the Union.* Indianapolis, IN: Bobbs-Merrill, 1952.

Wiley, Bell Irvin. *The Life of Johnny Reb, The Common Soldier of the Confederacy.* Indianapolis, IN: Bobbs-Merrill, 1943.

Willard, Frances E. *Woman and Temperance; or, the Work and Workers of the Woman's Christian Temperance Union.* Hartford, CT: Park Publishing Co., 1883.

Willard, Frances E., and Mary A. Livermore, eds. *A Woman of the Century: Fourteen Hundred-Seventy Biographical Sketches Accompanied by Portraits of Leading American Women in All Walks of Life.* Buffalo, NY: Moulton, 1893.

Wilson, Dorothy. *Stranger and Traveler: The Story of Dorothea Dix, American Reformer.* Boston: Little, Brown & Co., 1975.

Wittenmyer, Annie T. *A Collection of Recipes for the Use of Special Diet Kitchens in Military Hospitals.* N.P., 1864; reprint ed., Sara D. Jackson and John M. Carroll & Co., 1983.

Wittenmyer, Annie T. *History of the Woman's Temperance Crusade.* Boston: J. H. Earle, 1882.

Wittenmyer, Annie T. *Reports of Mrs. Annie Wittenmyer, State Sanitary Agent.* Des Moines, IA: F. W. Palmer, State Printer, 1864.

Wittenmyer, Annie T. *Under the Guns: A Woman's Reminiscences of the Civil War.* Boston: E. B. Stillings & Co., 1895.

Wittenmyer, Annie T. *Woman's Work for Jesus.* New York: Nelson & Phillips, 1873.

Wittenmyer, Annie T. *The Women of the Reformation.* New York: Phillips & Hunt, 1885.

Wittenmyer, Annie T. *The Woman's Relief Corps Red Book.* Boston: E. B. Stillings & Co., 1897.

Wood, Ann Douglas. "The War Within a War: Women Nurses in the Union Army," *Civil War History* 18 (September 1972): 197–212.

Woodward, Helen Beal. *The Bold Women*. Freeport, NY: Books for Libraries Press, 1971.

Woolsey, Jane Stuart. *Hospital Days*. New York: D. Van Nostrand, 1870.

Wormeley, Katharine P. *The Other Side of War with the Army of the Potomac*. Boston: Ticknor & Co., 1889.

Worthington, C. J., ed. *Story of the Civil War, Or, The Exploits, Adventures and Travels of Mrs. L. J. Velasquez*. New York: Worthington Co., 1890.

Yellin, Jean Fagan. *Women and Sisters: The Antislavery Feminists in American Culture*. New Haven, CT: Yale University Press, 1989.

Young, Agatha Brooks. *The Women and the Crisis: Women of the North in the Civil War*. New York: McDowell, Obolensky, 1959.

Zur, Ofer. "Men, Women and War: Gender Differences in Attitudes toward War." Ph.D. dissertation, Berkeley, Wright Institute, 1984.

INDEX

Adams General Hospital, 99
Allen, Dr., 98
Allen, Mrs. C. D., 74
American Medical Association
    (AMA), 107, 192–93
American Revolution, xvi
Ames, M. B., 152
Amigh, Mrs. O., 59
amputations, 39, 123–24
Anthony, Susan B., 165, 166
Antietam, Battle of, 28, 121
Armory Square Hospital, 30, 42

Bartholow, Roberts, 132–33, 134
Barton, Clara, xx
Battle Cry of Freedom (McPherson),
    xv
Bellows, Henry, 3, 11, 47–49,
    102–3, 156, 170, 172–73
Benedict, W. A., 151
Benton Barracks Hospital, 31–32
Bickerdyke, Mary Ann Ball
    ("Mother"), xx
Bingham, James, xiii–xiv
Bingham, Mary Warden, xiii–xiv
Blackwell, Elizabeth, 10–11, 106
Blackwell, Emily, 106

Bloomer, Amelia, 75–77, 109
bloomers, 109–10
"bonnet brigades," xviii
Brainerd, N. H., 78, 79
Breckinridge, Margaret E., 170, 171
Brockett, Linus P., *see Woman's
    Work in the Civil War*
    (Brockett and Vaughan)
Brown, E. O., 143–44, 145
Brownell, Kady, 173
Brown Hospital, 95–98
Bucklin, Almira, 25, 161
Bucklin, Sophronia E., xix,
    xxiii–xxiv, 186, 190
acceptance into nursing service,
    17
adjustment to war's carnage,
    12–13
centrality of wartime experiences
    to her self-understanding,
    162
Dix and, 17
dressing of wounds, 19
enthusiasm for war service, 3–4,
    5–6
gender relations among hospital
    personnel, 31, 34–39

Bucklin, Sophronia E. (*continued*)
at Gettysburg, 36–38
hardships of daily life, 13
historians' portrayal of, 180–82
information about nursing, search
for, 6, 11–12
"maternal" duties of nursing, 19
medical techniques, critique of,
38–39
memoir of, 3–4, 5, 33–34, 161,
162
photograph of, 2
postwar activities, 160–62
prewar private life, 5
privacy, lack of, 14–15
satisfaction of nursing work,
44–45, 46
wages issue, 24–25, 26–27,
29–30
women, professional relations
with, 41
Bull Run, First Battle of, 5, 8
Bull Run, Second Battle of,
120–21
Bureau of Refugees and Freedmen,
150
Burnside, Gen. Ambrose, 120,
121, 137
business-related activities, women's
involvement in, xvii–xviii
Byers, S. H. M., 51

Cameron, Simon, 7
Castle Thunder Prison, 140
Chafe, William, xvi
Chatham Square Methodist
Episcopal Church, 52
Chickamauga, Battle of, 129
City Point Hospital, 41
civilians in conquered areas, 136

Civil War:
as transformative event for
United States, xv
Victorian gender system and,
xxii–xxiv, 159–60, 197–99
see also women's roles in Civil
War
Clark, Catharine, 95, 96, 98, 100
Clark, Julia A., 95–98
clothing for women, 109–10
Collamer, J., 152
Congressional Act of August 1861,
24
Conklin, Cary, 145
Cooper, George E., 131–32,
149
Couch, Gen. Darius, 137
Council Bluffs Soldiers' Aid
Society, 76
Coyle, Lt. Col., 146

DeFoe, Edwin, 126
De Motte, W. H., 151
diet kitchens, *see* special diet
kitchen project
Dill, Col. Daniel, 147–48
Dillon, John F., 80
Divers, Bridget, 173, 174–75
Dix, Dorothea Lynde, xix, 11, 14,
29, 36, 93
Bucklin and, 17
limiting of her power, 20, 21,
22–23
moral standards, 15
nursing-related goals, 21
nursing service, appointment to,
7–8
requirements for prospective
nurses, 16–18
wages for nurses, 23–24, 25–26

INDEX

Eastman, Mary, 167
Edgerton, R. Curtis, xvii–xviii
education, 52, 62, 107
Emonds, Reverend, 77–78
Erva (Bucklin's niece), 186–87
espionage activities, 136–38
Etheridge, Annie, 173, 175

Fairleigh, Col., 145, 146
feminist movement, xvi
52nd Ohio Volunteers, 130–31,
    134–38
Finley, Clement A., 114, 116
Fredericksburg, Battle of, 122
Frietchie, Barbara, 168–69
Fryer, B. E., 97

Gardner, Brig. Gen. William M.,
    139
"Gender: A Useful Category of
    Historical Analysis" (Scott),
    195
Gender and the Politics of History
    (Scott), 195
gender systems, xx–xxi
    see also Victorian gender system
Geneva Medical College, 106
Gettysburg, Battle of, 36–37
Gettysburg hospital, 37–38
Gibbons, Mrs., 41
Gray, C. C., 147
Green, J. N., 115–16, 117–18,
    119
Griswald, Charles, 145

Hammond, Lt. Col. J. H., 144,
    146
Hammond, William, 20
Hammond General Hospital, 13,
    19, 36, 41

Hancock, Cornelia, 15, 17–18, 20,
    46, 47
Hancock, Gen. Winfield Scott, 137
Harris, Mrs. John, 170–71
Hasbrouck, Lydia Sayer, 126
Hawkins, Lewis, 25
historians' view of Civil War women:
    Bucklin and, 180–82
    complementary response of the
        sexes to war, depiction of,
        172–73
    ideal Union woman, 166–69
    laboring class women, 174
    nursing service, interpretation of,
        47–49, 172, 188
    postwar image of women's Civil
        War contribution and,
        169–70
    self-sacrifice, emphasis on, 171
    soldiers' aid, interpretation of,
        102–3, 184
    soldier-women, 173–77
    Victorian gender system and,
        xxiv–xxv, 160, 176–77,
        178–79, 196
    Walker's omission from historical
        record, 156–57, 177–78
    Wittenmyer's story,
        reconfiguration of, 179–80
    women chosen for portrayal,
        170–71
    women's postwar social position,
        redefinition of, 182–83
    *see also Woman's Work in the
        Civil War* (Brockett and
        Vaughan); *Women of the
        War* (Moore)
*History of the Woman's Temperance
    Crusade, The* (Wittenmyer),
    163

301

Holstein, Anna, 4, 28
Holt, J., 152–55
home missionary movement, 163
Hood, T. B., 32
hospital personnel, 20
Howell, Mrs. J. B., 65, 69
Hygeia Therapeutic College, 120

Indiana Hospital, 115–16, 117–18, 119
In Hospital and Camp (Bucklin), 3–4, 5, 33–34, 161, 162
Iowa in War Times (Byers), 51
Iowa Sanitary Commission, 80
Iowa State Army Sanitary Commission, 60–65, 70–71, 72–77, 79–80

Jackson, Gen. Thomas J. ("Stonewall"), 168–69
Jefferson Barracks Hospital, 45
"Jenny Wade of Gettysburg" (Eastman), 167–68
Jobes (ward master), 30
Johnson, Andrew, 131, 134, 150–52, 155
Judiciary Square Hospital, 19, 34, 45

Keokuk Ladies' Soldiers' Aid Society:
bookkeeping issues, 66–67, 68
coordination of Iowa relief effort, 55–56
defection of local societies to state agency, 75–77
distribution of supplies, 58–59
establishment of, 54
financial support for, 71–72, 74
hospital support program, 55

legitimization of women's wartime role, demand for, 63–64, 69–72
male standards of professionalism, adoption of, 66–68
merger with state agency, 79–80
military's support for, 68–69
"selling supplies" scandal, 77–78
state agency, criticism of, 74–75
state's efforts to supplant, 60–65, 72–77
transportation concerns, 69
USSC, conflict with, 57
Wittenmyer's positions with, 54, 59
women's support for, 65
"women's work" perspective on soldiers' aid, 58, 74–75
King, Preston, 122–23
Kirkwood, Samuel J., 60, 64–65, 70, 72, 73, 75
Knowles, Lucretia, 66, 68, 74
Kynett, A. J., 60, 64, 72, 73, 75, 78, 79, 80, 81

laboring class women, 174
Larcom, Lucy, xvii
Lawson, Thomas, 114
Lincoln, Abraham, 11, 69
Walker and, 129–30
Livermore, Mary Ashton Rice, xviii–xix, 8
Logan, Mary S., 105
Louisville Female Military Prison, 141, 142–49

McChesney, Fitzhough, 127–28
McCook, Col. Dan, 131, 135, 136
McPherson, James M., xv, xxii
Marsh, A. S., 65

INDEX

Meade, Gen. George, 137
Medical Department of Union
    Army:
  employment of surgeons, 119
  expansion at start of Civil War,
    114
  Walker's examination by,
    131–34
  Walker's pursuit of commission
    and, 112, 113, 116–17
medical profession:
  postwar changes, 190–93
  regular and non-regular
    practitioners, 107–8, 133,
    154
  Victorian gender system and,
    21–22, 107
  women, prejudice against,
    192–93
  women admitted to, 108–9
  women excluded from, 106–7
  see also nursing service; Walker,
    Mary E.
Mertz, Miss, 26
Michigan Relief Association, 9
Millard, D. E., 151
Miller, Albert, 111
Moore, Frank, see Women of the
    War (Moore)
Mound City Hospital, 39
Mt. Pleasant Hospital, 98, 100
Muir, James, xiv

Newcomb, Hiram A. W., 26
Newcomb, Mary, 4, 9, 25–26,
    39–40
New York Times, The, 178
Nightingale, Florence, 10, 187
nursing profession, postwar, 186–89
nursing service, xix–xx, 112

complexities of women nurses'
    experiences, 48
dismissals of nurses, 35–36
Dix's appointment to, 7–8
dressing of wounds, 19
eating arrangements, 32–33
enthusiasm of nurses, 3–6
federal program, 6–8, 11
gender relations among hospital
    personnel, 30–41
historians' interpretation of,
    47–49, 172, 188
immorality concerns, 14–15
information about nursing
    opportunities, shortage of,
    6, 11–12
maternal chores, similarity to, 19
medical techniques, critique of,
    38–40
movement restrictions on nurses,
    34
non-medical assignments for
    nurses, 35
pensions for nurses, 26, 32,
    160–61, 164
postwar status of nursing and,
    186–89
professionalization of women
    and, 21–30
recruitment of women, 6–7
regimental positions, 8–9, 18
requirements for prospective
    nurses, 16–18
resistance to women's
    involvement, 7–8, 12–15, 20
satisfaction of nursing work,
    44–47
single women and, 14–15
soldiers' appreciation of women's
    efforts, 45–46

nursing service (*continued*)
  special skills of nursing, women's
    demand for recognition of,
    40
  Surgeon General's takeover of,
    20–21
  surgeons-in-charge and, 35–36
  training for nurses, 10
  Victorian gender system and,
    12–15, 43–44
  visiting nonmedical women and,
    42–43
  WCRA and, 10–11
  women, conflicts between, 41
  women's determination to serve,
    18
  women's right to care for sick
    and, 38
  youth and beauty issue, 16–18,
    21, 23
  see also Bucklin, Sophronia E.
nutrition programs, *see* special diet
    kitchen project

Oliphant, Catherine, 9
Olnhausen, Mary Phinney von, 6,
    43
Orphan Asylum Association:
  establishment of homes, 84
  organization and administration
    of homes, 86–87
  professionalization of women
    and, 85–87
  state involvement, 83–84
  Wittenmyer's political skills and,
    84–85
  Wittenmyer's proposal for, 83

Palmer, Sarah, 4–5, 13–14, 29,
    40, 43

Parsons, Emily Elizabeth, 31–32,
    45, 46, 47
*Part Taken by Women in American
    History, The* (Logan), 105
pensions for nurses, 26, 32,
    160–61, 164
Phelps, E. E., 145, 147, 148–49
Point of Rocks Hospital, 90–92
Porter, Eliza Chappell, 45
Powers, Elvira J., 6, 30–31
Poynter, Lida, 157
prisoners of war, 138–41, 144–47
professionalization of women, xxiii
  in benevolence work, 71–72,
    85–87
  in nursing service, 21–30
  special diet kitchen project and,
    92–94, 98–99

reform dress, 109–10
Republican Motherhood, xvi
Ricketts, Fanny, 170
Ropes, Alice, 17
Ropes, Hannah, 30, 46
Rosa, A. J., 130
Rush, Benjamin, 108

Sample, Capt. J. B., 59
Sanford, Nettie, 81–82
sanitary supply collection and
    distribution, *see* soldiers' aid
Schneider, Dorothy and Carl J.,
    xvi
Schuyler, Louisa Lee, 16, 23
Scott, Joan W., 195, 196, 197
Semmes, Capt. B. J., 138–39
Sharpless, Harriet, 32
Shelton, Mary E., 83–84, 179
Sherman, Maj. Gen. William T.,
    141, 143

Sibyl, The (reform journal), 110, 126, 127, 137
Simpson, Matthew, 163
soldiers' aid, xviii–xix
    forms of aid provided by women, 54
    historians' interpretation of, 102–3, 184
    Iowa Sanitary Commission, 80
    Iowa State Army Sanitary Commission, 60–65, 70–71, 72–77, 79–80
    Victorian gender system and, 63, 81, 103, 186
    women's leadership, consequences of, 184–86
    as women's work, 58, 74–75, 81–82
    see also Keokuk Ladies' Soldiers' Aid Society; special diet kitchen project; United States Sanitary Commission; Wittenmyer, Annie
soldier-women, 173–77
special diet kitchen project, 87, 179
    accomplishments of, 89–90
    corrupt practices, managers' crusade against, 100–101
    establishment of, 88–89
    gender-related tension between managers and hospital personnel, 95–101
    goals of, 92
    need for, 87–88, 90
    operation of kitchens, 92
    opposition to women managers, 94–95, 99–100
    professionalization of women and, 92–94, 98–99

    qualifications and duties of managers, 92–94
    success, Wittenmyer's responsibility for, 101–2
    takeover of hospital kitchens, 90–92
    Victorian gender system and, 87, 99
    as women's work, 98
Spinner, F. E., 152
Springsteen, Capt. Alex, 128
Stanton, Edwin, 69, 128–29, 151, 152
Stanton, Elizabeth Cady, 165, 166
Stearns, Amanda, 30, 42, 46, 47
Stewart, Amanda Shelton, 23
Stewart, Nixon B., 135, 136
Stillé, Alfred, 192
Stone, William, 83, 89
Strong, Mary, 66–67, 72, 73, 74
suffrage movement, xvi, 164, 165–66, 183
Syracuse Medical College, 108, 133

temperance movement, 162–63, 164
Thomas, Gen. George H., 129, 130–31, 134, 136–37, 141–42
Townsend, E. D., 136, 155

Under the Guns: A Woman's Reminiscences of the Civil War (Wittenmyer), 52–53, 87–88, 90–91, 163
Underwood, Mrs., 98
Union Hotel Hospital, 30
United States Christian Commission (USCC), 88–89

United States Sanitary Commission (USSC), 60, 89, 170
  establishment of, 11
  Medical Department of Union Army and, 114
  national control of soldiers' aid effort, 57

Vance, S. E., 101
Vaughan, Mary C., see *Woman's Work in the Civil War* (Brockett and Vaughan)
Victorian gender system:
  assumptions of, xxi–xxii, 197
  Civil War's impact on, xxii–xxiv, 159–60, 197–99
  clothing and, 110
  complexity of gender system change, 197
  historians and, xxiv–xxv, 160, 176–77, 178–79, 196
  limits of Civil War era tolerance for gender system change, 190–94, 199–201
  medical profession and, 21–22, 107
  nursing service and, 12–15, 43–44
  postwar redefinition of gender boundaries, 186, 189–90, 196–97, 199–201
  soldiers' aid and, 63, 81, 103, 186
  special diet kitchen project and, 87, 99
  "spheres" of activity, 67, 197
  wage earning by women and, 27–28
  Walker's efforts against, 110–11, 165–66, 177–78, 190–94

visiting comforters, 42–43

Wade, Jenny, 167–68
wage earning by women, 27–28
  see also professionalization of women
Walker, Mary E., xx, xxiii, xxiv, 105, 199, 200
  acceptance by colleagues and patients, 118, 122–23, 129, 134, 141–42, 150–51, 152
  amputations, approach to, 123–24
  benevolent projects, 125–26
  civilians, care for, 136
  clothing preferences, 109–10
  commission as peacetime military surgeon, pursuit of, 150–55
  commission as wartime military surgeon, pursuit of, 112–17, 128–30, 141–42
  Congressional Medal of Honor for Meritorious Service, 154–56
  courage and persistence of, 194
  crying incident, 139
  "dynamic fluctuation" of Civil War medical career, 124–25
  early years, 106
  espionage activities, 136–38
  examination by Medical Department of Union Army, 131–34
  female self-sacrifice, belief in, 119
  financial compensation issue, 119, 122–23, 142, 143
  gender-related tensions surrounding, 148
  health problems, 140

INDEX

historians' failure to
acknowledge, 156–57,
177–78
liaison work, 127–28
marriage, attitude toward, 111
medical education, 106, 108–9,
120
photograph of, 104
popular postwar image, 178
postwar activities, 165–66
press stories on, 178
as prison contract surgeon,
141–49
as prisoner of Confederacy,
138–41
private medical practice in
Washington, 126–27
regiment, proposed organization
of, 128–29
as regimental contract surgeon,
130–31, 134–38
services performed by, 117–18
soldiers' attitude toward, 135,
136
termination by army, 149
transport of wounded soldiers,
121–22
Victorian gender system,
opposition to, 110–11,
165–66, 177–78, 190–94
volunteer work, 115–20, 122
women's housing project, 125–26
wars, gender systems and, xxi
Wheelock, Julia S., 9, 15, 46
Whittier, John Greenleaf, 168
Wilber, John, xviii
Willard, Frances, 164
Wittenmyer, Annie, xix,
xxiii–xxiv, 64, 65, 66, 70,
190

advantages enjoyed by, 53–54
bookkeeping issue, 68
distribution of sanitary supplies,
58–59
gender expectations, fight
against, 93–94, 102
historians' portrayal of, 179–80
with Iowa Sanitary Commission,
80
memoir of, 52–53, 87–88,
90–91, 163
photograph of, 50
political skills, 68–69, 74, 75,
82, 84–85
postwar activities, 162–65, 184
prewar involvement in
benevolence work, 51–52
professionalization of women
and, 85–87
public stature, 59, 78–79, 82
religious commitment, 52, 163
reports about troops, 59
"selling supplies" scandal, 77–78
soldiers' aid, entry into, 52–53
state agent, appointment as, 72,
80
state aid agency, cooperation
with, 73
temperance activities, 162–63,
164
women's role in society, views
on, 164–65
see also Keokuk Ladies' Soldiers'
Aid Society; Orphan
Asylum Association; special
diet kitchen project
Wittenmyer, William, 53
Wolf-street Hospital, 32–33, 35
Woman's Central Relief
Association (WCRA), 10–11

Woman's Christian Temperance
Union (WCTU), xvi,
162–63, 164, 186
Woman's Relief Corps of the Grand
Army of the Republic
(WRC), 161, 164, 186
Woman's Work for Jesus
(Wittenmyer), 163
Woman's Work in the Civil War
(Brockett and Vaughan), 3,
159, 169–70, 171–73, 175,
176, 177, 179–80, 182–83
as official version of history, 170
Women of the Reformation, The
(Wittenmyer), 163
Women of the War (Moore),
169–75, 176, 179, 180
women's colleges, 107
women's housing project, 125–26
women's roles in Civil War:
business-related activities,
xvii–xviii
martial spirit, adoption of, xvii
military participation, 173–77
postwar power relations and,
183–84
variety of roles, xvii
visiting comforters, 42–43
weeping widows of the dead,
xiii–xv
see also historians' view of Civil
War women; nursing
service; soldiers' aid; *specific
women*
Women's Trade Union League, xvi
Wood, R. C., 116–17, 129, 134,
143, 144, 146
Woolsey, Georgeanna, 43
working styles of men and women,
61–62
World War I, xvi
World War II, xvi
Wormeley, Katharine, 43, 47

Yeatman, James E., 8